Shifting the Ground

Shifting the Ground

AMERICAN WOMEN WRITERS'
REVISIONS OF NATURE, GENDER, AND RACE

Rachel Stein

UNIVERSITY PRESS OF VIRGINIA
Charlottesville and London

First published 1997

⊗ The paper used in this publication meets the minimum requirements of the American National Standard for Information Sciences—Permanence of Paper for Printed Library Materials, ANSI Z39.48-1984.

Library of Congress Cataloging-in-Publication Data

Stein, Rachel.
    Shifting the ground : American women writers' revision of nature, gender, and race / Rachel Stein.
       p.   cm.
    Includes bibliographical references and index.
    ISBN 0-8139-1741-7 (cloth : alk. paper)
    1. American literature—Women authors—History and criticism.   2. Dickinson, Emily, 1830–1886—Criticism and interpretation.   3. Silko, Leslie, 1948– —Criticism and interpretation.   4. National characteristics, American, in literature.   5. Hurston, Zora Neale—Criticism and interpretation.   6. Women and literature—United States. 7. Walker, Alice, 1944– Meridian.   8. Gender identity in literature.   9. Nature in literature.   10. Race in literature.   I. Title.
PS147.S74   1997
810.9'9287—dc21
                                                    97-9841
                                                       CIP

To my children, Joshua Reed and Anna Rose Stein

Contents

Acknowledgments

This book was written with the aid and support of a community of family, friends, colleagues, and teachers. I thank Marianne DeKoven, Cheryl Wall, and Harriet Davidson, my dissertation advisors in the Rutgers Graduate English program, for encouraging my pursuit of what was then a little-known theoretical position, and for shepherding this project through its initial incarnation. The diverse feminist communities at Rutgers University provided a stimulating context for my thought. In particular I thank Katie Hogan, Christy Jesperson, Wesley Brown, and April Lidinsky for friendship and impassioned discussion. The members of my dissertation group, Kathy Bassard, Ken Smith, and most especially Dawn Skorczewski, offered me valuable guidance in untangling my mental snarls during the first writing of this project. Several colleagues have offered insightful readings of portions of my manuscript: my thanks to Anne Rea, Christy Jesperson, and Jerry Dollar.

I have been greatly encouraged by the increasing numbers of scholars working in the fields of ecocriticism and ecofeminist theory, and I am especially grateful to those who created the Association for the Study of Literature and Environment, an organization whose publications and conferences have provided me a community of like-minded scholars within which to pursue my work.

Siena College has generously supported this project through a summer grant from the Committee on Teaching and a reduction in teaching responsibilities during my final months of revision.

Many thanks to my editors at the University Press of Virginia, Cathie Brettschneider and Gerald Trett, who have meticulously ushered this book into final form.

My family has offered me the invaluable support that made this project feasible. I thank my parents, Shirley and Larry Stein, for their generous and loving faith and aid. I thank my sister, Susan Stein, for her encouragement and for her provocative art which sometimes gives image to my ideas. Finally, I thank my children, Josh and Anna, who have grown so steadily while I have been writing, for their patience, (and impatience), humor, and daily companionship. My children have given me the incentive and determination to pursue my work, for they have reshaped my life in ways that I could not have predicted.

A portion of chapter 2 originally appeared under the title "Remembering the Sacred Tree: Nature, Black Women, and Voodoo in Zora Neale Hurston's *Tell My Horse* and *Their Eyes Were Watching God*," in *Women's Studies* 25 (1996): 465–482. It is reprinted with permission.

I am grateful to the following publishers and copyright holders for permission to reprint poems by Emily Dickinson. Poem #228, "Blazing in Gold and quenching in Purple;" Poem #334, "All the letters I can write;" Poem #339, "I tend my flowers for thee—;" Poem #352, "Perhaps I asked too large—;" Poem #441, "This is my letter to the World;" Poem #742, "Four Trees—upon a solitary Acre;" Poem #716, "The Day Undressed—Herself;" Poem #722, "Sweet Mountains—Ye tell Me no lie—;" Poem #790, "Nature—the Gentlest Mother is;" Poem #1170, "Nature affects to be sedate;" and Poem #1400, "What mystery pervades a well!" Reprinted by permission of the publishers and the Trustees of Amherst College from *The Poems of Emily Dickinson*, Thomas H. Johnson, ed., Cambridge, Mass.: The Belknap Press of Harvard University Press, Copyright 1951, 1955, 1979, 1983 by the President and Fellows of Harvard College.

Poem #334, Poem #339, and Poem #716 are also reprinted with permission from *Complete Poems of Emily Dickinson* by T. H. Johnson. Copyright 1929, 1935 by Martha Dickinson Bianchi; copyright renewed 1957, 1963 by Mary L. Hampson. By permission of Little, Brown and Company.

I am grateful to the following publisher and copyright holders for permission to reprint poems by Adrienne Rich. The lines from "An Old House in America", from *The Fact of a Doorframe: Poems Selected and New, 1950–1984* by Adrienne Rich. Copyright 1984 by Adrienne Rich. Copyright © 1975, 1978 by W. W. Norton & Company, Inc. Copyright © 1981 by Adrienne Rich. Reprinted by permission of the author and W. W. Norton & Company, Inc. The lines from "Dreams Before Waking", from *Your Native Land, Your Life: Poems* by Adrienne Rich. Copyright 1986 by Adrienne Rich. Reprinted by permission of the author and W. W. Norton & Company, Inc.

Shifting the Ground

Introduction

Our project must be to locate a nature which is within rather than without history, for only by doing so can we find human communities which are inside rather than outside nature.—*William Cronon*

The tools are often stories, retold stories, versions that reverse and displace the hierarchical dualisms of naturalized identities.—*Donna Haraway*

PROMOTIONAL LITERATURE ENTICING European settlers to North America often portrayed the continent as a woman, sometimes an Indian maiden, arms generously open, proffering the riches of the new land to the prospective immigrants.[1] Such images not only depicted the New World landscape as ready resource awaiting the settlers but also figuratively equated women and native peoples with nature and thus representationally bound such persons into servitude to the young nation. While cultural historians have long asserted that the Euro-American conquest of the New Land is a founding mythos of the United States of America, we have yet to examine fully the complex interconnections between the settlers' imperative to subdue the wild terrain and their contemporaneous subordination of those peoples such as women, Native Americans, and African Americans, whom they associated in differing ways

1

with wild nature.[2] Historian Patricia Limerick suggests that we Americans still live within this "legacy of conquest," those divisive geographical and social relations set in motion during the Euro-American subjugation of the places and peoples of the New World, but that we have yet to comprehend the intricate ways in which our current relations have been determined by that history.[3] This is in part because American identity has been so immersed within the mythos that we have for centuries assumed it to be a God-given mandate rather than an ideology that grounds its operations through recourse to the natural.

But those who have suffered the consequences of colonization may have been less blinded to the workings of its rhetoric. In a segment of a poem entitled "From an Old House in America" Adrienne Rich's speaker ponders her identity as an American woman against a historical backdrop of certain women's harsh fates in the New World. The poem portrays women of various ancestries "pressed" into the service of a dream they had not freely chosen. Moreover, the poem subtly suggests that the women's servitude and suffering had been endorsed by the equation of women with nature: the women in the poem are treated as part and parcel of the fertile ground that must birth the young American nation. An American woman writer such as Rich might well feel impelled to "turn over" this colonial equation:

> I am an American woman:
> I turn that over
>
> like a leaf pressed in a book
> I stop and look up from
>
> into the coals of the stove
> or the black square of the window
>
> Foot-slogging through the Bering Strait
> jumping from the *Arbella* to my death
>
> chained to the corpse beside me
> I feel my pains begin
>
> I am washed up on this continent
> shipped here to be fruitful

my body a hollow ship
bearing sons to the wilderness

sons who ride away
on horseback, daughters

whose juices drain like mine
into the *arroyo* of stillbirths, massacres

Hanged as witches, sold as breeding wenches
my sisters leave me

I am not the wheatfield
nor the virgin forest

I never chose this place
yet I am of it now[4]

While many female settlers certainly must have found fulfilling lives in the New World, Rich's speaker emphasizes the plight of those who struggled within the undercurrents of American history. All of the women whose stories and voices bleed into the speaker's—be they enslaved African, besieged Native American, or reluctant European immigrant—have been subsumed within the colonial mission to plow and people the wilds of America. Within the context of this mission, the women are no more than reproductive bodies, hollow vessels who bear sons to the wild land, rather than self-fulfilled persons who exist in their own right. Tellingly, these shards of colonial women's histories are framed in the poem between two natural references. The stories commence when the speaker turns over her identity "like a leaf pressed" and they conclude when the speaker disavows her conflation with "wheatfield" and "virgin forest." This ordering implies that the framing of these women as wild nature may be at the root of their struggles in the New World.

An American woman, such as Rich's speaker, might find in this history cause for consideration and question, might need to *turn over* this legacy as a necessary step in the process of self-definition. The phrase "I turn that over" inscribes a process of investigation, of turning something to varied angles in order to gain a fuller view of what has been hidden from sight.

It also implies an act of overturning, of upsetting and dislocating an old interpretation or position. Finally, it brings to mind the preparatory turning of soil, the shifting of ground that promotes a new planting, that enables the cultivation of a new relationship between speaker and nature, between speaker and history, one that might come to fruition in a new American mythos less burdensome to all those formerly identified with the wheatfield and the virgin forest.

Rich's poem raises a number of questions I have sought to answer in this book. Given that American women writers have inherited the difficult legacy Rich describes, have they in fact perceived a pattern of negative identification with nature? How did this detrimental association manifest itself in differing historical periods and social contexts? What social problems do the writers see as grounded in this conflation? How might the writers have *turned over* these problematic patterns, questioning assumptions that their contemporaries had viewed as natural fact? How do the writers' recastings of nature take on different meaning when read within the context of the history that Rich divulges? How might formal qualities of their writings stem from their reinscriptions of nature? Finally, how do their revisions of the intersections of nature, gender, and race shift the ground of problematic aspects of American identities and allow the writers to reimagine more fertile social/natural interrelations?

While I believe that many American women's writings address the assumptions that Rich questions in her poem, *Shifting the Ground* is a study of four writers whose revisions of nature, gender, and race strike me as particularly compelling in illuminating this ideological complex.[5] Although very different from one another, the works of Emily Dickinson, Zora Neale Hurston, Alice Walker, and Leslie Marmon Silko are united by a common critique of the dominant culture's map of America as what historian Perry Miller calls "nature's nation."[6] In varied ways the writers call into question the exclusionary function of the traditional mythos of America as a nation lodged in the wilderness, and they reveal that American conceptions of nature have always been deeply social, mirroring and reflecting hierarchic social relations, particularly those of gender and race, to the point where we cannot truly redress these social roles without reconceiving our notions of nature as well. While critics have often read the nature imagery of these writers apolitically, disconnected from any social critique, when the texts are reexamined within the context of the discourse of nature's nation, the writers' reconceptions of nature emerge as boldly polemic subversions of that ideological complex.

Because I am working from within a relatively new critical framework, I have chosen to discuss established writers who are recognized as important within American literature in general and who are considered major figures in their particular branches of literature. My hope is that readers will already be familiar enough with their works to evaluate the merit of my reinterpretations. I have also selected writers who approached the negative affiliation with nature from differing cultural and historical perspectives. Emily Dickinson, one of our most daringly experimental poets, led a cloistered life as a middle-class white woman dwelling in genteel, puritanical nineteenth-century New England. Zora Neale Hurston, raised in the first all-black incorporated town in Florida at the turn of the century, came into her own as a novelist and folklorist during the final flowering of the Harlem Renaissance. Alice Walker, daughter of black southern sharecroppers, began writing poetry, fiction, and essays addressing black women's complicated identities in the wake of the Civil Rights movement. Leslie Marmon Silko, who is of mixed Laguna, Anglo, and Mexican descent and who was raised within the tribe at Laguna Pueblo, wrote her first novel during the 1970s, a period of reawakened activism for American Indian self-determination. Writing from these diverse positions, the four writers examine particular historical instances in which the denigration of women, African Americans, and Native Americans was grounded in their negative conflation with nature. I have focused upon examples of their writings that not only expose the costs of this negative affiliation but, more importantly, refigure social/natural interrelations in a manner that calls the premises of the dominant discourse into question. In order to challenge prevailing assumptions, the writers incorporate alternative conceptions of nature from highly diverse popular and indigenous traditions, such as sentimentalism, Voodoo, African-American animism, and Laguna Pueblo story cycles. I demonstrate that by reinscribing less polarized social/natural relations, the writers are consequently able to envision more complex and fluid conceptions of gender and race as well as more reciprocal formal relations between knower, words, and world. Their revisions shift the ground of national identity and offer us a more richly comprehensive mapping of America.

In order to convey the full import of their works, I situate the writers against the general context of American formulations of nature and society to which they respond. It has long been a truism that American identity has traditionally been formulated in terms of nature, and much cultural criticism and cultural history has been devoted to examining this conver-

nature
&
nation

gence between nature and nation. My study builds upon the previous work of many scholars, no one of whom examines this paradigm of nature's nation from my particular perspective but from whose findings I have gathered the many threads from which I have woven my position.

Literary critic Myra Jehlen comments in *American Incarnation* that unlike Europeans who believed themselves to be the product of history, Americans believed their new society to be an incarnation of natural law, sprung full-blown from the earth of the North American continent. While the precepts infusing American society were actually inherited from the Reformation and the Enlightenment, Americans took these principles to be an expression of the supposedly vacant land. Jehlen explains: "Americans saw themselves as building their civilization out of nature itself, as neither the analogue nor the translation of Natural Law, but its direct expression. Fusing the political with the natural, human volition with its object, and hope with destiny, they imagined an all-encompassing universe that in effect healed the lapsarian parting of man and his natural kingdom."[7]

But how was civilization to be built out of nature? As Americans fused the political with the natural, what sort of relation was enacted between new society and natural continent? The writers I discuss will assert that the American formulation of nation out of nature was actually a propriative paradigm in which all that is identified with the natural will be subsidiary. As a number of historians and cultural critics suggest, it was the *conquest* of the natural continent that was to be the fundamental ground of American identity, for through the *mastery* of the new land, European settlers recreated themselves as denizens of a new nation.[8] Cultural historians such as Perry Miller and Henry Nash Smith note that Americans conceived of the uniqueness of their national character as the result of their domestication of the vast wilds of the New World; having left behind the crowded civilizations of Europe for the reaches of America, settlers entered a vacant continent, a virgin land that offered them the space and natural resources to start afresh and fulfill their destiny to create a new civilization in the wilderness.[9] Within this conceptualization of nature's nation, nature was contradictorily construed as the very ground of nation and yet also the converse of human civilization, Roderick Nash explains in *Wilderness and American Mind*. On the one hand, nature was the abundant source of physical and economic sustenance that promoted the settlers' inhabitation of the new land. Yet during the onset of each wave of settlement, nature was, for the most part, viewed as the antithesis of civilization, as the threatening wilderness that must be tamed and transformed for progressive development to thrive. Leo Marx notes in *The Machine in the Garden* that not until civilization had been imposed upon the wild landscape and Euro-American methods of cultivation had transfigured much of the wild continent into a productive garden would nature be romanticized as the source of spiritual sustenance, the soul as it were, of the American republic. In a repeated cycle, progressive development led invariably to rampant despoliation of the natural world—such as clear-cutting of ancient forests, extermination of animal species and native plants, depletion and erosion of soils— prompting successive waves of westward movement in search of still-unspoiled, open and free land. Paradoxically, settlement inevitably de-stroyed the rich natural resources that had sustained it. Wild or undisturbed nature could only be valued in hindsight, note Nash and Marx, once the sprawl of civilization threatened it with extinction. In this contradictory manner, nature was conceived as the ground upon which the American nation rested; as resource and impediment, the natural continent would be refashioned to serve the needs of the new nation, and through this struggle to reshape the land, American men would redefine themselves as citizens of a new social order. In an essay elaborating his now-classic 1893 thesis formulating the crucial impact of the frontier in forming American charac-. ter, Frederick Jackson Turner eloquently imagined an impassioned ex-change between feminized land and male citizen:

> Into this vast shaggy continent of ours poured the first feeble tide of European settlement. European men, institutions, and ideas were lodged in the American wilderness, and this great American West took them to her bosom, taught them a new way of looking upon the destiny of the common man, trained them in adaptation to the conditions of the New World, to the creation of new institutions to meet new needs. . . . She opened new provinces and dowered new democracies in her most distant domains with her material treasures and with the ennobling influence that the fierce love of freedom, the strength that came from hewing out a home, making a school and a church, and creating a higher future for his family furnished to the pioneer.[10]

In this fashion, the conquest of the land came to be seen as the source of democracy; taming the land, American men would develop their unique political and social identities.

With the hindsight of an ecologically sensitive perspective, we may recognize the problematic views of nature inhering within the paradigm of nature's nation, a paradigm that the four writers I discuss will interrogate and challenge in differing ways. Clearly, nature was subsidiary to nation in the North American enterprise. Environmental historian Carolyn Merchant and cultural historian Frederick Turner both point out that the conquest imperative blended the biblical mandate to seize dominion of the lower orders of the natural world with the scientific-progressive vision of nature as the raw matter to be mastered and made productive by the active human will.[11] Christian settlers must "plant, possesse and subdue" the virgin territories of America because God did "create lande, to the end that it shold by Culture and husbandrie, yeeld things necessary for man's life," claimed Sir George Peckham, a backer of one of the first English forays to the New Land in 1583, whom Turner quotes in *Beyond Geography*.[12] By establishing dominion, the Euro-American white male settler proclaimed himself separate from and superior to the natural order. Arguably, the Puritan's ordained mission to transform the heathenish wilderness into the Lord's garden without falling prey to the lures of the physical world set the pattern for settlers' alienated manipulation of the natural terrain. In *Errand into the Wilderness*, Perry Miller describes the Puritans' willed detachment from their natural surroundings: "A society dispatched upon an errand . . . could go forth to possess a land without ever becoming possessed by it."[13] Turner extends Miller's formulation, arguing that Euro-Americans' stance of "estrangement" from the natural world required that they "take possession without being possessed . . . never to merge, to mingle, to marry" with the lands they came to inhabit.[14] Turner notes that Puritans imposed penalties on those who lived beyond the lines of settlement in the reaches of natural world, for fear that settlers would fall under nature's spell and go wild. For example, under Puritan law bestiality—a certain sort of "mingling" with the wilderness—was punishable by death, and Merchant documents that several men were executed for this crime during the early period of settlement.[15] Close attachment to nature violated the colonial mission and was proscribed God's minions in the new land.

In fact, estrangement was at the heart of the Euro-American epistemological model of human/natural relations. Merchant suggests that within the practices of national conquest, as within the new sciences, the human subject was believed to be essentially divided from his natural object; knowledge, will, and agency were attributed only to the human actors, and any claim of nature's active participation in this exchange was categorically denied. Nature was deemed knowable and controllable, mere spiritless matter subsidiary to human needs and desires. In this formulation of nature and national identity, Euro-Americans were sovereign subjects taking nature as the *natural* object of their expansionist desires.[16] Dickinson, Hurston, Walker, and Silko will point out the dangerous social consequences of this paradigm; the instrumental view of nature as what Silko terms a "dead thing" carries over into sexist and racist constructions of women, African Americans, and Native Americans.

A number of scholars have suggested that the ideology that endorsed the conquest of nature also held sway in the social sphere, where interrelations were often dictated by the project of colonization. European beliefs that women, Native Americans, and African Americans were more closely related to the lower animals and less civilized than men were often acted out in America yet were at the same time conveniently masked within the rhetoric of nature's nation. Feminist theorists in a range of disciplines have examined the predominant conflation of women with nature in European scientific, religious, and literary writings. In *The Death of Nature*, Merchant traces the conventional figurative feminization of nature in tropes such as regal Dame Nature, nurturant Mother Nature, or more negatively as an unpredictable and dangerous seductress. Christian doctrine, particularly Puritanism, had preached that women, as descendants of Eve, were ensnared within the fallen material realm of the natural world. Within the new mechanistic paradigms of the scientific revolution, the negative Baconian conception of nature as wanton female justified increasingly intrusive human control of natural phenomenon, Merchant notes.[17] Ludmilla Jordanova demonstrates in *Sexual Visions* that proponents of scientific advances frequently described interactions with nature in overtly sexual and violent imagery, envisioning human progress beyond natural conditions as a male struggle to subdue rampant women. She concludes that "human history, the growth of culture through the domination of nature, was represented as the increasing assertion of masculine ways over irrational, backward looking women."[18]

During the conquest of America, this metaphoric framework took on new life as male settlers called upon visions of the land-as-woman to legitimize their colonization of the continent. In her wittily titled *The Lay of the Land*, Annette Kolodny explains that this metaphor became literalized in the American ideology of the new nation born out of the womb of the natural continent: "What had by then degenerated into the dead conven-

tions of self-consciously 'literary' language . . . suddenly with the discovery
of America, became the vocabulary of everyday reality. . . . If the American
continent was to become the birthplace of a new culture and, with it, new
and improved human possibilities, then it was, in fact as well as in metaphor, a womb of generation and provider of sustenance. Hence, the heart
of American pastoral—the only pastoral in which metaphor and the patterns of daily activity refused to be separated."[19] From the time of early
exploration and settlement and on into the twentieth century, American
male writers consistently imagined themselves sensually gratified by entering a maternal and erotic landscape. Kolodny suggests that the symbolic
feminization of the land created a psychological bond between male settlers and this foreign and otherwise ominous new territory. But such imagery also masked the violence done to the continent by posing nature as
willing lover/mother whose overtures initiated conquest. For example, in
1632 Thomas Morton's "New English Canaan" described New England as
an eager virgin awaiting the marital embrace of her lover, the colonist:
"Like a faire virgin longing to be sped/and meete her lover in a Nuptiall
bed."[20] Similarly, Crèvecour's *Letters from an American Farmer*, written in the
following century, portrays nature as nurturant female spread wide before
the settlers: "Here nature opens her broad lap to receive the perpetual accession of new comers."[21] In these images, nature willingly opens herself
to the settlers, offering them free access to her private bodily territories.
But there are troubling overtones to this idyllic story. In this imagined encounter with nature, the pioneer protagonists are exclusively male, erasing
women's participation in the drama of nationhood, and, more ominously,
even though the relationship between male settler and nature-as-woman is
described in familial, nearly erotic terms, the pioneer's self-development is
predicated on his use and despoliation of nature, when, as Frederick Jackson Turner described above, he hews "out a home" upon her lush body.
Nature-as-woman fulfills the settler's every need but is progressively more
ravaged for the sake of his advancement. Kolodny concludes that because
civilization is predicated upon despoiling the wilderness and "laying waste
her fields of plenty," the male settler inevitably "rapes" and incestuously
"violates" the land-as-woman.[22]

The conflation of women and nature within this paradigm often boded
poorly for actual American women who, like nature, were generally subordinated to male mastery and denied the full rights and responsibilities of
citizenship. Construed as closer to nature than men, more immersed in the

bodily cycles of reproduction and mothering, women were, for the most part, believed to be lacking in the higher mental and spiritual powers through which men asserted themselves over the natural world and raised themselves beyond mere physical existence.[23] Believed to be deficient in such characteristics as rationality, political and social leadership, artistic genius, and spiritual authority, women were second-class citizens who were precluded from owning property, attaining higher education, participating actively in public life, or voting. American women were legal minors, virtual children, whose function in national development was comparable to that of the natural continent; women were to birth and nurture the men who would actively produce the nation. For example, Dickinson's poetry links nineteenth-century white women's secondary social status and domestic confinement to Puritan and Transcendentalist views of nature's subservience to the will of God and man. White middle- and upper-class women, like Dickinson, were to be policed from their carnal natures, safely ensconced in a domestic haven, away from the dangers of the exterior wild and public world. Lower-class white women, enslaved black women, and Native American women were viewed in various ways as improper, nonfeminine creatures naturally suited to brute labors and filled with carnal sexuality—with no means of transcending their animal physicality.

The imperative to conquer the virgin land had devastating consequences for Native Americans, whose ancestral lands were, of course, the very territories that settlers encroached upon in their advances upon the continent. Cultural historians Roy Harvey Pearce and Frederick Turner have traced the contrasting views of inhabitation underlying the conflicts between these peoples. They note that Euro-Americans grounded their claim to Indian lands in the divine mandate to spread Christendom to the New World by peopling the wilderness. God's plan for the New World obliged Christian settlers to work the land and convert the Indians. God would reward this Christian missionizing service with the rich territories of the new lands, wrote the Reverend Samuel Purchas in 1625: "All the rich endowments of Virginia, her Virgin-portion from the creation nothing lessened, are wages for all this worke; God in wisedome having enriched the Savage Countries, that those riches might be attractive to Christian suters."[24] In Purchas's self-serving logic, God had sagely placed the savages in the virgin land so that missionizing colonists might be richly recompensed in their quest to impose civilization upon nature and native inhabitants.

Pearce explains that, ironically, Euro-American claims to Indian lands rested on the belief that Indians lived in a "state of nature," ignorant of the divine law of Christian settlers that ordered man to take dominion over the land. Indians were savage heathens who wasted and misused the lands through nonintrusive hunting and farming practices, rather than subjecting the natural world to the European mode of clearing forests and applying intensive agricultural methods. Pioneers insisted that Indians selfishly squandered large territories that could easily sustain dense settlement. In 1629, John Winthrop lamented: "The whole earth is the Lord's garden, and he hath given it to the sons of Adam to be tilled and improved by them. Why then should we stand starving here for the places of habitation . . . and in the mean time suffer whole countries, as profitable for the use of man, to lie waste without any improvement." Even on into the nineteenth century, President Andrew Jackson used a similar argument to authorize the removal of the Cherokee and other tribes from Georgia. Indians must give ground before the advances of the nation: "What good man would prefer a country covered with forests and ranged by a few thousand savages to our extensive Republic, studded with cities, towns, and prosperous farms, embellished with all the improvements which art can devise or industry execute, occupied by more than 12,000,000 happy people, and filled with all the blessings of liberty, civilization, and religion?"[25]

Furthermore, because Indians failed to establish dominion over the natural world, Euro-Americans viewed them as subhuman beasts who blended into the landscape rather than lording over it. Repeatedly, in the literature and letters of the early colonial period, the Indians are negatively equated with wild animals. For example the sixteenth-century explorer Frobisher writes that northeastern Indians "live in caves of earth, and hunt for their dinners or praye, even as the beare or other wild beastes do." Writing in 1609, Richard Johnson describes the Indians of Virginia as "wild and savage people that live and lie up and downe in troupes like heards of Deere in a Forrest: they have no law but nature. . . . They have no Arts nor Sciences."[26] Frederick Turner notes that in the Euro-American perspective, only by distinguishing oneself from nature, only by establishing clear dominion, did one assume full human status. To live in a state of nature, was to live as an animal. Turner and Richard Slotkin have argued that such views gave settlers free reign to implement genocidal policies toward native inhabitants—to enslave them, forcibly remove them from ancestral lands, war against them, confine them to reservations, and eventually to exterminate vast populations—all in the name of God and civilization.[27] Silko's novels track the miseries of contemporary Indian reservation life and the sick consumerism poisoning mainstream culture back to the settlers' stories of nature and of native peoples as dead things to be feared and destroyed. In her fiction, the story of nature's nation is a form of witchery that poisons all within its reach.

African Americans, too, were ensnared within the establishment of nature's nation. In *White over Black*, historian Winthrop Jordan notes that the Euro-American seizure of Native American lands created vast farming territories and that, ironically, this very abundance of productive land spurred the colonists' participation in the slave trade; too few indentured white workers willingly remained in service on other men's land when the "vacant" continent was theirs for the taking. Thus, nature's nation required another source of captive workers, colonist Emmanuel Downing explained in 1645: "I doe not see how wee can thrive untill wee get into a stock of slaves sufficient to doe all our business, for our children's children will hardly see this great Continent filled with people, soe that our servant will still desire freedom to plante for themselves, and not stay but for verie great wagcs. And I suppose you know verie well how wee shall mayneteyne 20 Moores cheaper than one Englishe servant."[28] Enslaved Africans would provide the colonists with the inexpensive labor to grow the new cash crops, such as tobacco and cotton, that would reap profit from the wilderness.

Much the same way that colonization of Indians was justified by equating them with wild nature, Winthrop Jordan explains that enslavement of Africans was condoned through the view of them as a barbaric, debased form of humankind, more closely related to apes than to white fellow homo sapiens. Such supposedly hybrid, subhuman beasts could justifiably be captured, purchased, and transported to the West Indies and the Americas as perpetually enslaved workers.[29] In a dreadful cycle, the slave trade enforced this association of blacks with beasts; while suppositions of African bestiality and brute endurance served as justifications for black enslavement, the practices of slavery institutionalized this subhuman status, robbing Africans of legal and social identity and employing blacks as beasts of burden, thus further reinforcing this association of Negroes and animals in the minds of white slave owners. African slaves were legally termed *chattel personal*, or human cattle, and were treated as such. Like livestock, slaves were publicly displayed, oftentimes naked, for physical examination before being sold at auction. Like beasts of burden, they were forcibly worked at brutal physical labor, frequently whipped, beaten, maimed, and killed with no legal or social recourse.[30] Like farm stock, slaves were bred to produce additional *chattel personal* for the slave owner.[31] Like stock, slaves were sold away from kin, severing family relations. Slaves were collectively stripped of many of the Western signs of humanity, such as history, shared language and literacy, traditional religions, and common culture.[32] Even after abolition of slavery, the racial segregation of the South was still predicated upon the idea that subhuman Negroes were not fit to mix with whites in any situation that might imply social equality. Hurston's ethnography and fiction trace the negative colonial identification of black women with animals that predominated during the centuries of chattel slavery and that, even in the early decades of the twentieth century, still endorsed black women's miserable social station and their misuse as beasts of burden and sexual objects. Similarly, Walker's characters challenge the historical subterfuge through which racial inequities instituted during slavery continued to masquerade as natural facts within the racial divisions of the twentieth-century Jim Crow South.

How might we reinterpret women writers' inscriptions of nature against this historical backdrop? Two previous works of feminist scholarship have already begun this task. *Lay of the Land*, Kolodny's first study of gender and American pastoral, discussed above, argued that the paradigm of male settler embracing the land-as-woman imaginatively excluded American women from the drama of conquest. In her 1984 companion volume, *The Land before Her*, Kolodny turned her attention to women's writings about the American frontier. She concluded that these authors responded to their exclusion from the masculine paradigm by creating a more hospitable alternative image of the land-as-garden, an extension of domestic space: "Massive exploitation and alteration of the continent do not seem to have been a part of women's fantasies. They dreamed, more modestly, of locating a home and familial human community within a cultivated garden."[33] Vera Norwood's 1993 *Made from This Earth: American Women and Nature* extends the scope of Kolodny's project, analyzing American women's engagement in a wide range of naturalist pursuits. Acknowledging that nature study has primarily been considered a masculine domain, Norwood considers the influence of gender roles upon women's naturalist activities, some of which, such as flower painting, birdwatching, and gardening, were considered

[handwritten: critique of Norwood & Kolodny]

[handwritten: separate female tradition vs subversive (?)]

properly feminine, others of which, such as big game hunting and primate studies, challenged gender boundaries. In an all too brief chapter on women's fiction, Norwood also examines how racism complicates African-American and Native American women's treatment of nature. She argues that the prevailing negative stereotypes depicting them as animals may have made it more difficult for women of color to claim a positive identification with nature but that their fiction challenges these negative portrayals and reimagines powerfully subversive bonds to nature.[34] While both she and Kolodny argue for what Norwood calls a "distinctly female tradition in American nature study,"[35] they believe that women's treatment of nature is largely influenced by their exclusion from the dominant masculinist tradition and by prevailing gender roles rather than by any essential female response to nature.

While I find Kolodny and Norwood's formulations of a women's tradition convincing, I view the women's writings under discussion in my book not so much as a separate tradition, a safe haven within a hostile world, but as a powerfully dialogical intercultural altercation in which the women talk back to the dominant culture from the position of those taken as the ground of nation, voicing cultural perspectives counter to the prevailing mythos. While numerous men have also penned objections to the dominant American stance toward nature, canonical white male nature writers such as Henry David Thoreau, John Muir, and Edward Abbey have generally been less cognizant of the social repercussions that this framework has had upon those persons deemed nature incarnate, and they occasionally unwittingly rely upon the rhetoric of nature's nation even as they rail against the appropriative vision of nature.[36] In contrast, the four women writers under discussion here make clear that the appropriative view of nature also endorses gender and racial oppressions. Once they have exposed the mechanisms through which these social hierarchies are naturalized, the women writers "turn over" this paradigm by incorporating alternative models of social/natural relations from the very cultures that the dominant discourse has served to marginalize. While the authors write as women and people of color, they do so in order to question the very premises through which gender and race have been defined in America. Thus, if we view these writings as a separate female tradition, we may diminish the force of their challenges. But when we recontextualize them against the dominant paradigm, their subversive intent resounds clearly.

Dickinson, Hurston, Walker, and Silko emphasize that the equation

of women and people of color with lower nature translated the American
conquest of the natural continent into analogous hierarchic social relations
of gender and race through which women, particularly women of color,
were similarly construed as social objects rather than as full and independent persons. I have found in the fledgling fields of ecocritical and ecofeminist theory a general framework for analyzing the conjunctions between
cultural conceptions of nature and social categories that I find operating in
the women's literary texts. Spurred by current ecological crises and concerns, ecocritics examine what Larry Buell has called the "environmental
imagination," tracing literary inscriptions of human relationships to the encompassing natural world in the hopes that such analysis might aid us in
reframing our position within an increasingly fragile natural environment.[37]
Ecofeminists working in a variety of disciplines argue that the treatment
of nature is always, in fact, deeply entangled with other social issues and
power relations. They suggest that in a mutually reinforcing cycle, attitudes
toward nature are colored by social beliefs, and social relations are justified
through conceptions about humans' position within the natural order.[38]
While the particulars of these intersections vary widely in differing cultures
and in differing historical instances, philosopher Val Plumwood explains
the general dynamic through which the prevailing Western stance of mastery of nature might translate into subordination of those persons deemed
most immersed in the natural sphere:

> The category of nature is a field of multiple exclusion and control,
> not only of non-humans, but of various groups of humans and as-
> pects of human life which are cast as nature. Thus racism, colonial-
> ism and sexism have drawn their conceptual strength from casting
> sexual, racial and ethnic difference as closer to the animal and the
> body construed as a sphere of inferiority, as a lesser form of human-
> ity lacking the full measure of rationality or culture. . . .
>
> To be defined as "nature" in this context is to be defined as pas-
> sive, as non-agent and non-subject, as the "environment" or in-
> visible background conditions against which the "foreground"
> achievements of reason or culture (provided typically by the white,
> western, male expert or entrepreneur) takes place. It is to be defined
> as *terra nullius*, a resource empty of its own purposes or meanings,
> and hence available to be annexed for the purposes of those sup-
> posedly identified with reason or intellect, and to be conceived and

moulded in relation to these purposes. It means being seen as part of a sharply separate, even alien lower realm, whose domination is simply "natural," flowing from nature itself and the nature(s) of things.[39]

Plumwood and a number of other ecofeminists argue that Western social hierarchies are often grounded in this Platonic model of unequal binarisms. Within this paradigm, paired terms are defined in opposition to each other, with one term elevated over and against the other, which is relegated to the negative status of empty background for the primary term. When nature is viewed in this manner as the "terra nullius," or empty background for culture, as a passive resource for human domination, those persons equated with nature may analogously be treated as natural inferiors, and ensuing inequitable and divisive social interrelations may be cast as natural rather than humanly created, as inevitable rather than open to question and reform. Thus Donna Haraway, a feminist theorist of science, concludes: "Constructions of nature (are) a crucial cultural process for people who need and hope to live in a world less riddled by the dominations of race, colonialism, class, gender and sexuality."[40] Throughout this book, I draw upon the premises of ecofeminist theory as a fruitful framework for explaining the social import of women writers' inscriptions of nature.

Although their concerns vary, the writers understand prevailing forms of social oppression to be a legacy of conquest, reinforced through the continuing negative identification of certain groups of people with nature. Dickinson's poetry links the highly regimented Victorian gender segregation that confined white women within the strictly domestic sphere to the appropriative mastery of nature-as-woman. Hurston's *Tell My Horse* and *Their Eyes Were Watching God* trace the abject poverty and sexual abuse suffered by Afro-Caribbean and African-American women back to the colonial denigration of them as "donkeys" fit only to serve as beasts of burden. In *Meridian*, Walker argues that black mothers' desperate attempts to raise their children within the savage inequalities of the Jim Crow South result from their treatment as "chattel personal," or self-reproducing property, during the reign of slavery. Silko suggests in *Ceremony* that the alienation, alcoholism, and cultural loss that her Laguna characters undergo is the cumulative effect of centuries of dispossession from the lands that had sustained their tribe. In her more recent dystopian epic, *Almanac of the Dead*, numerous devastating contemporary problems are shown to be rooted in the Conquistadors' brutal destruction of all those they considered to be natural object of their consumptive lust. Understanding that these damaging formations of race and gender are rooted in the conquest of the continent, the writers begin to denaturalize prevailing social stratifications by reinscribing alternative, nonpolarized interrelations between human and natural world.

In order to accomplish this revision, each of the writers incorporates an alternative conception of society/nature that she reclaims from a marginalized popular or indigenous tradition. Dickinson playfully adopts the positive feminization of nature from Victorian women's sentimentalism. As an ethnographer, Hurston discovers the subversive sacralization of nature and black women's bodies within Afro-Caribbean Voodoo religion. Walker finds images of human/natural collectivity within Native American and African-American animistic spirituality. Silko's novels build upon Laguna Pueblo story cycles of human kinship with natural entities. While the traditions that the writers employ operate variously, each replaces the paradigmatic conquest of nature with a version of what Haraway terms "social/natural co-construction" in which human and nature are both viewed as actors whose mutual interactions produce the world as we know it:

> Historically specific human relations with "nature" must somehow—linguistically, ethically, scientifically, politically, technologically, and epistemologically—be imagined as genuinely social and actively relational; and yet the partners remain utterly unhomogenous. . . . Curiously, as for people who came before us in Western discourses, efforts to come to linguistic terms with the nonrepresentability, historical contingency, artifactuality and yet spontaneity, necessity, fragility and stunning profusions of "nature" can help us refigure the kind of persons we might be. These persons can no longer be, if they ever were, master subjects, nor alienated subjects, but—just possibly—multiply heterogeneous, inhomogeneous, accountable and connected human agents.[41]

She suggests that we might begin this process of reconceptualization by figuring nature as "coyote," a playful "coding trickster" with whom we must learn to "converse," and by reimagining human knowers as monstrous "cyborgs"—part human, part machine, part animal amalgams—who defy traditional polarities and who embrace the "partiality" and "situatedness" of all knowledge claims.[42] Haraway's alternative paradigms replace the predominant bifurcation of subject and object, self and other, human and nature, with a mode of relationality in which all entities are understood to impinge upon each other. In such alternative systems, the conquest model of hierarchic division and domination is replaced with more slippery and shifting identifications across difference, as well as with "cyborgian" hybridity based upon the interpenetration of supposed oppositions.

In this vein, Dickinson, Hurston, Walker and Silko utilize "monstrous" reconfigurations of nature in order to replace the model of conquest and domination with more interactive and egalitarian social/natural relations. In various manners each of the writers represents a form of human/natural amalgamation and collectivity that defies the appropriative bifurcation of subject and object inhering in the conquest paradigm. Through these reconstructions of nature, the writers emphasize the constructedness and the destructiveness of that paradigm; the story of nature's nation is only one story among many, but it is a story that has wrought deadly consequences for all that has been despised as merely natural. Yet, the writers insist, once we realize the fictiveness of this paradigm, we are freed to replace the mythos of forced dominion with other, more mutually enlivening stories of social/natural relations.

Crucially, the writers illustrate the ways that such reciprocating interrelations between human and nature promote the construction of more fluid and shifting racial and gender identities and encourage belief in transformative possibility and social movement rather than static and unequal divisions. Through alternative inscriptions of nature, the writers' speakers and characters transform themselves from social objects to expansive, active subjects who develop self-determined identifies and who institute personal and political change: Dickinson's identification with nature's mysterious female powers fuels her heterodox defiance of the constrictions of Victorian decorum; the Voodoo-derived pear-tree vision of marriage in Hurston's *Their Eyes Were Watching God* inspires Janie to resist being treated as "the mule of the world"; Meridian's legacy of African-American and Native American animistic collectivity provides Walker's character the vision and determination to bodily defy the racial divisions of Jim Crow segregation; Silko's Tayo reconstructs Laguna stories about the kinship between human and nature as a means of halting the destructive animosity between whites and natives that is decimating his world. Thus, in reimagining nature, these writers shift the ground of colonialist assumptions and cultivate more complex, fluid, and egalitarian social identities.

writing
style as
subversive

Furthermore, the writers' formal innovations may also be interpreted as an aspect of their interrogation and revision of colonial modes of mastery. In each case, the writer eschews the traditional realist model of a masterful subject describing a fixed, passive, and transparent natural object in favor of formal strategies that promote partiality, movement, and an interactive identification of narrator with nature. The writers' techniques emphasize the artful constructedness of their stories and foreground their belief that human/natural relations should be reconstructed. They illustrate how Other stories perform other modes of interrelation, and in this way they once again shift the ground of conquest, textually cultivating the possibilities of positive change.

In chapter 1, I argue that Emily Dickinson complicates the predominant American relation to nature by questioning the certitudes of Puritan typology and challenging the Emersonian view of nature as the feminized "not me," or transparent screen, through which the male poet knows the truth of God. Dickinson insists that nature, language, and gender are much more complex than that, and her poetry demonstrates these elusive and shifting relations. Emphasizing the slippery possibilities of language through the nonlinear movements of her infamous gaps, elisions, equivocations and contradictions, Dickinson writes of nature as unknowably mysterious, wilder and more variable than human comprehension would permit. Dickinson represents nature as an omnipotent female figure who defies human mastery and overturns realist doctrines of nature's passive submission to men's control. Redeploying the standard sentimental association of women and nature, Dickinson presents a fluid mutual identification of female speaker with feminized Nature, and thus, in describing Nature's rich elusiveness, she also argues that actual women exceed the limits of Victorian gender roles. Dickinson's nature poetry enacts the "conversational" relationship with nature as "witty actor" proposed by current feminist theorists of science, Donna Haraway and Evelyn Fox Keller.

Chapter 2 explores Zora Neale Hurston's revisions of the colonial representation of black women as animals. I argue that *Tell My Horse*, her critically neglected ethnographic study of Caribbean culture and religion, reveals Hurston's contradictory position as an authoritative black woman observing a society in which black women are treated as "donkeys," sexual objects, and beasts of burden. Hurston's bitterly ironic and exaggerated use of natural tropes to describe these women makes clear the harsh effects of this negative identification of black women with lower nature. In contrast,

Hurston describes Afro-Caribbean Voodoo spirituality as offering a more unbounded concept of gender and race, based upon a worship of nature as an interpenetration of opposites that is analogous to Haraway's notion of cyborgian intermixed polarities. I suggest that the same dynamic structures *Their Eyes Were Watching God*, in which Janie escapes her society's view of black women as "mules of the world" through Voodoo-like visions of the pear tree and the hurricane as fecund and overpowering convergences of supposed oppositions.

In chapter 3, I suggest that Alice Walker—a late twentieth-century writer who has participated in numerous social movements such as civil rights, feminism, American Indian rights, and ecology—turns the revision of nature, gender, and race that she finds in the work of her proclaimed foremother Hurston toward direct political contest and social reform. In *Meridian*, Walker transposes the individual black woman's quest for self-possession that Hurston had described in *Their Eyes* into the collective social struggles of the civil rights movement. In Walker's novel the southern landscape is a burial ground of the Native American and African-American cultures decimated by the dominant society. Meridian comes to question the god-given authority of the racist southern order when she exhumes alternative histories and spiritual traditions from two historically marked natural sites, the Sacred Serpent mound and the Sojourner tree. She uncovers animistic visions of human/natural collectivity and kinship that contest the unequal racial divisions of the Jim Crow South. Through acts of civil disobedience, Meridian defies these false boundaries and transforms herself from social object to political objector.

Chapter 4 discusses Leslie Marmon Silko, a writer of partial Native American descent, who uses Laguna Pueblo storytelling and spiritual traditions to reframe the history of the European conquest of America. In her first novel, *Ceremony*, Silko reinterprets what cultural historian Slotkin has called the "fatal opposition" between Native Americans and European settlers as a battle between contrasting "stories" of human relations to nature; the Laguna story of reciprocal kinship between tribe and nature has been besieged by the fatal European story of division and domination. Tayo begins to heal the ills of the ravaged land and the displaced native inhabitants through a ceremonial reconstruction of traditional stories that reassert the spiritual union of tribe and natural world. In her recent novel, *The Almanac of the Dead*, Silko expands this complex circuit of story, history, and nature as the piecing together of fragments of an ancient Indian almanac foments an undeclared war for the American continents, waged between dispossessed and indigenous peoples and their European-derived conquerors. The uprising hinges upon opposing conceptions of nature; the native view of nature as a living, inspirited entity battles the European conception of the world as a dead resource for consumption.

Dickinson, Hurston, Walker, and Silko show us the vested and fearsome power of our dominant mythologies. They remind us that the story of nature's nation is a flawed and dangerous tale and that the social configurations that we perceive as only natural are culturally created and forcibly maintained. Although the dominant culture has done its best to silence and suppress minority cultures, the writers remind us that those voices have continued to murmur and roar, transmitting other stories that counter the words of the masters. When we recontextualize the works of these four authors against the backdrop of the rhetoric of nature's nation, we can reinterpret their representations of nature as instances of bold intercultural conflict in which indigenous and popular cultures subvert the assumptions of hegemonic ideology and prove to us that alternative mythologies could offer us other, less violent social/natural geographies. Such revisions of nature encourage us to imagine and institute more egalitarian and life-sustaining social identities and geographic interrelations. The writers offer us a sense of the more hopeful possibilities that could be achieved through a courageous reimagining of the nature of our identities and of the social/ natural world that our stories spark into existence.

1

Nature Is a Haunted House: Emily Dickinson's Reconstruction of Nature and Gender

> Too often, constructionists presume that the category of the social automatically escapes essentialism, in contradistinction to the way the category of the natural is presupposed to be inevitably trapped within it. But there is no compelling reason to assume that the natural is, in essence, essentialist and that the social is, in essence, constructionist. —*Diana Fuss*

> Nature is a Haunted House—but Art—a house that tries to be haunted. —*Emily Dickinson*

RESIDING IN AMHERST, Massachusetts, a stronghold of patriarchal Puritanism, caught within the strictly domestic sphere allotted to women in the Victorian age, Emily Dickinson produced the most dramatically experimental poetry of the nineteenth century. In her nature poetry Dickinson addresses this tension between containment and rebellion by drawing upon the sentimental trope of "nature's house," which poses nature as a feminized domestic realm, only in order to undermine the very premises of Victorian propriety. For Dickinson cannily employs sentimental discourse in order to demonstrate that nature's house is a *man-made* cultural conception, built, rather than natural, which produces unfortunate social consequences for women and nature. Dickinson's nature poetry strategically rebuilds nature's house, subversively rewriting feminized nature as an omnipotent, powerful, defiantly playful and uncontainably

romanticized domestication

mysterious subject in her own right, rather than man's servant and God's minion. In Dickinson's trope, nature is a haunted house, possessed of supernatural and disturbing presences that elude masculine control and defy the conventional conception of the domestic as a safe space within the public order. Moreover, by taking the conventional association of women and nature to its logical conclusion, Dickinson is then able to claim nature's defiantly expansive qualities for women. Dickinson's formally innovative verse also rebuilds the formal relations between writer and nature, rearticulating knowledge, authorship, and gender as nonpolarized, shifting interactions between mutually participating partners.

Dickinson wrote within the context of the nineteenth-century domestication of the eastern American landscape and the related domestication of middle- and upper-class white women. By the early 1800s, the lands of New England had been transformed from the original Puritans' image of the region as a wilderness inhabited by savages into a landscape composed primarily of domesticated farmlands and woodlands inhabited predominantly by Euro-Americans. In the writings of the era this landscape was most frequently conceptualized as a tranquil garden, as nature under cultivation and in the service of civilization, even as an endangered Eden threatened by the incursions of industrialization.[1] Now that the wilds had been transformed into a more human-centered landscape and the native inhabitants had largely been displaced from the region or confined to reservations, a tamed nature could be idealized, and in the case of the wilderness and wildness of the western frontier romanticized from afar.

Certain American women were subjected to a similar process of romanticized domestication. Carolyn Merchant explains that as New England agriculture became consolidated and technologically advanced during the 1800s, middle-class women were more and more removed from outdoor farm labor and relegated to domestic tasks, thus effectively severing them from their former working relationship with the land.[2] As the natural landscape was increasingly placed under cultivation, so too, argues Vera Norwood, middle- and upper-class white women were more deeply enclosed within the domestic space of home and garden mandated by Victorian gender ideology. Paradoxically, because they were viewed as innately closer to nature, proper Victorian women were believed to need more protection from the wilds of the landscape, which might tempt them into untoward, unladylike behavior. Norwood notes: "Since the Victorian period, Euro-

American women's confinement to the landscape of home has been symbolic of their 'nature.' Biological models of women's reproductive functions
have been used to tie them more closely to animals and 'explain' their perceived lack of rationality and heightened emotionalism. Women's dangerous links to nature seemingly justified bounding middle class females within
the domestic sphere."[3]

While Victorian ladies were excluded from most sorts of encounters
with the wilder aspects of the American landscape, they were encouraged
in tamer naturalist pursuits such as gardening, botanizing, flower painting,
and sentimental nature writing—all of which positioned them as caretakers
or teachers of nature's moral lessons.[4] For example, the Puritan-derived
"natural theology" that permeated Dickinson's scientific education asserted
that natural systems could safely be studied as evidence of God's teleologi-
cal design writ large upon the natural world. Edward Hitchcock, the fore-
most natural theologian at Amherst College, who blended geology with
religious thought, believed that natural phenomena "teach many a moral
lesson with great clearness and force."[5] Women were thus expected to use
their naturalist pursuits in order to promote a greater social morality. Dickinson herself was grounded in scientific theology and pursued the approved
feminine study of horticulture, keeping a greenhouse and extensive garden,
whose flowers and produce were regularly shared with friends and neigh-
bors, yet her poetry rails against the assumption that nature is subject to
divine control and scientific scrutiny.[6]

As nature was assumed to be a source of moral teaching, so Victorian
women's *natural* sphere was defined as that of moral virtue, caretaking and
service, thus precluding most forms of public activity. Cynthia Griffin
Wolff notes: "Mid-nineteenth-century America offered women few oppor-
tunities to reap the full rewards of a 'successful' life. They might have marriage and children. However, membership in the larger community was
severely limited. They could not vote; under many circumstances they
could not even hold property in their own right. The arena allowed to a
woman for the exercise of her talents was mostly defined by the domestic
sphere. . . . The public code of dress for females—floor length skirts and
inflexible corsets—is probably a telling index of the freedom and encouragement they were given."[7]

Women's talents and desires were to be directed toward service to others, toward domestic nurturance, toward moral service. Joanne Dobson

amplifies: "The cultural ideology of respectable womanhood in mid-nineteenth-century American was structured on the assumption of women's innate and unique morality. It defined ideal feminine morality in large part as altruism, selflessness and reticence."[8]

Victorian womanhood entailed, in Adrienne Rich's image, a "corsetted" life, circumscribing not only a woman's actions but also her verbal expression; sexual passion, personal anger, worldly aspiration, intellectual and theological authority were all considered to be outside of women's proper concern.[9] There was, then, no acceptable nineteenth-century public discourse for women beyond the sentimental discourse of virtue and domesticity, and so it is this discourse that Dickinson's nature poetry strategically employs in order to revise the very premises underlying Victorian codes of female confinement.

In much of her apparently sentimental nature poetry, Dickinson wields the standard generic identification of women and nature in order to rewrite the exclusion of women from positions of public power and their relegation to the subsidiary domestic realm. In *Sensational Designs*, Jane Tompkins suggests that sentimental discourse performs the "cultural work" of inscribing pertinent social issues in images and types readily accessible to the general reading public.[10] While Dickinson uses sentimental discourse in order to sanction her authorial power, she then proceeds to dismantle the sentimental framework from within, by taking common tropes to their logical conclusion in such a way as to endorse female voice and female creative primacy, thus rebuilding nature's house into a structure much more hospitable to both nature and women. Similarly, Dickinson's formal experiments begin with common hymn form, only to radically challenge verse conventions, thereby discovering more fluid and mutual relations between knower and nature.

As a woman writing lyric nature poetry that expressed passion, intellect, and heterodox theological assertions, Dickinson undertook a traditionally masculine enterprise.[11] Her nature poetry addresses and undermines the prevailing masculinist assumptions about women and nature espoused by the Romantic and Transcendentalist writers and by Puritan theologians of her day. While numerous feminist critics have discussed Dickinson's problematic relationship to her male predecessors and contemporaries, many of these critics overlook the full extent of Dickinson's challenges to such traditions. They read her nature poetry as seeking, and failing to gain, entry to this exclusively male domain, whereas the poems under discussion here defiantly subvert realist readings of nature and gender.[12]

It has been widely argued that realist nature writing, including Romantic and Transcendentalist literature as well as Puritan typology, is inherently gendered. Such writings assume a male speaking subject and a female object of discourse, and further assume a hierarchical relationship between this subject and object in which the masculine subject appropriates the feminine object to his own purposes. Margaret Homans argues that Western literary tradition, beginning with Genesis, assumes an Adamic male speaker and namer whose "words have a portion of God's own verbal powers, whereby words create the things they name." She explains that Romantic poets such as William Wordsworth and, particularly, the Transcendentalist essayist and poet Ralph Waldo Emerson believe writing to be a form of Adamic naming of the world. For Emerson, "the poet is the sayer, the namer and represents beauty. He is sovereign and stands on the center . . . emperor in his own right." According to this view, poetry is a gendered enterprise; the speaker is male and his words reenact God's Logos that named the world into existence.[13]

The relationship between poet and nature is a gendered, at times even sexualized, relationship.[14] Homans notes that Emerson calls the bond between words and the natural objects "a marriage." This marriage is, as Homans explains, an appropriative relationship, wherein nature is subsumed by masculine desire and will: "This use of nature as the ground for human meaning is also propriative . . . because it subjects nature to human usage and denies it separate identity." Where Emerson envisions the speaker as male sovereign, he imagines nature as his servant. He writes: "Nature is thoroughly mediate. It is made to serve. It offers all its kingdoms to man as the raw material he may mould into what is useful. . . . More and more, with every thought does his kingdom stretch over all things, until the world becomes, at last, only a realized will." Throughout such writings, nature is represented as Other to the masculine self: nature does not exist in its own right and for its own purposes but acts solely as the mirror in which the male speaking subject sees himself writ large. In Emerson's dualist system, nature exists as the "not me" that serves to delimit human subjectivity, or the "me." Woman and nature exist only as objects of the poet's vision, as Homans explains: "When Mother Nature and other feminine figures are objectified as the Other, they may then be possessed or become the property of the subject. Explicitly linking the two sexually charged aspects of literary tradition above, language and the theme of nature, appropriation is the relationship between the self-centered Romantic speaker or poet and the feminine objects about which he writes."[15]

Not only is this relationship propriative, but such an epistemological model further assumes that nature is transparently decipherable and ontologically penetrable. In the emblematic system of interpretation that Emerson describes in the essay "Nature," nature in general and particular embodies unchanging human ideas which the poet retrieves through attentive perception and which he then conveys in his writing. Emerson explains the system of mirroring through which nature symbolizes human truths: "The world is emblematic. Parts of speech are metaphors because the whole of nature is a metaphor of the human mind. The laws of moral nature answer to matter as face to face in a glass." In this system, nature is the transparent medium transmitting fixed spiritual truths that the poet condenses into transparent language, as Emerson describes: "The universe becomes transparent, and the light of higher laws than its own shines through it." Attending to these "higher laws" believed manifest in natural phenomena, Emerson's poet claims to discern and voice the patterns of God's transcendent design: "This relation between the mind and matter is not fancied by some poet, but stands in the will of God."[16] Thus for Emerson nature exists as a divinely determined system of emblematic signs through which the male poet reads God's moral laws.

Emerson confidently proclaims the poet's role as definitive interpreter of nature in "The Apology," a poem describing nature as a series of "words," "letters," "thoughts," and "histories" that the poet will "gather in a song":

> I go to the god of the wood
>   To fetch his word to men.
>
> Tax not my sloth that I
>   Fold my arms beside the brook;
> Each cloud that floated in the sky
>   Writes a letter in my book.
>
> Chide me not, laborious band,
>   For the idle flowers I brought;

Every aster in my hand
    Goes home loaded with a thought.

There was never mystery
    But 'tis figured in the flowers;
Was never secret history
    but birds tell it in the bowers.

One harvest from thy field
    homeward brought the oxen strong;
A second crop thine acres yield,
    Which I gather in a song.[17]

While "nature" is often feminized in Emerson's essays, the natural phenomena in this poem, such as woods, clouds, and asters, are not explicitly gendered, although the poet-speaker is assuredly male, fetching to fellow men the word of the masculinized god of the woods.[18] More important is the speaker's confident equation of nature with human language and interpretive systems and his role as "harvester" of nature's messages; eternal transcendent meanings are conveyed from god to man through natural phenomena and are translated directly into language through the poet's perceptions. Certainty, constancy, and transparency of both nature and language are presumed by the male speaker in Emerson's "Apology." Dickinson's nature poetry will undermine such confident masculine authority, emphasizing instead the multiplicitous complexities of both nature and language.

As a writer of religious nature poetry, Dickinson also addressed an additional system of realist readings of nature, the Puritan tradition of allegorical typology, wherein natural phenomena are read as emblems of transcendent biblical truths. Jonathan Edwards, leader of the eighteenth-century Puritan revival called the Great Awakening, developed a system of Christian typology that equated natural phenomena with fixed religious meaning. In "Images or Shadows of Divine Things" he argues that the physical world mirrors divine images and lists material phenomena and their proper interpretations. For example, Edwards believes that hills and mountains signify heaven, rivers symbolize the "endless goodness of God," ravens represent "devils who prey on the dead," serpents are emblem of the "devil snaring us," and the sun equals "God's bounty and goodness."[19] In this allegorical system natural phenomena are subordinated to the transcendent meanings they bear, and while nature is not always explicitly represented as feminine, the transcendent Will that infuses nature is gendered male, and the theological authority who reads nature as text is also male. Puritans believed women to be secondary and sinful, while men authoritatively interpreted and disseminated God's inspiration. Puritan typology is explicitly dualistic, dividing the fallen, material world from the transcendent spiritual realm and associating women with the former and men with the latter. The physical world, including nature, is scorned as the realm of sin and temptation that believers should mistrust, fear, and deny for the sake of eternal salvation.

While many realist novelists were of course women (oft-times publishing under male pseudonyms in order to preserve tradition and female propriety), this literary model is inherently problematic for the woman writer, as Homans argues; its very premises deprive her of the powers of speech and language, because her gender is equated with passivity and silence. In such a model, women supposedly exist only as silent Other, as "not me," as passive nature awaiting the poet's mastery and desire.[20]

Dickinson's nature poetry challenges the realist appropriation of nature and women in several ways. First, Dickinson refashions the traditional trope of nature-as-woman into an image of omnipotent and self-possessed female power that will sanction Dickinson's own transgressive literary creations. Through this figure Dickinson rewrites the reaches of nature as female space and positions woman as the privileged nature poet, thus undermining the Victorian ideology of female subordination and separate gender spheres. While these figures have been read even by most feminist critics as merely sentimental, they are also polemical reappropriations that revise the standard trope of nature-as-woman to argue against the confines of gender ideology and to resist the forced domestication and destruction of nature.

Furthermore, through her playful exaggerations of this standard trope, Dickinson exposes the constructedness of gender and reality and thus gains the freedom to reimagine and reconstruct both. Clearly, Dickinson disbelieves interpretations of nature that confuse human inscription with intrinsic message, and much of her writing programmatically denaturalizes such readings. Thus, while her frequent use of the standard feminization of nature may appear merely traditional, it is instead consciously deployed, as a figurative construct that enables her to interrogate the way nature has been made to ground social formations of gender and to rewrite the relations between gender, nature, and knowledge. As Margaret Homans notes: "Dickinson is not taking Mother Nature to be a personification of nature, but a figure imported from tradition. . . . The concept of Mother Nature is only a fiction among other fictions."[21] Yet it is for Dickinson an empowering fiction; as she rewrites nature-as-woman, she emphasizes the writtenness, rather than the naturalness, of the trope, even while she utilizes it to refigure gender, nature, writing, and epistemology. Dickinson's interrogation and refiguration of the trope nature-as-woman is a circular and mutually reinforcing system: her denaturalization of prevailing views provides her the freedom to reimagine other configurations of gender, nature and art; and her refigurations of nature-as-woman further challenge the cultural assumptions that masquerade as natural truths. Too often she is read as literal when she is being slyly polemic.

Through her formal experimentation, Dickinson also rewrites prevailing assumptions about the literary relation between human and nature. Her radical style challenges prevailing realist certainty about the knowability of nature and undermines the standard duality between human authorial subject and natural object. Dickinson's language trades realist certainty for open-ended possibilities. Christanne Miller describes Dickinson's formal strategies: "The poet's metaphors and extended analogies, her peculiar brevity, lack of normal punctuation, irregular manipulation of grammar, syntax and word combination all invite multiple, nonreferential interpretations of what she means. . . . All of these transformations or disruptions of what is normally expected in language work toward creating multiplicity of meaning and an indeterminate reference, two characteristics that open questions of meaning but frustrate the referential or informative communication most language provides."[22] As Miller notes, Dickinson's poetics thwart realist desires to fix meaning and limit interpretative movement of poems. Her stylistic experimentation emphasizes nonlinear progression; multiple and contradictory possibilities of meaning; confusion of subject and object, self and other. Some of her stylistic techniques include omission and irrecoverable deletions of syntactic and logical connections between parts of poems; disjunctive connections between phrases and stanzas; compression of language; dense metaphors and highly associative words; syntactic doubling, or phrases that may function twice, creating links between disparate things or between subject and object, or self and other; contradiction and numerous variant editions of poems. This poetics produces a multiple yet uncertain sense that subverts the realist epistemology in which an autonomous subject objectively determines the meaning of his object.[23]

Rather than the realist paradigm of a subject separated from his object, discovering a set transcendent reading of nature, Dickinson's poetics emphasizes the complex interdependence of knower and nature and the active yet indeterminate production of meaning. Her poetic forms prefigure Donna Haraway's and Evelyn Fox Keller's calls for feminist or dynamic objectivity which is located, partial, and which acknowledges the mutual production of subject and object. Haraway describes this form of objectivity: "Feminist objectivity is about limited location and situated knowledge, not about transcendence and splitting of subject and object. In this way we might become answerable for what we learn how to see." Keller amplifies: "Dynamic objectivity aims at a form of knowledge that grants to the world around us its independent integrity, but does so in a way that remains cognizant of, indeed relies on, our connectivity with that world." She explains how such objectivity might alter our views of nature: "I am suggesting that questions asked about objects with which one feels kinship are likely to differ from questions asked about objects one sees as unalterably alien. Similarly, explanations that satisfy us about a natural world that is seen as 'blind, simple, dumb' ontologically inferior, may seem less self-evidently satisfying for a natural world seen as complex and, itself, resourceful."[24]

Dickinson's poetics enact this located, interactive, non-transcendent epistemological model. Her techniques also invite, if not demand, this same interactive relationship between text and reader in which meaning is mutually produced, rather than given, and changeable and cumulative, rather than reductive and static: "Dickinson is a poet of 'consent,' of the shifting transformation rather than the authoritative establishment of meaning."[25]

Dickinson's "Four Trees" offers a clear example of her radical departure from realist readings of nature such as Emerson's "Apology" or Edwards's typology, which claim transcendent, fixed, and knowable truth. Dickinson emphasizes instead the lack of given meaning, the view that nature bears no single correct message, and that any reading of nature is therefore a human construction:

Four Trees—upon a solitary Acre—
   Without Design
   Or Order, or Apparent Action—
   Maintain—

The Sun—upon a Morning meets them—
   The Wind—
   No nearer Neighbor—have they—
   But God—

The Acre gives them—Place—
   They—Him—Attention of Passer by—
   Of Shadow, or of Squirrel, haply—
   Or Boy—

What Deed is Theirs unto the General nature—
   What Plan—
   They severally—retard—or further—
   Unknown—(742)

The poem declares the absence of definititive interpretations of natural phenomena and rejects recourse to transcendent designs. Relationships between particular material beings and the "plan" or "General nature" remain unknown, undermining typological, transcendentalist visions of nature. The poem stylistically performs the absence of ontological interconnection; the abrupt brokenness of phrases marked by equivocal dashes rather than clearly directive punctuation or connective words formally enacts the indeterminate relations between God, sun, trees, wind, boys, and acre in the absence of some overarching plan. The formal fragmentation of the poem and the syntactic doubling that permits slippage of phrases between different contexts demonstrates the slippage of meaning that occurs once transcendent certitude disappears.

As Wolff describes: "The coherent relationships that are conventionally stipulated by grammar and diction are repeatedly denied in this poem. In the end, the accrued slippage—the carefully orchestrated series of failed relationships—acquires its own divisive meaning. The same linguistic structures that usually assert order are deployed here to assert separateness.

Instead of interacting in harmony, the words militate against one another."[26] Defying logic, many phrases may be read as connected or disconnected to either, or both, the preceding and subsequent phrases, for example: "Without Design" the trees may "maintain" themselves, or they may maintain "The Sun"; both "God" and "the Wind" may be the nearer "Neighbor." Notably, God, rather than divine master directing nature from behind the scenes, becomes only one more phenomenon drifting within the indeterminate relations of this poem. As such, he no longer authoritatively anchors realist readings of nature's book. Griffin Wolff concludes: "As God's power diminished and died, intrinsic order died with it. In 'Four Trees' . . . all the elements . . . stand in a perpetual state of existential isolation."[27]

As the above comment illustrates, "Four Trees" has most often been read as a poem of modernist lament for God's retreat. Yet I suggest that while elsewhere Dickinson does mourn God's absence or does rage against his absconding, here she simply, neutrally, and blasphemously rejects transcendent order, and this very absence of divine "Design" opens the way for her experimental revisions of nature and gender.[28] The deletion of fixed logical connections in this poem implies also a certain freedom from patriarchal systems of interpretation. While nature is not gendered female here, as it frequently is throughout Dickinson's work, the acre, the boy, and God are male, suggesting that the lack of "apparent" meaning is more of a dilemma for the male nature reader who, like Emerson, sees in nature a mirror for the social systems that bolster his masculine powers, while for a radically experimental woman writer the lack of fixed meaning grants an opening through problematic prevailing ideas about the nature of gender. If the relations between the beings in the poem occur "haply," or by chance, instead of by divine mandate, relations between beings and between knower and known might then also occur more equitably, more mutually, more "happily" for women. If nature has no one transcendent design, then perhaps the woman writer can rewrite nature in such a fashion as to wrest nature and women from patriarchal orders. The breakdown of apparent order within the stylistic progression of Dickinson's poem and within her reading of nature signals her experimental rebellion from systems problematic to the woman writer, a rebellion Paula Bennett describes as "her willful rejection of the laws upon which her culture was based. . . . In the unconventionality of her grammar as in the unconventionality of her thinking,

Dickinson was striking at the foundations supporting Western phallocentric thought."[29]

I begin with this poem in order to argue that Dickinson disbelieves interpretations of nature that confuse human inscription with intrinsic message and to show that much of her writing programmatically denaturalizes such readings. I read Dickinson's figures of nature as strategic polemical responses to traditional nature writing and traditional conceptions of woman and nature. She reappropriates nature-as-woman to her own ends, taking on as well as taking off from masculinist traditions.

In a poem often interpreted as a manifesto of her poetics, Dickinson reclaims the traditional figure of nature-as-woman in order to deconstruct women's exclusion from the production of serious poetry; the speaker of this poem implicitly allies herself with feminized Nature and utilizes their shared gender to propose the woman writer as a proper poet:

> This is my letter to the World
> That never wrote to Me—
> The simple News that Nature told—
> With tender Majesty
>
> Her message is committed
> To Hands I cannot see—
> For love of Her—Sweet—countrymen—
> Judge tenderly—of Me (441)

Nature is here set forth as source and sanction for Dickinson's poetry; as nature's ordained messenger, Dickinson claims "Majestic" authorization for her social transgression as woman writer. The production of poetry is here implicitly feminized, in direct contrast with literary, especially the Romantic and Transcendentalist, tradition where the Adamic male poet approximates God's primal Logos, the act of naming the world into being. Through a "simple" sex change, Dickinson's "letter" conveys a message originally "told" by feminized nature; Dickinson wittingly replaces God's logos with nature's "News," reversing standard gender roles. (And this would surely have been news to Puritan theologians such as Jonathan Edwards or Transcendentalists such as Ralph Waldo Emerson!) Dickinson's seemingly humble letters, or verses, are, by association, endowed with nature's regal powers. In the closing lines Dickinson chides the countrymen who "Judge" her writings according to masculinist biases, and she commands them to reconsider her "tenderly," for love of feminine "Nature." The speaker's self-proclaimed identification with feminized nature serves here to endorse the creative powers of both females, refiguring poetic and natural creation as womanly powers, and thus exploding the masculinist paradigm of creation as male prerogative.

Functionally, as described above, the poem accrues meaning through associations and slippages instead of clear separations and opposed subject/object relations. Dickinson's words refer forwards and backwards, permitted movement by the use of dashes and the omission of other marks that replace the fixed direction of standard punctuation. Whereas in "Four Trees" the syntactic inconclusiveness implied the failure of masculinist divine orders, in "This is my Letter" the same slippage permits a fluid identification between woman writer and nature-as-woman. In the motion of this poem Dickinson and nature overlap, confounding clear subject/object distinctions. Dickinson inscribes a reciprocal and fluid identification between speaker and nature based on their shared gender—Nature as self rather than Other. The slippage of words and lines that may refer to both Dickinson and nature emphasizes this identification. "Tender Majesty" may be read as referring backward to the previous line and also forward to the next stanza, describing both nature's news and Dickinson's transmission. The final lines also merge Dickinson with nature: "Me" must be judged tenderly in recognition of "Her" sweetness. Dickinson's poetics emphasizes a mutual, nonhierarchical relationship between female speaker and nature, based on identification rather than opposition, similar to the relations called for by Keller and Haraway. Such fluid identification between speaker and nature permits Dickinson to topple the strictures of Victorian propriety, her poetic voice now endorsed by the joint feminization that had erstwhile, in masculinist literary models, mandated female silence.

Given the isolation of the woman poet from an indifferent if not hostile social "world," transmission of meaning becomes an act of faith, a commitment to the existence of unseen readers who will grasp her message; poetic authority is posed as direct contrast to social powerlessness. In the presentation of multiple, discoverable rather than fixed, meanings, Dickinson's poetic acknowledges both her hostile countrymen and the possibility of unseen "Hands." Certain readings are there for those who reach but invisible to those who look away. Meaning is socially created, a mutual, contextually controlled interaction rather than a transcendentally fixed given. Instead of referring to God's fixed transcendent Logos whose message is available only to the Elect, Dickinson's poetry presents nature's immanent "simple News," democratically committed to all willing to read this letter for themselves.

This substitution of nature's news for God's Logos is continued in a number of poems in which nature's maternal presence, rather than God's paternal power, is represented as the constant, sustaining force of life. While these poems have often been dismissed, even by feminist critics, as cloyingly sentimental, they employ a naively sentimental stance for polemical ends, much as William Blake did in *Songs of Innocence and of Experience*, in order to criticize by default the cruelty of Puritan visions of a masculinized God's willful absence.[30] By inscribing nature as nurturant mother who provides us everything that God denies, the innocent voices of the poems expose the cruelty and hypocrisy of Puritan doctrines. As in "This is my letter," the poems substitute nature's active, omnipotent female presence for God's problematic absence and thus also implicitly argue for a revaluation of gender roles in which the primacy of mothering, female nurturance, and creativity be given their due. The placid sentimental surface of these poems masks the subversiveness of this revision. Bennett observes: "Dickinson is not subverting an androcentric concept of God. She is jettisoning it altogether and reconstructing God in woman's image. . . . For Dickinson God *could* be loving and lovable, but only in a female or immanent form. . . . Dickinson's nature poetry is a testament to this love. Given its emphasis on female, and in particular, on 'domestic' values, it is also a testament to the positive effect that woman-centered sentimentalism had upon her."[31]

Yet such reconstruction *is* in itself an acerbic subversion of Puritan realist values. Rather than jettisoning God, who remains a strong, if often problematic, presence throughout her work, Dickinson displaces his parental authority onto nature in a clear subversion of patriarchal dominance. Her positive, albeit sentimental, images of a deified nature bitterly, polemically imply the failures of the masculinist theology they replace; Dickinson's characterizations of nature as fond mother stand in rich contrast to her characterizations of God as inaccessible, absent father in cutting ironic lines such as "Of course I prayed and did God care," or "He has hid his rare

life / From our gross eyes."[32] In response to the Puritan conception of a
cold, unyielding, unknowable God, Dickinson repeatedly portrays nature
as idealized mother, constantly and tenderly ministering to her children.
One such sentimentally polemic poem deifies female domesticity even as
it defies the limits of the Victorian domestic sphere:

> Nature—the Gentlest Mother is,
> Impatient of no Child—
> The feeblest—or the waywardest—
> Her Admonition mild—
>
> In Forest—and the hill—
> By Traveller—be heard—
> Restraining Rampant Squirrel—
> Or too impetuous Bird—
>
> How fair Her Conversation—
> A Summer Afternoon—
> Her Household—Her Assembly—
> And when the Sun go down—
>
> Her Voice among the Aisles
> Incite the timid prayer
> Of the minutest Cricket—
> The most unworthy Flower—
>
> When all the Children sleep—
> She turns as long away
> As will suffice to light Her lamps—
> Then bending from the Sky—
>
> With infinite Affection
> And infiniter Care—
> Her Golden finger on Her lip—
> Wills Silence—Everywhere—(790)

The childlike speaker of this poem replaces the judging and ineffable
male God with a female deity of loving presence, implying that nature is

the more responsible and kind parent.[33] Rivaling God's stature, nature is omnipresent: her household is the earth itself and reaches to the heavens where the stars are her lights. In contradiction to prevailing realist views of nature as God's handmaid, no mention is made of a godly Father directing nature from behind the scenes. In fact, nature offers what, in Dickinson's view, the Calvinist God fails to provide; she is constantly accessible, turning away from her children only momentarily in order better to guard their sleep, while God is unavailable to all but the Elect. Her conversation is "fair" in both meanings of the word, as beautiful and, more importantly, just, while God is silent as well as erratic and undependable in judgment. As a "waywardest" believer, unwilling to accept much contemporary theological doctrine, Dickinson creates an alternative maternal deity who revises God-the-Father's failings; this beneficent maternal image, projected throughout nature, embraces the wayward, transgressive behaviors of the nonconforming woman poet who knows herself damned within prevailing Christian doctrine, and this figure interrogates by ironic contrast our acceptance of a grim and absent male God.[34]

Substituting nature for God, Dickinson consequently refigures female power. Bennett explains that "by defining God in terms of nature, Dickinson was able to assert a fully separate and autonomous source for female power. . . . Immanent in nature, this image of God became Dickinson's answer to the killing transcendence of the biblical deity and, at the same time, a basis on which to claim a (female) power of her own."[35] Whereas I differ from Bennett in arguing that in Dickinson's view nature remains distinct from God, I concur with her idea that nature affords Dickinson an image of autonomous, nontranscendent female power. While Victorian culture assumed women's subsidiary status, Dickinson's poetic vision of nature's maternal ascendancy implies that female creativity and caregiving are not subordinated to male desires or God's orders but are instead primary and self-originating.

Further, through characterization of nature as fond mother, Dickinson radically extends the typically female domestic sphere. In this poem nurturant domesticity assumes deified proportions, defying Victorian confinement to private interior space; Dickinson describes the reaches of nature, from earth to stars, as proper female realm. The poem vindicates domesticity, inscribing maternal care as the principle of nature that insures survival of all creatures, a point that nineteenth-century sciences, such as Darwinism, denied, to the detriment of female status within those systems. Susan Gubar calls such revision of the domestic "a theology of the ordinary, the homely, the domestic, a theology that constitutes a uniquely female version of the philosophy Thomas Carlyle called 'natural supernaturalism' . . . sacraments of the household, the hearth, the garden."[36] Yet this "theology" also entails a radical revaluation of just such diminutive terms as *homely* and *domestic* that renders problematic their confinement to "household" and "hearth."

Many of Dickinson's poems rewrite domesticity by representing nature, or aspects of nature, as feminine figures in domestic roles. In "Whose are the little beds, I asked" (142) nature rocks the cradles of flower bulbs as they sleep the winter away. "She sweeps with many-colored Brooms" portrays an aproned nature weeping jeweled shreds of color across the evening sky. She is addressed as "Housewife in the Evening West" (219). The poem "It sounded as if the streets were running" describes a spring wind storm so powerful that some citizens believe Judgment Day has arrived, but they find that this is just the work of nature, in an "Opal Apron / Mixing fresher Air" (1397). All such poems enlarge domesticity so that it wreaks notable natural events such as seasonal changes, fecundity, beauty, instead of menial household tasks. With these images Dickinson vindicates domesticity and rewrites the reaches of nature as women's home, thus unsettling ideological oppositions between home and world, domestic and wild, female and male that become meaningless within such a radically expanded view of the domestic.

In contrast to contemporary views of nature as God's servant and man's dominion, Dickinson repeatedly emphasizes nature's independent self-sufficiency. Rather than being subservient to God, she is active, self-directed agent. Rather than resource for man, she is assuredly self-possessed. The following poem lightly ridicules the appropriative male gaze that subsumes nature to men's desire:

> The Day undressed—Herself—
> Her Garter—was of Gold—
> Her petticoat—of Purple plain—
> Her Dimities—as old

Exactly—as the World—
and yet the newest Star—
Enrolled upon the Hemisphere
Be wrinkled—much as Her—

Too near to God—to pray—
Too near to Heaven—to fear—
The Lady of the Occident
Retired without a care—

Her Candle so expire
The flickering be seen
On Ball of Mast in Bosporus—
And dome—and Window Pane (716)

In describing the close of day as a striptease, Dickinson both literalizes and mocks the view of nature as erotic temptress performing for a voyeuristic male gaze, which Kolodny traces throughout American letters.[37] This poem denaturalizes the eroticized relation between man and nature by playfully taking the image of nature as vamp to such an extreme that we see it as a cultural construct.[38] "The Day undressed Herself" emphasizes the sexual voyeurism of this male fantasy of the land as "lay"[39] by detailing features of the sky and land as Day's undergarments, even as the poem patently frustrates that dream of nature's sexual display; rather than being a servant of male pleasure, Dickinson's Day is a self-possessed grand mistress who undresses "—Herself—" by herself, for herself, under her own command, and for her retirement rather than for men's titillation. "Too near to God—to pray," Day is omnipresent, eternal, and too cognizant of her own powers to implore or fear any male, even God himself, and as God's celestial neighbor and equal she assuredly dispels the Puritan notion of women and nature's lowly stature and inherent sinfulness. Through this insouciant "Lady," Dickinson blithely inscribes the self-sufficiency and sovereignty of women and nature, disclaiming the traditional subservence of both to men's desires.

Women's resultant enlarged stature is exemplified in a poem wherein the speaker herself assumes a position of omnipresence and infinite desire:

> Perhaps I asked too large—
> I take no less than skies—
> For Earths grow thick as
> Berries, in my native town—
> My Basket holds—just—Firmaments—
> Those—dangle easy—on my arm,
> but smaller bundles—Cram (352)

The speaker's titanic and self-satisfying desires are graphically con-
trasted to the limited scale of proper feminine expectations. She gathers
immensities of nature—"Earths," "skies," "Firmaments"—and refuses the
"smaller bundles" that would, ironically, "Cram" her within the constricted
scope of feminine norms. Rendering the speaker as an infinite and omnipresent figure, the poem defies female diminution and argues that universal
scope is woman's "just" portion. Like the images of nature's grandiose self-
sufficiency in the poems above, the immense speaker offers a vision of
women's enlarged ambition and fulfillment, beyond their cramped stature
in service to men's appropriative desires.

In opposition to the masculine voyeuristic gaze that subsumes and pos-
sesses nature to its own ends, Dickinson reimagines the relations between
female worshiper and feminized nature deity as egalitarian, reciprocal, and
nonappropriative. This relationship is located, moving, and noncentered,
resembling the relationship between knower and nature that Haraway and
Keller articulate. This homosocial, even homoerotic, mutually sustaining
recognition between female figures polemically rewrites prevailing hierarchical and appropriative relations between man and nature, man and
woman.

> Sweet Mountains—Ye tell Me no lie—
> Never deny Me—Never fly—
> Those same unvarying Eyes
> Turn on Me—when I fail—or feign,
> Or take the Royal names in vain—
> Their far—slow—Violet Gaze—
>
> My Strong Madonnas—Cherish still—
> The Wayward Nun—beneath the Hill—

> Whose service—is to You—
> Her latest Worship—When the Day
> Fades from the Firmament away—
> To lift Her Brows on You— (722)

In this revision of Psalm 121—"I will lift up mine eyes unto the hills, from whence cometh my help. My help *cometh* from the Lord, which made heaven and earth,"[40] Dickinson's speaker invokes a female power immanent within the surrounding mountains. As in "Nature—the Gentlest Mother is," the constancy of the feminized mountains, who "tell . . . no lie—Never deny . . . —Never fly," even as the "Wayward" speaker fails to satisfy social decorum, implicitly chastises God, who embraces only the strictly devout. As in the poems above, the constant presence of the mountains condemns and corrects God's judgmental erraticism.

More importantly, the poem inscribes an interactive mutual gaze that flows between speaker and mountains. Unlike God's gaze which turns against the wayward believer, the mountains' steadfast gazes "Turn on," or pivot upon and surround, the speaker as focal point for their "slow," "Sweet," "violet" regard. Unlike the appropriative male gaze, described in Emerson's poem quoted above, which subsumes nature for its own aggrandizement, here the speaker's eyes meet and reciprocate the mountains' gaze in the closing line, "To lift Her Brows on You." These feminine gazes are in motion, turning and lifting in response to each other, inscribing a subject and object mutually produced, entwined, and in accord; in fact, the words *subject* and *object* lose polarity and fixity within this relation, as mountains and speaker switch roles and position, each in turn acting as source and recipient of the gaze in a reciprocally sustaining reflective dance. Interestingly, while the first stanza describes the mountains from the speaker's standpoint, the second stanza presents the mountains' view of the speaker: the "I" of the first stanza becomes "she" in the second. This poem gracefully performs the mutuality of knower and known that Keller described above, in which both parties are engaged as resourceful players. The poem also enacts Haraway's notion of situated vision in which a particularly located speaker looks at a world that looks back. Haraway explains that this interconnected subject/object relation requires "conversation" rather than monologue: "Accounts of a 'real' world do not, then depend on a logic of 'discovery,' but on a power-charged social relation of 'conversation.' The world neither speaks itself nor disappears in favor of a master decoder. The codes of the world are not still, waiting only to be read. The world is not raw material for humanization. . . . The world encountered in knowledge projects is an active entity."[41]

In Dickinson's poem this interactive and nonappropriative circuit occurs between female entities. It is a "Sweet" homosocial, even homoerotic,[42] economy of shared female service and loyalty; in fact, as a "Wayward Nun," the speaker may have forsworn other more worldly heterosocial and heterosexual ties in favor of this devotion. She finds a succor in this mutually reproducing same-sex relation apparently unavailable within the hierarchical patriarchal systems that judge her wanting. As in "This is my letter," the same-sex identification of female speaker with feminized mountains fosters the fluctuating cross-positioning within the poem. While Homans has argued in regard to other Dickinson poems that same-sex relations are figured as stultifyingly similar and thus deadly and that heterosexual relations are inscribed as differentiated and productive,[43] I insist instead that the same-sex cross-identification of speaker and nature within the poems I discuss encourages a positive female identity based on that shared gender; in "Sweet Mountains" as elsewhere in these poems, gender sameness permits the "constant" movement of subjectivity and identity between speaker and mountains that "serves" to nourish both female entities.[44] Perhaps, in fact, within the loving bond between speaker and feminized nature Dickinson can give expression to a mutually nurturant same-sex eroticism that, as Martha Smith and Paula Bennet argue, she strongly desired but also feared as inappropriate or impossible between herself and female friends.[45]

The eroticism of this relationship between female speaker and nature becomes very clear in a poem where this cross-identification plays upon the literary association of flowers with women's sexual favors, using this association as means of expressing active female desire considered inappropriate to women's virtue. Again, Dickinson wittingly exaggerates this trope, emphasizing its artfulness, even as she uses it to express female desire in terms highly unorthodox to Victorian femininity:

> I tend my flowers for thee—
> Bright Absentee!
> My Fuchsia's Coral Seams
> Rip—while the Sower—dreams—

Geraniums—tint—and spot—
Low Daisies—dot—
My Cactus—splits her Beard
To show her throat

Carnations—tip their spice—
And Bees—pick up—
A Hyacinth—I hid—
Puts out a Ruffled Head—
And odors fall
From flasks—so small—
You marvel how they held—

Globe Roses—break their satin flake—
Upon my Garden floor—
Yet—thou—not there—
I had as lief they bore
No Crimson—more—

Thy flower—be gay—
Her Lord—away!
It ill becometh me—
I'll dwell in Calyx—Gray—
How modestly—alway—
Thy Daisy—
Draped for thee! (339)

Dickinson literalizes and revises this standard trope of flower as female sexual symbol; an avid gardener, horticulturist, and botanist, Dickinson knows well that flowers are literally the sexual organ of plants, and she uses flowers here to inscribe metonymically active female desire in sensuous detail scandalous to Victorian feminine propriety. Identification of the female speaker and flowers, through the repeated possessive article "my" and her naming of herself as "Thy flower" and "Thy Daisy," permits the speaker simultaneously to displace this indecorous and uncontainable sexual energy onto the flowers and yet also indirectly to claim it as her own.

The poem plays upon the impossible attempt to contain irrepressible female desire as the flowers shamelessly flaunt their overflowing erotic energy in an accumulating spill of active verbs—"Rip," "tint," "splits," "tip," "Puts out," "fall," "break"—refusing confinement, much as the French term *jouissance* describes female pleasure as that which defies enumerative bounds and disrupts clear distinctions, so that "You marvel how they held." The pungent homoerotic or autoerotic details of the speaker's descriptions sensuously savor the flowers' active insurrection against fixed borders as they rip their seams, break, and flake open their globes and spill themselves out of flasks. They exceed gender categories as the cactus "splits her Beard," the hyacinth exposes a vulval yet phallic "Ruffled Head," and their collective energy supplants the accepted Victorian distinction between male sexual aggressiveness and female passivity.

The ending of the poem, which pretends to suppress, or at least "modestly" cloak the speaker's own erotic bloom within a gray calyx, or sheath, can't in fact neatly reseal the disruptive flowering of female desire, but only reemphasizes that it already lies unfurled beneath her nunnish exterior. The use of "lief," which puns with leaf, to express the speaker's desire, further allies "Thy Daisy" with her plants even while she feigns distinction from them, and her deployment of the ambiguous term "Draped," which inscribes modest veiling even as it also implies immodest posturing, emphasizes the ambivalence of her disclaimer. The confusion in this poem between feminized flowers and speaker enables the expression of her transgressive erotic desire even as it allows her to don propriety—knowing full well that after the earlier chaotic profusion of the flowers, such distinctions can no longer hold. Having literalized the trope of flower as female sexuality, Dickinson prevents us from again disguising female erotic energy behind a veil of sentiment in this image, but more importantly, the insistent outpouring of the flowers argues against confinement, fixed borders, firm separations and images another more interpenetrating, moving, and eruptive female subjectivity and sexuality.

A flower again represents overlapping female desire and an identification of woman and nature that fosters communion in the following poem, which, acknowledging the customary exchange of garden flowers and garden produce, plays upon the conceit of flower as emissary of the poet:

>   All the letters I can write
>   Are not fair as this—

> Syllables of Velvet—
> Sentences of Plush,
> Depths of Ruby, undrained,
> Hid, Lip, for Thee—
> Play it were a Humming Bird—
> And just sipped—me— (334)

Through the "Play" of metamorphosing identifications whereby flower and letters, petals and syllables, lips and hummingbirds, speaker and flower become imaginatively merged, Dickinson offers herself, by means of literal and literary flower, to the addressee of the poem. Semantic slippage and multiplicitous reference create the overlapping layers of identifications in which the "it" of the penultimate line may be read as simultaneously signifying "Lip," "humming Bird," flower, and letter. This playful accretion of possible identities allows the communion in which the speaker is "sipped" by the recipient of this floral message.[46] Nature serves as medium for this moment of union when the identification of woman with flower permits the meeting of speaker and recipient, thus paradoxically representing presence even in absence, and consummation even despite physical distance.[47]

In another group of poems, nature's mysterious and fluid power is posed as a direct challenge to the problematic enclosures and exclusions endemic to a masculinist culture based on notions of hierarchic duality. In these poems, nature's mysterious undecidability and unrepresentability defy epistemological determination and problematize fixed social categorizations. Through inscriptions of nature's elusive powers, Dickinson argues for "other" less objectifying ways of knowing nature and other more fluid social relations; in ascribing to nature the resourceful agency that Keller and Haraway advocate, Dickinson also reclaims such resourceful self-determination for those humans who have been negatively identified as nature incarnate.

Much as "I tend my flowers for thee" plays upon the impossibility of containing female desire, a number of Dickinson's nature poems wittily describe nature as an irrepressible,uncontainable, and ultimately unknowable female whose freedom questions normative Victorian social boundaries. "Juggler of Day" throws convention to the wind. The poem is a vision of female energy outside the bounds of propriety—a public, active, lower-class, carnivalesque performer:

> Blazing in Gold and quenching in Purple
> Leaping like Leopards to the Sky
> Then at the feet of the old Horizon
> Laying her spotted Face to die
> Stooping as low as the Otter's Window
> Touching the Roof and tinting the Barn
> Kissing her Bonnet to the Meadow
> And the Juggler of Day is Gone (228)

Like the bursting blooms in "I tend my flowers," the bounding female energy of the "Juggler of Day" drives this poem, as the juggler's kinetic movements continually circulate across socially constituted boundaries. The poem performs her flights across categorical limits, as she leaps up and down, from the celestial to the terrestrial, moving between animal and human domains, bringing both fire and darkness. Her energetic freedom erupts in decidedly improper, "stooping," unfeminine, physical and public display that juggles static Victorian categories and expectations into flux, into play, into the air.

Victorian femininity is shown to be artificially imposed, rather than a natural, innate condition; nature exceeds any such cultural definition. In fact, she leaves such definitions an empty show, and juggles cultural certainties into disarray:

> Nature affects to be sedate
> Upon occasion, grand
> But let our observation shut
> Her practices extend
>
> To Necromancy and the Trades
> Remote to understand
> Behold our spacious Citizen
> Unto a Juggler turned—(1170)

Nature's affectation questions Victorian gender expectations and ways of looking that limit our knowledge of nature by misprizing and misrepresenting her larger and more complex scope. The first three lines of the poem insist that our constructed and constricted view of nature's gentility are refracted back to us when, under our "observation," nature enacts only those roles we have scripted for her. As in "Blazing in Gold," nature is a performer, but one who appears to sedately affect the roles of proper femininity required by her observers. "Observation" here shrewdly conflates both meanings of the term in a closed solipsistic cycle, as our acts of perception are revealed to be nothing more than blind reflections of customary practices: we see only what we expect to see, and so nature necessarily conforms to our observations.

Yet when freed from methods of "observation" that "shut" her into "sedate" or even "grand" propriety, nature's practices disrupt gender roles, disturb polarities, and destroy neat epistemological mirrorings. There is an ominously unfeminine and uncontrollable side to nature that our observations don't wish to acknowledge: she practices "Necromancy," or haunting arts of witchery and dark magic in which boundaries such as those between life and death, creation and destruction, citizenry and circus no longer hold, thus destroying the certainty of "civilized" dualist distinctions. As I will argue in the next chapter, Afro-Caribbean Voodoo religion disturbs Western polarities in just this manner. Interestingly, the word *necromancy* is of Latin origin and in Middle English it took the form of "nigromancie," or the black arts. While Dickinson is making no overt mention of race, perhaps the word *necromancy* covertly subverts white, supposedly "civilized," hegemony. "Remote" from our fixed systems of understanding, nature practices "Trades," or unladylike, lower-class productions and transactions; she commerces in exchanges, displacements, transformations, transmutations, even transmogrifications, all of which employ economies of circulation and movement "Remote to understand" because we lack fluid enough epistemological systems to follow her constant reformations and instabilities. Nature's necromancy, her continual and even indistinguishable cycles of creation, growth, and destruction, destabilize any fixed system of taxonomic classification. Nature juggles all assumptions and turns epistemological fixity against itself. The poem makes it clear that our methods of observing and knowing are incompatible with nature's complexity. Haraway suggests that rather than imposing false fixity upon nature, we must allow some "unsettling possibilities" into human/nature relations:

Acknowledging the agency of the world in knowledge makes room for some unsettling possibilities, including a sense of the world's independent sense of humor. . . . The Coyote or Trickster, embod-

ied in American Southwest Indian accounts, suggests our situation
when we give up mastery but keep searching for fidelity, knowing
all the while we will be hoodwinked . . . (by) the world as witty
agent and actor. Perhaps the world resists being reduced to mere
resource because it is—not mother/matter/mutter—but coyote, a
figure for the always problematic, always potent tie of meaning and
bodies . . . with whom we must learn to converse.[48]

A final example of Dickinson's portrayal of nature's ultimate impenetra-
bility, "What mystery pervades a well!," brings us full circle in examining
Dickinson's revision of the sentimental figure of nature's house, for in this
poem nature is a "haunted house," a domestic yet carnivalesque space possessed by mysterious and ghostly presences that unsettle the over familiar
delusions of realist certitudes:

>   What mystery pervades a well!
>   The water lives so far—
>   A neighbor from another world
>   Residing in a jar—
>
>   Whose limit none have ever seen,
>   But just his lid of glass—
>   Like looking every time you please
>   In an abyss's face!
>
>   The grass does not appear afraid,
>   I often wonder he
>   Can stand so close and look so bold
>   At what is awe to me
>
>   Related somehow they may be,
>   The sedge stands next the sea—
>   Where he is floorless
>   And does no timidity betray
>
>   But nature is a stranger yet;
>   The ones that cite her most
>   Have never passed her haunted house,
>   Nor simplified her ghost,

> To pity those that know her not
> Is helped by the regret
> That those who know her, know her less
> The nearer her they get. (1400)

We can trace Dickinson's reconstruction of nature and gender in the movement of this poem, which begins by considering the awe-inspiring mystery of a masculinized well, but concludes with a wider focus upon the ultimate strangeness of feminized nature. While the speaker initially appears daunted by the immeasurable depths of the well and seems somewhat enviously taken aback by the brash proximity of the masculinized grass to the abysslike waters, the closing two stanzas call into question this initial scene of male bonding and male knowledge claims. For, as in the foregoing poems, nature's final strangeness eludes such falsely assumed familiarity. Ironically, those who "cite her most," who claim authority over nature or who use her as evidence to ground their views, turn out to be those least familiar with her more elusive realms of "haunted house" and "ghost." As in "Nature affects to be sedate," nature's mysterious or supernatural aspect reveals the inadequacy of realist certitudes, be they scientific, poetic, or theological. Notably, nature is here identified with a house, a domestic, typically feminine domain, albeit haunted rather than cozy. Yet this haunted house is finally an impenetrable and unknowable domain, eluding and riddling even those who "know her." In fact, in contrast to the presumptuous grass, those who know her recognize that nature cannot finally *be* known; her elusiveness is her defining quality. We can "pass" her house, but we cannot presume to enter her premises. Once again, nature's ultimate, haunting mystery evades simplification, and once again her elusiveness serves to dislodge Victorian gender ideology, throwing doubt upon patriarchal presumptions grounded in references to the naturalness of separate spheres. If we are ultimately estranged from nature's haunted house, what are we to make of our own houses and of the physical and social walls that both hem us in and lock us out?

In this chapter I have argued that we must read Dickinson's sentimental nature poems as canny reappropriations and calculated reconstructions of the standard literary figure of nature-as-woman. Dickinson's refigurations of nature-as-woman strategically open up the interlocking nineteenth-century determinations of nature and gender. By emphasizing nature's indeterminacy, Dickinson suggests that women, as well, may slip out of the patriarchal strictures that diminish their powers and scope and might then reimagine more egalitarian and expansive roles and relations. Dickinson reconstructs nature's house as a space of possibility rather than predetermination, as a realm that is hospitable to the woman writer, but that defiantly destabilizes the boundaries of Victorian separate spheres.

2

Rerooting the Sacred Tree: Nature, Black Women, and Voodoo in Zora Neale Hurston's *Tell My Horse* and *Their Eyes Were Watching God*

These sitters had been tongueless, earless, eyeless conveniences all day long. Mules and other brutes had occupied their skins. But now, the sun and the bossman were gone, so the skins felt powerful and human. They became lords of sounds and lesser things. They passed nations through their mouths.—*Zora Neale Hurston*

BORN IN 1891 and raised in the first incorporated Negro town of Eatonville, Florida, Zora Neale Hurston inherited a firm pride in rural black culture and accomplishment, despite the extreme prejudice and discrimination reigning full sway just beyond the town borders.[1] Although Hurston left the sheltering atmosphere of Eatonville at an early age and bore the brunt of racism as she supported herself by working as a maid, manicurist, and personal assistant while she completed her education, she retained her belief in the vibrancy of black people and black culture. After training at Barnard with the anthropologist Franz Boas, Hurston returned to Florida to begin documenting the African-American folk life and folklore that she treasured. While other Harlem Renaissance artists and advocates announced the advent of the New Negro who had migrated to northern cities to escape the shackles of racism, Hurston's fiction and ethnography traced the roots of African-American resistance within the folk culture of the rural South. *Mules and Men*, the title of Hurston's first folklore collection, insists that even though the dominant society treated African Americans as subservient "mules," within their own songs, dances, stories, and folk beliefs, blacks had creatively and subversively redefined themselves as men and women.[2]

Long dismissed as a work of uneven anthropology,[3] Hurston's second ethnographic text, *Tell My Horse: Voodoo and Life in Haiti and Jamaica* deserves recognition as a pioneering study of Afro-Caribbean society and religion, notable, in particular, for Hurston's biting analysis of the harsh effects of colonialism upon black women and for her presentation of Afro-Caribbean Voodoo religion as countering these oppressive social relations.[4] As Hurston delineates in her study, Caribbean racial and sexual inequities are grounded in the representation of black women as animals; because black women are viewed as subhuman "donkeys," their sufferings in "this man's world" can be dismissed as inevitable, and the social pyramid that rests upon their backs can be justified as natural. However, as Hurston describes it in *Tell My Horse*, Voodoo presents an alternative spiritual model that reframes the binary hierarchies operating within the denigration of black women as nature incarnate. Through rituals that locate the sacred within nature and within female sexuality, Voodoo challenges the degradation of black women as donkeys. Furthermore, spirit-possession offers black women an opportunity for self-possession in the midst of a hostile social order; when "donkeys" become "horses" ridden by the loas, colonial class, color, and gender lines are called into question, and black women may finally talk back to otherwise invulnerable social superiors.

Beyond its import as ethnography, *Tell My Horse* provides an invaluable context for rereading Hurston's classic novel of a black woman's quest for self-fulfillment, *Their Eyes Were Watching God*. Hurston wrote *Their Eyes* while undertaking her Caribbean field study, and I argue that she "embalmed" her growing knowledge of Voodoo spirituality within the nature imagery of this novel. Much as Caribbean black women are transformed by Voodoo ritual, Janie, the protagonist of *Their Eyes*, is inspired to resist her society's conception of black women as "mules of the world" through her Voodoo-informed vision of the blossoming pear tree as a fecund "marriage" of polarities. In this chapter, I will first trace Hurston's analysis of black women, nature, and Voodoo in *Tell My Horse*, and I will then reread *Their Eyes* in the context of this ethnographic material in order to suggest that Hurston's novel develops the full revolutionary potential she perceived within Afro-Caribbean spiritual belief.

The Caribbean conception of black women as donkeys is of course only one instance of the historic representation of blacks, particularly black women, in terms of animals. Winthrop Jordan notes that, beginning with early European explorations of the African continent, European popular and scientific speculations upon the relations between Africans and Europeans generally posed Africans as a questionable form of humanity, ranked along the Great Chain of Being between whites and apes, below fully intelligent life and suspiciously close to animals. The simultaneous European contact in Africa with Negroes and tailless apes such as orangutans further spurred the European belief in the close generic or evolutionary association between Negroes and apes, an association that was cemented in the European imagination by the belief that sexually aggressive orangutans sometimes engaged in intercourse with African women. Jordan comments that Europeans always imagined this transgressive sexual coupling as occurring between ape and black woman: "The sexual union of apes and Negroes was *always* conceived involving *female Negroes* and *male apes*. Apes had intercourse with Negro *women*."[5] Consequently, pseudoscientific representations of black women's animalistic sexual behavior were then evoked as a key indication of essential racial differences between whites and blacks, proving Negro proximity to lower nature. In this defining racist image of black women as sexual beasts, both race and gender were simultaneously naturalized, based on the belief in fixed rank categories: man was defined over and against woman, white over and against black, human over and against nature, with the animality of black women serving to affirm the higher humanity of white men.

Furthermore, animalistic sexual desire was attributed to slave women, and they were then held responsible for the sexual relations frequently forced upon them by white men. As chattel, black women could not legally resist overt rape or other forms of forced sexual relations with designated black or white men. White interpretations of black women's sexuality reveal the contradictions within prevailing constructions of racial differences. The representations of black women's wild, bestial sexuality and brute physical strength were used to distinguish the white and black races, conflating blacks with animals rather than humans.[6] Yet the very desire of whites to engage in *animalistic* sexual relations with black women contradicted and ironically undermined clear racial distinctions, producing offspring who literally intermixed black and white, making essential racial distinction clearly impossible, even though society attempted to enforce racial categories by continuing to class a person of partial Negro ancestry as black.[7] Conceptions of black women's sexuality served as vector here: sign of essential racial difference yet also site at which such distinctions become totally absurd as the line between races is crossed and complicated through interracial sexual relations.[8]

The prevailing white representation of African women as sexual beasts was epitomized in the treatment of Sarah Bartman, a Hottentot woman captured in Africa in 1810 and exhibited in Europe as the "Hottentot Venus." Medical scientists were fascinated with Bartman's "primitive" genitalia, which they compared to those of the female orangutan as sign of the distinct and debased nature of the Negro race. The scientists further speculated that such primitive genitalia demonstrated black women's likeliness to couple with apes, which led them to conclude that blacks were closer to animal than human. As Sander Gilman notes, all medical discussions of Bartman were limited to her genitals, which were removed during the autopsy performed after her early death, and which still remain on display at the tellingly named Musée de L'homme in Paris. In art, literature, and the popular imagination as well, "Sarah Bartman's sexual parts . . . serve as the central image for the black female."[9]

It is this image of the black woman as sexual beast and beast of burden that Zora Neale Hurston overturns through her radical refigurations of nature and of black women's sexuality in Tell My Horse and Their Eyes Were Watching God. Tell My Horse commences with a chapter entitled "The Rooster's Nest" in which Hurston emphasizes the unnaturalness of the colonial social relations that prevailed at the time of her visit to Jamaica. Hurston sees the conjunction of racism, sexism, and classism in the social powerlessness of poor black women who are considered the dregs of Caribbean society. Ironically, through the adoption of colonial values, black colonials themselves reinforce the European derogation of blackness, particularly as embodied by black women, and they continue the conflation of black women with lower nature as opposed to higher, whiter, European culture. Hurston acerbically describes the colonial values of Caribbean Negroes who regard English manner and appearance as the key to social advancement and who thus prize any infusion of white blood and paler skin into their family lines, shunning darker Negroes as retrograde. Color lines in the Caribbean, Hurston reports, tend to be drawn not between white and all other colors, but between black and any shade of lighter mulatto.

Consequently, race becomes a fluid rather than essential category in this colonial situation because those mulattoes with adequate white blood, status, and money may have themselves declared legally white in the official census records, thus literally erasing their black ancestry. As Hurston states, tongue in cheek: "Everywhere else a person is white or black by birth, but it is so arranged in Jamaica that a person may be black by birth but white by proclamation" (7). In this situation, race becomes a matter of social rank and legal fiction rather than an innate or historical identity.[10]

Unfortunately, this aspiration toward whiteness necessitates the unnatural denial and legal erasure of black forebears, usually, as Hurston perceives it, of the black mothers who bear children to white or lighter skinned fathers. In the rush toward whiteness, English paternity is overemphasized while black maternity is hidden from sight: "When a Jamaican is born of a black woman and some English or Scotsman, the black mother is literally and figuratively kept out of sight as far as possible, but no one is allowed to forget that white father, however questionable the circumstances of birth. You hear about 'My father this and my father that, and my father who was English, you know,' until you get the impression that he or she *had* no mother. Black skin is so utterly condemned that the black mother is not going to be mentioned nor exhibited" (8). Hurston's observations about the erasure of black mothers are strikingly similar to those of French feminist Luce Irigaray, who argues in "Plato's Hystera," her parodic recasting of Plato's parable of the cave, that the patriarchal model of selfsame replication entails systematic denial of the mother, or womb, in favor of the father, or phallus. In this parable, the womb is associated with darkness, while the phallus is linked with light.[11] While Irigaray's essay, like Plato's, uses light and dark imagery metaphorically, Hurston's discussion emphasizes the literal racial politics of this light/dark opposition in which the black mother is "kept out of sight" in order to sustain the son's illusory whiteness.

Hurston ends this passage on Caribbean racial politics with an explanation of the metaphoric figure of the rooster's nest, which serves as the title and theme of this chapter: "You get the impression that these virile Englishmen do not require women to reproduce. They just come out to Jamaica, scratch out a nest and lay eggs that hatch out into 'pink' Jamaicans"

(8–9). By using this ridiculously unnatural figure of the rooster's nest to frame her analysis of the colonial erasure of black mothers, Hurston emphasizes the painful absurdity and sterility of colonial race relations that destroy the natural familial connections of mother and child and of people of color to their own history and heritage. Through this figure Hurston underscores the questionable nature of European virility, which usurps the actual sources of Jamaican life—black mothers and black cultural heritage—in the false image of its own self-creating powers, and she exposes the elevation of Englishmen at the expense of black women as a travesty of actual, or *natural*, productive and reproductive relations. By describing the Englishmen as roosters, Hurston also subjects them to the same sort of animal analogies that they have historically used against black women, and thus, through this ironic trope, Hurston begins to expose the way that the discourse of nature has functioned in conceptions of race and gender.

The Caribbean notion of English superiority has severe effects upon poor black women, who are seen as outside the pale of progressive whiteness and who therefore have absolutely no legal or social status. In the chapter entitled "Women in the Caribbean," Hurston makes clear through observations and anecdotes that the colonial disavowal of blackness leads to severe oppression of black women. Hurston describes them as donkeys, in a clear parroting of European constructions of black women as beasts. The term *donkeys* emphasizes that black women's social disempowerment is rooted in their conflation with animals, and Hurston pointedly uses the image of the donkey to unsettle this colonial association:

> If she is of no particular family, poor and black, she is in a bad way indeed in that man's world. She had better pray to the Lord to turn her into a donkey and be done with the thing. It is assumed that God made poor black females for beasts of burden, and nobody is going to interfere with providence. Most assuredly, no upper class man is going to demean himself by assisting one with a heavy load. If he were caught in such an act he probably would become an outcast among his kind. It is just considered down here that God made two kinds of donkeys, one kind that can talk. The black women of Jamaica load banana boats now, and the black women used to coal ships when they burned coal. (58)

By literalizing the figure of the woman-as-donkey, Hurston demonstrates the way this negative identification has been used to justify the mistreatment of black women. By exposing the cyclical process through which black women, assumed to be donkeys, are forced to perform brute labors and are consequently perceived as no better than talking beasts, Hurston undercuts the circular logic upholding Caribbean social divisions.

Hurston describes in painful detail the crippling effects of the back-breaking labors, such as loading boats, transporting loads down mountain paths, or hammering large rocks into piles of gravel, that these talking donkeys must perform for their meager sustenance. Through these descriptions, Hurston further delineates the circular process through which the brute labors "distort" the women into pathetic, subhuman forms, de-creating them into the prevailing image of black-women-as-animals. Her tone in this passage is strikingly ambivalent, mingling repulsion at the women's "wretched" bodies with ironic outrage at their bitter fate:

> She can do the same labors as a man or a mule and nobody thinks anything about it. In Jamaica it is a common sight to see skinny-looking but muscular black women sitting on top of a pile of rocks with a hammer making little ones out of big ones. They look so wretched with their bare black feet all gnarled and distorted from walking barefooted over rocks. The nails on their big toes thickened like a hoof from a life time of knocking against stones. All covered with the gray dust of the road, those feet look almost saurian and repellent. . . . It is very hard, but women in Jamaica must eat like everywhere else. And everywhere in the Caribbean women carry a donkey's load on their heads and walk up and down mountains with it. (59)

By emphasizing the causal connection between hard labor and the women's hooflike, or saurian, feet, Hurston attacks the prevailing assumption that black women are innately subhuman, and she demonstrates that social stigma, rather than divine intent, is responsible for their miserable condition.

Aside from brute laborer, the other role assigned to Caribbean black women is that of sexual object. Early on, Hurston relates her argument with a Caribbean man who proclaims that women's only God-given role is

to exist as *women*, loving and serving men. Western career women, he declares, have desecrated their natural function: "He said we insulted God's
intention so grossly that it was a wonder that western women had not given
up the idea of mating and marriage altogether" (17). But the black woman
in Caribbean society is not even considered properly marriageable to men
of higher rank; while all women are viewed primarily as sexual companions
of men, black women are seen as disposable sexual commodities to be used
and abandoned by men of higher class or paler color who bear no legal
obligations to women below their rank. Hurston describes the utter powerlessness of the black woman seduced by a higher ranking man: "She has no
rights which he is bound to respect. What is worse, the community would
be shocked if he did respect them. Fatherhood gives no upper class man
the license to trample down conventions and crash lines, nor shades of
color lines, by marrying outside his class" (59). Caribbean social arrangements depend upon the sexual misuse of black women: class and color lines
are preserved at her expense. Hurston repeats several tragic tales of dark
women whose lives are destroyed when they are seduced and cavalierly
abandoned by mulatto men. Such women have no legal recourse, no fi-
nancial security, no social protections because they are regarded as no more
than available sexual prey. Like the "Hottentot Venus," black women in
these stories are seen as sexualized, subhuman curiosities whose fate is irrel-
evant to Caribbean society. "But what becomes of her is unimportant" (61).
Hurston comments ironically upon the Caribbean response to the death of
a woman who was tricked into marriage by a man who abandoned her
immediately after consummating the union: "Perhaps she suffered some,
but then he was a man and therefore sacred and his honor must be pro-
tected even if it takes forty women to do it" (61).

Much of *Tell My Horse* concentrates upon Hurston's research into Afro-
Caribbean Voodoo religion, and many of the spiritual beliefs and practices
that Hurston describes directly challenge the colonial denigration of black
women. Voodoo, the Caribbean transposition of the African religion Vodun, which was brought to the islands by enslaved blacks, is, at the time of
Hurston's research in the 1930s, the unofficial national religion of Haiti.[12]
Hurston argues against previous researchers who had interpreted Voodoo
as an aberrant form of Catholicism or dismissed it as barbaric superstition.
She insists that Voodoo reconstructs a pantheon of African-derived deities
to which have been added lesser deities, or loa, particular to the Caribbean.[13] Hurston notes that at the time of her study Voodoo is a religion

most openly practiced by the black lower classes, but it is somewhat of an embarrassment to upper-class believers, who attempt to hide their faith from Western eyes. Clearly, Voodoo is a retention of African culture, more widely preserved among the least Westernized black underclass than among the English-aspiring mulatto upper crust. Crucially, Voodoo spirituality contests the binary hierarchies within colonial structures that prove so damaging to black women. Hurston repeatedly insists that all religions are a reflection of the worshipers: "Gods always behave like the people who make them" and certain Voodoo gods are a "deification of the common people of Haiti" (219).[14] Voodoo refracts the terms of colonial racism and sexism and offers Afro-Caribbean women a mirror reflecting their self-worth and full humanity.

In contrast to male-dominated Western religions, in Voodoo women and men have equal stature, and mambos and houngans (priestesses and priests) have comparable and often shared authority. Unlike most Western religions in which ranks of authorities mediate between worshipers and deities, Voodoo is a decentered religion that grants spiritual authority to all worshipers.[15] Voodoo is a highly participatory spiritual practice in which worshipers enact ceremonies, feed the loa, and are instructed by them, dance, and undergo spirit-possession. The pantheon of Voodoo deities is, similarly, metaphysically decentered, composed of numerous male and female loa, who have independent spheres of authority over particular sacred sites and manifestations. Hurston notes that both male and female attributes of the deity are primary to Voodoo spirituality (113). Furthermore, Voodoo is a syncretic religion, constantly evolving through the creation of new loa, new sacred rites, and new sacred objects in response to changing cultural and social conditions.[16] A religion of re-creation and transformation rather than of stasis, the very fluidity of Voodoo ritual and belief encourages a view of human transformative possibilities, rather than of externally fixed, eternally static identities.

In contrast to prevailing colonial stratifications in which one term is defined as over and against the other—such as male over and against female, white over and against black, spiritual over and against sexual, and culture over and against nature—Voodoo practices and beliefs emphasize a border-crossing intermingling of polarities, paradigmatic of feminist theorist Donna Haraway's cyborg myth of "transgressed boundaries, potent fusions and dangerous possibilities."[17] Haraway imagines her "cyborg"—a creature part human, part animal, part machine—as symbolizing a vital alternative to the increasingly deadly Western divisions between those deemed fully human and those who are seen as less-than-human resources for profit and consumption. She argues that in breaching assumed boundaries, the cyborg has the potential to disrupt stratified colonial orders that depend upon binaristic differentiation. I suggest that Voodoo works in just this fashion, breaching colonial class, color, and gender lines by refiguring the negative association of black women and nature as a promising cyborgian interpenetration that disrupts racial and sexual hierarchy. Voodoo offers black women a spiritual framework that contests the terms of colonial ideology, and it is thus a powerful means of indigenous Afro-Caribbean resistance to colonial strictures.

Voodoo refigures the very representation of black women as sexual beasts exemplified by the "Hottentot Venus." While Christianity, the prevailing Western religion, generally condemns nature and carnal existence as antithetical to the transcendent spiritual realm, in Voodoo, nature and the sacred interpenetrate, as followers worship natural phenomena and hold ceremonies at particular natural sites. Hurston explains: "Voodoo is a religion of creation and life. It is the worship of the sun, the water and other natural forces" (113). Natural elements, such as water and fire, are central to many Voodoo rituals, and throughout Haiti ceremonies are held at sacred trees, stones, and, in particular, springs, grottos and waterfalls inhabited by loa. For example, the "Tete l'eau," or "Head of the Water" ceremony, is conducted at the head, or "source," of a stream. During this ceremony the followers bow to the source while the priest intones a liturgic song Hurston translates as "Master . . . we ask your protection. The water, which is able to hear mortals, we ask protection for all of us children" (227).[18] Voodoo adherents approach the loa through ritual communion with nature. While in Western theological tradition worshipers must forswear the natural world and carnal existence in order to gain the transcendent realm, in Voodoo, bodily proximity to nature is a means to the divine, and this positive revaluation of body and nature serves to contest the colonial denigration of black women.

Voodoo adherents, many of them black women, make a yearly pilgrimage to the most famous waterfall, Saut D'Eau, even though the local priest has had police stationed at the falls to discourage this pagan practice. In contradiction to the church's disparaging view, Hurston presents the celebratory ascension of the falls as a transfiguration of the worshipers from "sordid" objects to "ecstatic" beings: After discarding their clothes, "hundreds of people entering the eternal mists from the spray and ascending the sacred stones and assuming all possible postures of adoration made a picture that might have been painted by Doré. It was very beautiful and fitting. Whether they had the words to fit their feelings or not, it was a moving sight to see these people turning from sordid things once each year to go into an ecstasy of worship of the beautiful in water forms" (232). The bodily, ecstatic reentry into the sacred waters of nature ceremonially frees the black worshipers from their "sordid" existence as "things" within the colonial order and transforms them into a beautiful tableau rivaling even Doré's classic representations of Western sacred transport.[19] It is as though in stepping into the waters the participants depart from the colonial frame of reference, which casts them as "things," and enter the Voodoo perspective, which reframes them as members of a sacred order of nature. This sacralization of body and nature clearly challenges colonial objectification. Little wonder, then, that the Western church wishes to prohibit this yearly escape.

The clash between colonial-Christian and Voodoo views of nature and of black women is also evident in the history Hurston relates of a legendary sacred palm tree that became a national shrine:

A beautiful, luminous virgin lit in the fronds of a palm tree there and waved her gorgeous wings and blessed the people. She paused there a long time and the whole countryside saw her. Seeing the adoration of the people, the Catholic Priest of the parish came out to drive off the apparition. Finally she sang a beautiful song and left of her own accord. She had not been disturbed at all by the priest. People came to the palm tree and were miraculously cured and others were helped in various ways. The people began to worship the tree. The news spread all over Haiti and more and more people came. The Catholic Church was neglected. So the priest became so incensed . . . at the adoration of the people for the tree that he seized a machete and ran to the tree to cut it down himself. But the first blow of the blade against the tree caused the machete to bounce back and strike the priest on the head and wound him so seriously that he was taken to the hospital in Port-au-Prince, where he soon died of his wound. Later on the tree was destroyed by the church and a church was built on the spot to take the place of the

palm tree, but it is reported that several churches have burned on
that site. One was destroyed by lightning. (230–31)

The people's worship of the miraculous tree poses a clear threat to Catholic
authority, and the priest's animosity toward the tree leads to his attempts
to destroy this source of Afro-Caribbean spiritual nourishment and bodily
healing. The priest's religious jealousy becomes a literal battle against nature, and while the palm tree is eventually destroyed, nature continues,
through fire and lightning, to thwart church suppression.[20] The battle between tree and church is clearly a power struggle between African heritage
and Western religious domination; the tree represents the resurgence of
Voodoo worship of nature and also indicates the powers of Voodoo spirituality to unsettle Western dominance.

The tree, like the waterfall, heals and reaffirms the black bodies so despised by the colonial order. The spot, now marked by the blackened ruins
of a church, remains a site of Voodoo worship and bodily healing. Hurston
notes the physical assurance of the black women anointing their bodies at
the shrine: "They anointed their faces and legs and their bare breasts. Some
had ailing feet and legs, and they anointed them. Several women were rub-
bing their buttocks and thighs without any self consciousness at all" (230).
The tree-shrine affords these women an opportunity for affirming their
bodies and for healing physical ailments that sound remarkably like the
painful physical "distortions" of the donkey women described above. The
worship of nature overturns church fears of the flesh and soothes colonial
distortions of black women's bodies.[21] As Hurston also comments, the
women are remarkably unselfconscious about their nakedness and about
publicly touching sexual areas of their bodies. Unlike standard Christian
asceticism, which abhors sexual pleasure, the ritual of the tree embraces
female sexuality as a natural manifestation of spirit.

The tree, as Hurston would have known, is a central Voodoo symbol
and often signifies the sexual and spiritual union of the primary male and
female deities. Trees, as Hurston notes, are sacred to Legba, a major loa in
the Voodoo pantheon. In *Tell My Horse*, Hurston describes families who
have sacred trees that are the abode of their ancestors, and particular trees
are feared or worshiped as sources of spiritual knowledge for Voodoo
priests. One man even claims a tree as lover. While Hurston does not explain the significance of the tree to Voodoo belief, I will argue below that

she incorporates this imagery into the pear-tree figure in *Their Eyes Were Watching God*. Robert Thompson, a later scholar of African art and images, notes that the tree is central to many Voodoo ceremonies and religious icons. The tree is symbolized by the center post of the hounfort, or place of worship, which is circled in ritual dancing. Thompson also traces the recurring Voodoo image of a palm tree entwined by two serpents, representing the sacramental sexual embrace of the primary deity, Damballah and his wife, Ayida Hwedo, joined in an "ecstatic union" of male and female principles.[22] The sacred tree, then, as an image of spiritual and sexual ecstasy, contradicts the Judeo-Christian images of the tree-of-knowledge and the crucifix-tree, which represent the dangers of bodily knowledge and the painful renunciation of physical existence. Whereas Christian dogma would forswear the sexual, and whereas colonial structures would despise black women as repositories of sexuality, in the image of the serpent-twined sacred tree, the sexual embrace manifests divine union. This tree-and-serpent emblem symbolizes a spiritual healing of the damaging divisions of body and soul, sex and spirit, male and female, animal and divine.

Whereas Western views despised black women as the repository of bestial sexual desire, and even as in the case of Sarah Bartman, regarded their genitals as scientific evidence of their kinship with apes, Voodoo ceremonially worships black women's sexuality as the female aspect of the deity. Hurston describes a Voodoo ceremony in which the Mambo, or priestess, is questioned. "What is truth?" "She replies by throwing back her veil and revealing her sex organs. The ceremony means that this is the infinite, the ultimate truth. There is no mystery beyond the mysterious source of life. . . . It is considered the highest honor for all males participating to kiss her organ of creation, for Damballah, the god of gods, has permitted them to come face to face with truth" (113–14). While Sarah Bartman's genitals were made into Western emblems of black women's sexual debasement, the priestess's sex organs are ritually venerated as the "face of truth,"[23] and while black women's maternity is socially erased in Caribbean "rooster's nest" aspirations toward whiteness, the priestess's "organ of creation" is the literal focus of this Voodoo ritual. What colonial values discount is, in Voodoo, the center of attention and veneration. What Caribbean men use and then discard is here made the object of male worship. Most importantly, Voodoo does not permit the sorts of literal and symbolic dissections that Western science inflicted upon Sarah Bartman. The ceremony radically refigures the

Western image of black woman, replacing deadly oppositions with a cyborgian model of transgressive interconnections that unsettle normal colonial relations.

The challenge that such cyborgian relations pose to the colonial order is most clearly illustrated in the history of Celestina Simon. Celestina, called by the populace "the Black Joan of Arc," is a peasant woman and Voodoo priestess, famed for her spiritual prowess, which propelled her father from lower-class military officer to Haitian president. In her legendary history, Celestina's magical powers drove her father's soldiers to victory and intimidated the ruling-class elites who had installed her father as president in the hopes of using him as a puppet for their own control. The source of Celestina's spiritual authority is her ceremonial Voodoo "marriage" to Simalo, a goat, who is also her father's best friend. Such bonds between adepts and their animal familiars, such as Marie Leveau's snake, are readily accepted in this spiritual tradition in which animals are messengers of the gods.[24] While Celestina's marriage to Simalo may be symbolic more than actual, her father pridefully has this marriage "annulled" so that Celestina will be free to take a human husband, but the eligible upper-class men are horrified and Celestina is subsequently humiliated as well as partially bereft of her Voodoo powers. Simalo dies of grief, and the Black Joan of Arc and her father are soon deposed from the palace.[25]

In this historical tale, two members of the black lower class assumed national power and superiority to the mulatto elite through Celestina's Voodoo marriage; while this story, as Hurston tells it, verges dangerously close to the Western view of black women's bestial sexuality, it is most clearly a parable of the disruptions to colonial hierarchies brought about by Voodoo's transgressive sacralization of nature and black women's sexuality; Celestina's marriage to an animal is the direct source of her spiritual and political influence. Perhaps this Voodoo "marriage" might best be read as illustrating Donna Haraway's "cyborg myth" of "potent fusions and dangerous possibilities" (152) that breach assumed oppositions between human and animal, human and machine. Haraway explains: "The cyborg appears in myth precisely where the boundary between animal and human is transgressed. . . . Cyborgs signal disturbingly and pleasurably tight couplings. Bestiality has a new status in this cycle of marriage exchange."[26] While Haraway's cyborg is mythic rather than historical, and while Haraway does not take into account the way that the "old status" of bestiality was frequently turned against women of color, still, her cyborgian dissolution of animal/human boundaries offers a dangerous disruption of fixed social and zoological ranks that is analogous to Celestina's rupture of the colonial order.

A similar challenge to colonial ideology is posed by spirit-possession, in which the Voodoo worshiper, or "horse," is "ridden" by a spirit, or loa. Again this Voodoo rite complicates the negative conception of black women as animals, when the women's bodies denounced as donkeys, or mere laboring flesh, become manifestations of spirit, "horses" of the loa. Possession is a common Caribbean religious experience, the most forceful instance of communion between Voodoo spirit and human.[27] In possession the spirit enters the "horse" who is then transfigured by the visitant, becoming impervious to physical pain, gesturing, moving, and speaking in ways characteristic to the loa and performing extraordinary physical feats.[28] Possession challenges belief in fixed identity and crosses dichotomies between flesh and spirit, self and other, in that during possession the spirits become incarnate in the bodies of the believers, temporarily replacing the individual subjectivity with the character of the loa and inducing striking behavioral changes. Spirit and body interpenetrate, and fixed, essential identity is transgressed by the transformative presence of the gods.

Possession crosses other boundaries as well, pointedly transgressing the normative social divisions of race, gender, and class that confine Caribbean black women to the lowest social ranks. Gender is complicated when worshipers are possessed by loa of the opposite sex: thus a body of one gender becomes receptacle for a differently sexed spirit. Certain loa, such as the "facetious" Baron Samedi, make a burlesque of gender; he requires his "horses" to cross-dress: "Women dressed like men and men like women. Often the men, in addition to wearing female clothes, thrust a calabash up under their skirts to simulate pregnancy. Women put on men's coats and prance about with a stick between their legs to imitate the male sex organs" (224). Race and color divisions are also crossed since loa of one racial background may possess believers of a different racial composition. For example, because the primary female loa Erzulie is mulatto, when blacks impersonate her they cover their faces with white powder (122).[29]

Hurston explains that the black lower classes have their own particular loa, the "boisterous Guede," who is "as near a social criticism of the classes by the masses as anything in all Haiti" (219). She comments: "The people who created Guede needed a god of derision. They needed a spirit who could burlesque the society that crushed him" (220). During possession,

Guede ventriloquizes through his "horse" all sorts of impermissably bold and pointed social comments prefaced by the phrase "tell my horse." Possession by Guede permits the despised lower-class blacks to talk back to their otherwise invulnerable social superiors. In fact, Hurston suspects that peasants at times feign possession in order to speak their minds: "The phrase '(Tell my Horse)' is in daily, hourly use in Haiti and no doubt it is used as a blind for self-expression. . . . A great deal of the Guede mounts have something to say and lack the courage to say it except under the cover of brave Guede" (221). Possession is, then, a means of self-possession in the midst of extremely limiting social structures. It is a means of black women's self-redefinition, a reformation of identity and self-image, and a means of voicing social protest and criticism. It is also a means of retaining and reformulating an African-derived cultural identity in the midst of colonial domination.

Voodoo confounds other crucial Western cultural assumptions as well, further problematizing fixed binary oppositions. For example, good and evil are inevitably intertwined within Voodoo. The beneficent Rada loa are mirrored by maleficent Petro counterparts, but some priests and priestesses serve both tribes of gods, or cannot always control which set of spirits will appear when summoned.[30] Divisions between human and nature are crossed by the belief that adepts may take animal forms and that animal loa may possess humans.[31] The boundary between life and death is confused by Zombies, whose bodies are called back from death to act as enslaved laborers, yet who retain no individual consciousness.[32]

Not only does Voodoo defy Western binary division, it also confounds realist objectivity and conclusive knowability. In Hurston's discussion of Zombies we can see the conflict between the realist conventions of anthropological description that she brings to her study and the uncontainable vagaries of Voodoo that she witnesses in Haiti. Rather than being poor ethnography, on which grounds it has oftentimes been dismissed, *Tell My Horse* demonstrates Hurston's authorial waverings between differing notions of truth and representation—the anthropological dependence upon realist objectivity and causality versus the Voodoo dissolution of such certitudes.[33] Analagously, Hurston's confrontation with the Zombie Felicia exemplifies Hurston's own fluctuating narrational position throughout this text. As a black woman and social scientist studying a colonial society in which black women are objects, Hurston's authorial position is complex and contradictory. Her authority is partially dependent upon her academic training and on her status as a Westerner not subject to the Caribbean derogation of black women. At times Hurston herself appears clearly implicated in the colonial deprecation of black women, as I have noted in regard to certain of the passages quoted above. Yet, simultaneously, Hurston is clearly disturbed by the women's desperate situations and her observations generally forego objective impartiality in favor of partisan commentary on their behalf.

Her authorial waverings demonstrate her struggle with the way that Western objectivity is implicated in the colonial objectification of Caribbean women. As speaker and observer Hurston is trying to use the tools of Western science to describe the effects of Western ideology, and she is also trying to use realist observation to document a religion that subverts realist certitudes. These struggles can clearly be seen in her attempts to document and explain the phenomenon of Zombies, for Zombies defy Western credibility and confound Western science. In Hurston's discussion of this phenomenon, we can see the struggle between the practices of social-scientific observation and explanation and the inexplicability of Voodoo, and we can also see the insufficiencies of the traditional observational position of subject detached from one's object. Hurston at times utilizes an objective, realist perspective in order to give credence to the most incredible aspects of Voodoo, even as she admits that these mysteries exceed medical explanation.

Hurston understandably utilizes demonstrable proofs in order to establish the existence of Zombies for dubious Western readers, pointing to her empirical observation and photographic record as conclusive evidence: "I had the rare opportunity to see and touch an authentic case. I listened to the broken noises in its throat, and then, I did what no one else had done, I photographed it. If I had not experienced all of this in the strong sunlight of a hospital yard, I might have come away from Haiti interested but doubtful. But I saw this case of Felicia Felix Mentor, which was vouched for by the highest authority. So I know that there are Zombies in Haiti" (182) In order to validate her belief in Zombies, she presents Felicia as a case study, citing hospital authorities and relating the facts of her history, gathering medical explanations for this uncanny phenomenon. Yet in a passage describing the process of photographing Felicia, Hurston moves away from Western objectivity, which poses Felicia as the passive object of empirical scrutiny, and she instead assumes a vexed and emotional interrelation with this destroyed woman. Hurston represents the moment of photographing

Felicia as a painful and impossible struggle between science and mystery reminiscent of the fatal battle described above between the priest and the sacred palm tree. Although Hurston does "take" Felicia's face, she is devastated by the sight and, ironically, rather than solving this mystery, Hurston's visual "proofs" instead make its horror more pronounced. Rather than demonstrating the superior clarity of Western science, this struggle reveals the limitations of the classical empirical subject/object divide, in which the object is supposed to passively reflect the views of the observer.[34]

In *Woman, Native, Other* Trinh Minh-Ha argues that traditional anthropological studies tend to pose native peoples, in particular native women, as Others whose exotic difference serves, by contrast, to reinforce the contours of the anthropologist's Eurocentric culture. Yet Hurston's interaction with Felicia exposes the violent insufficiency of this model. Felicia clearly defies such objectification, and Hurston clearly refuses the role of disinterested observer: "Finally the doctor forcibly uncovered her and held her so that I could take her face. And the sight was dreadful. That blank face with the dead eyes. The eyelids were white all around her eyes as if they had been burned with acid. It was pronounced enough to come out in the picture. There was nothing that you could say to her or get from her except by looking at her, and the sight of this wreckage was too much to endure for long" (197). Hurston can "get" nothing besides her image from Felicia, and the process of attaining this image is not described as a triumphant capture by a detached observer; it is instead an emotionally devastating struggle with a horrifically intractable enigma. Felicia is here what Minhha terms an "inappropriate/d Other,"[35] who troubles rather than reinforces the sureties of medical expertise and the social-scientific explanations of the anthropologist. Hurston and the doctors cannot conclusively explain Felicia's damaged state and can only speculate that the Voodoo practitioners have medicinal secrets unknown to Western science.[36] Mystery, finally, exceeds the limits of scientific certitude and undermines the realist stance of masterful subject scrutinizing passive object that Hurston finds implicated in the traditionally appropriative ethnographic stance toward native peoples.[37]

Overall, *Tell My Horse* presents Voodoo as a powerfully transformative means of countering the denigration of Caribbean black women, in particular by revising the terms of their negative Western association with nature. Voodoo, as Hurston describes it here, exemplifies the powerful resistance that indigenous Afro-Caribbean culture offers against colonial disempow-

erment; Voodoo undermines the ground of racist and sexist colonial hierarchies and provides black women a means of redefining themselves in
positive and defiantly fluid terms. The revisionary potential of Voodoo
spirituality becomes even clearer in Hurston's classic novel of a black woman's struggle for self-creation, *Their Eyes Were Watching God.*

Hurston wrote *Their Eyes Were Watching God* during her first trip to the
Caribbean, while she was collecting the material that would later be published as *Tell My Horse.* For seven weeks she wrote late into the night after
her day's work collecting information about culture and Voodoo, compos-
ing the novel in order to calm her feelings about a tumultuous relationship
she had broken off when she left the United States.[38] Hurston recalled in
her autobiography, *Dust Tracks on a Road:* "So I sailed off to Jamaica. But I
freely admit that everywhere I set my feet down, there were tracks of
blood. Blood from the very middle of my heart. So I pitched in to work
hard on my research to smother my feelings. But the thing would not
down. The plot was far from the circumstances, but I tried to embalm all
the tenderness of my passion for him in *Their Eyes Were Watching God*" (260).
While Hurston admits to having "embalmed" her passion within this novel,
I argue that she also "embalmed" her knowledge of Voodoo spirituality
within the novel's nature imagery and the plot of Janie's development. *Embalm* is a curiously ambivalent word, implying both death and preservation,[39] and it aptly describes Hurston's use of Voodoo in this novel, which
is dismissive of Voodoo on a conscious level but is suffused imagistically
and formally with Voodoo belief.[40] In *Their Eyes,* as in *Tell My Horse,* black
women are defined as "the mules of the world," and it is Janie's Voodoo-
informed vision of the blossoming pear tree that offers her the means of
rewriting her life beyond the narrow terms of her culture. In the pear tree,
Hurston has embalmed the transgressive possibilities of the sacred Voodoo
tree that she described in *Tell My Horse.*[41]

From the start of Janie's recitation of her story to Pheoby it is clear that
she finds foreign the sorts of firm racial identities and separations observed
by her society. Like the mulattoes of the Caribbean who complicate racial
classifications, Janie is herself of mixed racial heritage and is described as
light-skinned with long silky hair.[42] As a young child being raised by her
black grandmother, who is caretaker to a white family, Janie feels akin to
the other children until shown a photograph of herself that makes obvious
her darker skin; her racial difference appears to her as an effect of photographic representation rather than innate identification.[43] She is unaware

of racial divisions until schoolchildren tease her for associating with whites and her grandmother decides to move to the black community to avoid such conflicts. Janie's early naïveté challenges the enforced racial separations of her society.

As Janie matures, Nanny further reinforces racial and gender boundaries in an attempt to teach Janie colonial values for her own protection. Like the black women in *Tell My Horse*, Nanny has experienced the treatment of black women as sexual objects and human chattel, for she has been used as both a "work ox or a brood sow" (31). As a slave she bore a daughter to her white master and then fled from the plantation when his wife threatened to whip her to death for producing such a "white" child. Having gained her freedom, Nanny later refused to marry for fear that a black man might abuse such a light-skinned child, who was indeed later raped and ruined by a black schoolteacher. Nanny believes that black women's sexuality allows their abuse at the hands of white and black men and thus must be carefully confined, if not completely denied, for their own self-protection. She also believes that property and money provide women the only protection against lives of brute labor. In order to shield Janie from the ravages of the larger world, she arranges for her to marry an unattractive older man who owns the requisite property. Nanny explains racial and gender politics to Janie in words highly reminiscent of the description of black women as donkeys in *Tell My Horse*: "Honey, de white man is de ruler of everything as fur as Ah been able to find out. . . . So de white man throw down de load and tell de nigger man tuh pick it up. He pick it up because he have to, but he don't tote it. He hand it to his womenfolks. De nigger woman is de mule uh de world so fur as Ah can see. Ah been prayin fuh it tuh be different wid you" (29).[44] Nanny's vision of black women as mules, or less than fully human, will be borne out by many other members of the black communities of the novel, who frequently refer to women as mindless or laboring farm animals. Janie's first husband associates her labor with the purchase of a new mule, while her second husband insists that she must docilely follow his dictates since women are as irrational as cows and chickens. The porch talkers, too, swap remarks and tales that represent women as sexual objects and dumb animals provided for male amusement.

Yet while Nanny would have Janie confirm and negotiate her powerlessness as mule, Janie instead resists this role through her vision of the blooming pear tree that she internalizes as self-image and metaphoric emblem of her desires.[45] Like the sacred tree in *Tell My Horse*, the pear tree refigures black women's association with nature as healing rather than debased. Janie uses this figure of the tree as a standard to direct and measure the stages of her life against the social limits she encounters; the tree affords Janie a Voodoo vision of the transformative possibility beyond the confines of racist and sexist social relations, and thus it spurs her growing resistance to confining external definitions of black women as mules. The first occurrence of this figure opens Janie's recitation of her life history to Pheoby and presents her life as encompassing a mingling of opposites: "Janie saw her life like a great tree in leaf with the things suffered, things enjoyed, things done and undone. Dawn and doom was in the branches" (20). As Missy Dean Kubetschek notes, the passage indicates "a balance of opposites . . . perhaps even the union of opposites, since the singular verb 'was' indicates a singular subject in 'dawn and doom.'"[46] Such a union or intermingling of opposites derived from Voodoo spirituality will constitute Hurston's narrative of Janie's development.

The actual pear-tree scene is central to Hurston's revision of black women's sexuality and to Janie's rejection of the colonial view endorsed by Nanny. Like the sacred tree in *Tell My Horse*, the pear tree image radically revises the binary oppositions informing the definition of black women as mules by refiguring nature as the interpenetration of dichotomies:

> Janie had spent most of the day under a blossoming pear tree in the back-yard. She had been spending every minute that she could steal from her chores under that tree for the last three days . . . ever since the first tiny bloom had opened. It had called her to come and gaze on a mystery. From barren brown stems to glistening leaf-buds; from leaf-buds to snowy virginity of bloom. It stirred her tremendously. How? Why? It was like a flute song forgotten in another existence and remembered again. . . . This singing she heard that had nothing to do with her ears. The rose of the world was breathing out smell. It followed her through all her waking moments and caressed her in her sleep. It connected itself with other vaguely felt matters that had struck her outside observation and buried themselves in her flesh. Now they emerged and quested about her consciousness.
>
> She was stretched on her back beneath the pear tree soaking in the alto chant of the visiting bees, the gold of the sun and the panting breath of the breeze when the inaudible voice of it all came to

her. She saw a dust-bearing bee sink into the sanctum of a bloom;
the thousand sister-calyxes arch to meet the love embrace and the
ecstatic shiver of the tree from root to tiniest branch creaming in
every blossom and frothing with delight. So this was a marriage!
She had been summoned to behold a revelation. Then Janie felt a
pain remorseless sweet that left her limp and languid (22–24).

In this passage the sexual is mingled with the sacred, the physical with the
immaterial, the human with the natural, pain with pleasure, and gender
division all but disappears in Janie's revelation of marriage.[47] Much of the
language is overtly ceremonial and biblical: "mystery," "snowy virginity,"
"rose," "alto chant," "gold," "the sanctum," and "revelation." At the same time
the revelation is sensuously physical and explicitly sexual: "matters that had
. . . buried themselves in her flesh," "the thousand sister-calyxes arch to
meet the love embrace and the ecstatic shiver of the tree . . . creaming in
every blossom and frothing with delight," "pain remorseless sweet." This
mingled description mixes the sexual with the sacred and locates both
within nature, as in the Voodoo image of the serpent-twined tree, symbolic
of Damballah and his wife in sacred intercourse. As in that Voodoo icon,
Janie's profound identification with this sacred tree, which culminates in
her empathetic orgasm, works metonymically to inscribe Janie's desire as
revelatory. Like the Voodoo ceremony described above, during which the
priestess's vagina is revealed as source of sacred truth, this passage presents
black female sexuality as sacred mystery, as the "rose of the world." Janie's
vision of the pear tree gives her a sense of life's pleasure and fulfillment that
counters Nanny's vision of inevitable degradation and drudgery. As in *Tell
My Horse*, the tree vision affirms black women's erotic energy as vital source
of life.

Like Voodoo, this inscription of the sacred tree unsettles normative
Western dichotomies underlying the derogatory conception of black
women. Nature, rather than being base object of scientific scorn, is sacralized. Female sexuality, rather than being bestialized, is revelatory. The
tree's desire, which is rendered female through the implication of the word
sister (although the passage is actually largely gender-neutral) is presented
as both active sensuality and engaged receptivity. Human and natural are
merged, not hierarchically separated. Pain and pleasure are indivisible. This
image of the tree unifies the supposed opposites that cast women as mules.

Janie internalizes this commingled image, overtly identifying her own desire with that of the tree: "Oh to be a pear tree—*any* tree in bloom! With kissing bees singing of the beginning of the world! She was sixteen. She had glossy leaves and bursting buds and she wanted to struggle with life but it seemed to elude her. Where were the singing bees for her?" (25). Janie's identification with the tree corresponds to the spiritual convergence of adept and nature loa in Voodoo worship. This identification offers Janie a sense of ripening possibilities and the strong desire to "struggle with life" rather than concede. Desire recreates the world.

Janie claims kinship and communion with nature much like that of a Voodoo priestess: "She knew things that nobody had ever told her. For instance, the words of the trees and the wind. She often spoke to falling seeds and said, 'Ah hope you fall on soft ground,' because she had heard seeds saying that to each other as they passed" (44). Throughout the novel, Janie will use the image of the tree as a vision of possibility that opens up the limiting assumptions of her culture. The blossoming pear tree will act as what Henry Louis Gates calls "Janie's master trope on her way to becoming" (187).

Through this master trope the blighting limitations of Nanny's views become strongly apparent. Janie sees her as a ravaged tree: "the standing roots of some old tree that had been torn away by storm. Foundation of ancient power that no longer mattered" (26). While Janie believes that Nanny has betrayed her foundation by valuing property and security over dreams and fulfillment, she also realizes that Nanny's powers have been torn from her by the storms of history that she has survived; it is significant that Nanny named the daughter whom she was later unable to protect, Leafy. Janie later explains to Pheoby that because of the hardships of slavery and reconstruction, Nanny has forsaken her "roots" and adopted white people's preference of "things" over "people." And even more dangerously, Nanny has acceded to the white view of black women as "things," or mules, rather than people, by setting Janie "in the marketplace to sell" instead of allowing her to quest after her dream tree (138). Paralleling Hurston's description of the sacred waterfall's transformation of Caribbean women from "sordid things" to beatific beings in *Tell My Horse,* Janie fights Nanny's objectification through a folk-derived image of herself as God's infinitely precious creation: "She had found a jewel down inside herself and she had wanted to walk where people could see her and gleam it around" (138). Similarly, Janie utilizes the tree to measure the shortcomings of her first two marriages. Because the physically repulsive Logan Killicks "was desecrating the pear tree" (28), Janie eventually flees this loveless marriage. She next elopes with self-important and domineering Jody Starks, who spoke of horizons rather than bees and blossoms, but years of his oppressive pomposity have killed her "petal-openness": "She had no more blossomy openings dusting pollen over her man, neither any glistening young fruit where the petals used to be" (111–12).

After Jody's death, the vision of the tree prompts Janie to look for another mode of relations that is more life-affirming, more satisfying, and less bound by arbitrary social inequalities and divisions. Her marriage to Tea Cake (Vergible) Woods, fulfills her vision: "He could be a bee for her blossom—a pear tree blossom in the spring. . . . He was a glance from God" (161). As Wall observes, Tea Cake is a "man of nature" embodying an alternative definition of manhood independent of the white attributes of power and property.[48] By marrying Tea Cake, Janie attains her pear-tree vision of nonhierarchical marriage and she literally becomes Janie Woods, realizing her identification with the tree.[49] Describing Janie's relationship to Tea Cake, Barbara Christian emphasizes the role of play in Janie's pear-tree vision of marriage: "Hurston characterizes this relationship as play, pleasure, sensuality, which is for her the essential nature of nature itself, as symbolized by the image of the pear tree that pervades the novel. . . . Hurston used metaphors derived from nature's play to emphasize the connection between the natural world and the possibilities of a harmonious social order."[50] The pear tree symbolizes playful, harmonious, sensuous relations— a Voodoo-informed vision of lively interconnectedness that vexes the dominant social order and directs Janie toward the freer, more playful, less rigidly defined life with Tea Cake on the muck.

Following Tea Cake to the muck, Janie participates in an agricultural folk community that defies many of the limiting divisions of the dominant society, much as in her vision of the pear tree.[51] Although the community of the muck is still implicated in the racism, sexism, and classism of the surrounding social order and although Hurston does not hide the violence or hardship of the migrant farmworkers' lives, her emphasis is on the relative freedom of this vagrant life and on the cultural richness of this lowest class of blacks. Like spirit-possession, which defies the bounds of race, class, and gender, on the muck the oppositions that structure the surrounding society are loosened: men and women dress, work, flirt, and fight alike, diminishing gender distinctions; ethnic and racial groups meet and mingle, sharing cultural traditions and rites; and all participate in the folk-culture games, music, dances, and stories that challenge white dominance. The muck is primal site of the play of the folk process that Hurston cherished as the core of black culture. Like the constant metamorphosis of Voodoo practices and philosophy, on the muck folk culture is constantly recreated: "All night now the jooks clanged and clamored. Pianos living three lifetimes in one. Blues made and used right on the spot. Dancing, fighting, singing, crying, laughing, winning, and losing love every hour. Work all day for money, fight all night for love. The rich black earth clinging to bodies and biting the skin like ants" (196–97). Like Voodoo services, the folk process of the muck is prompted by immersion in nature, when the people are coated with the "rich black earth," which re-emphasizes and revalues their own blackness. The earth of the muck, both "rich" and "biting," symbolizes the harsh potential of life on the muck and signifies the commingling of opposites beyond dichotomies, much like Janie's earliest orgasmic "pain remorseless sweet." On the muck Janie comes into her own as a person actively engaged in the folk community—dancing, playing, telling stories, even fighting over Tea Cake as well as with him. Within her marriage to Tea Cake, she asserts herself as equal, active partner, refusing stereotypes of gender, class, and color.

Yet, as Wall observes, the relatively nonhierarchical relations within the muck community are finally disturbed by Mrs. Turner's insistent class and color consciousness.[52] Like the Caribbean mulattoes in *Tell My Horse*, Mrs. Turner argues that light-skinned blacks should "class off" and aspire toward whiteness. Janie refutes Mrs. Turner's divisive racial categorization by noting that "we'se ah mingled people and all us got black kinfolks as well as yaller kinfolks" (210). Although Janie is propertied and light-skinned, her allegiance remains with Tea Cake and the multiethnic working-class community. For Janie, race is not a fixed and final matter of color so much as it is a chosen community and common culture. Notably, whereas at the commencement of the novel Janie identified with the white children, now she identifies with the itinerant blacks.[53] Unfortunately, Tea Cake and his cohorts distrust Janie's heterogeneous views on class and color. The idyll on the muck falters with Tea Cake's beating of Janie and his semicomic but destructive revenge against the Turners. The beneficent pear-tree vision of harmonious and "mingled" relations is not, finally, impervious to the antagonisms of colonial divisions.

If the muck exemplifies a beneficent Voodoo disruption of the white culture's false oppositions, the hurricane enacts a destructive rupture of the colonial order that is reminiscent of the malevolent Petro Voodoo loa, whom Thompson describes as "stern, hard, fierce," offering "salvation through extremity and intimidation."[54] Whereas the more benign Rada loa respond to supplicants' gifts of prayer and food, the fearsome Petro gods require sacrifices, even, it is rumored, death of their subjects.[55] It is this devastatingly chaotic face of divine power that is manifest in the storm, wreaking havoc with the artificial bounds of colonialism. The storm literally washes away the screen of white values that stands between the black community of the muck and the face of divine power. While Tea Cake and his friends stubbornly imitate the white bosses' resistance to the hurricane rather than the wise retreat of the Indians and the Bahamanians, the storm eventually forces them to look to God, rather than to false white authority. As the storm gathers strength, the narrator comments, "The time was past for asking the white folks what to look for through the door. Six eyes were questioning *God*" (235). And in the title passage the darkness of the storm replaces the image of white domination: "They seemed to be staring at the dark, but their eyes were watching God." Colonial ideology is driven awry by the hurricane.

The power of the wind and lake soon overthrows the normal order, causing all sorts of frightful reversals and transgressions much like the disruptive border-crossings of Voodoo spirit-possession, in which boundaries between classes, genders, races, human and nature, living and dead no longer hold. Nothing remains as it was, nothing appears unchanged. Nature rages out of control, ferociously destroying the complacencies of human domination. The placid lake becomes a menacing beast, freed from human restraint by the hurricane winds: "He seized hold of his dikes and ran forward until he met the quarters; uprooted them like grass and rushed on after his supposed-to-be conquerors, rolling the dikes, rolling the houses, rolling the people in the houses along with other timbers" (239). Nature, rather than whites, takes the upper hand, and chaos reigns, refusing normal polarities of life and death: "The wind and water had given life to lots of things that folks think of as dead and given death to so much that had been living things" (236). The separation of humans and animals, too, disappears before the storm: "They passed a dead man in a sitting position on a hummock entirely surrounded by wild animals and snakes. Common danger made common friends. Nothing sought a conquest over the other" (243). Apparent racial differences are erased by the ravages of death: decomposing white and black corpses are essentially indistinguishable to the men forced to attempt to sort them into segregated mass graves."[56] The city of Jacksonville, symbol of progressive human dominion over nature and site of extreme racial segregation, is decimated by the hurricane, while the more adaptable and fluid community of the muck survives the ravages more or less intact.[57]

The devastating extremities of the storm also overtake Janie and Tea Cake's marriage when Tea Cake contracts rabies while rescuing Janie from the attack of a rabid dog during the flood. Tea Cake's ensuing illness and mania translate the external destructions of the storm into a tempestuous and deadly internal struggle in which the violence and confusions of the hurricane contort Tea Cake's body and behavior. As the rabies progresses, Tea Cake is possessed by the "blank ferocity" of the dog (269), much in the way that Hurston had described Voodoo adherents whose faces and movements are terrifyingly distorted while "ridden" by the malevolent Petro loa. It is as though through this disease the disturbances of the storm infect Janie's pear-tree "vision of marriage," revealing love and violence, union and death, rescue and destruction, self-sacrifice and self-protection to be inextricably intertwined—the "things suffered, things enjoyed, things done and undone . . . dawn and doom" (20) in the branches of Janie's life-tree. Like spirit-possession, Tea Cake's rabies attacks comfortably false binaries. Driven by crazed malevolence, Tea Cake demonstrates the violence of overpossessive love, as he professes affection for Janie one moment and rails against her, threatening her with his pistol, the next. The disease is described as an alien spirit possessing his body, from which Tea Cake can be saved only through his death; as Tea Cake repeatedly fires upon her, Janie believes that the only way to preserve herself and her lover is by killing him: "She threw up the barrel of the rifle in frenzied hope and fear" (272). At the final moment of his death, nurture and destruction coexist in pained embrace: "She was trying to hover him as he closed his teeth in the flesh of her forearm. They came down heavily like that. . . . She had wanted him to live so much and he was dead" (273).

Throughout her relationship with Tea Cake, Janie has acknowledged the interpenetration of polar extremes, professing her willingness to risk pain in order to approach bliss. As she told him at the onset of the hurricane: "If you kin see de light at daybreak, you don't keer if you die at dusk" (236). In leaving the closed safety of her high seat for this unconventional marriage, Janie has ventured into the realm of Derridian freeplay beyond the closed circle of Western values, entering the rough and rich life on the muck, surviving the horrendous trials of the storm, and enduring the final trauma of Tea Cake's death. She has, as she tells Pheoby, been to the "far horizon," that place at which all lines of distinction converge into a single point, where seeming oppositions meld into new complexities. In the final moment of the novel, Janie "pulled in her horizon like a great fishnet. Pulled it from around the waist of the world and draped it over her shoulder" (286). She enfolds herself within the meshes of all the vast and contradictory array of existence.

Having pursued her vision of the tree even through the turbulence of the storm, Janie has fulfilled her desire to "utilize herself all over"—not only to actualize every imagined aspect of herself but also to refuse the bounded visions of her culture, to grasp that horizon where everything is inextricably intermingled and one may roam "all over," free of imprisoning demarcations. Janie's original Voodoo vision of nature's profuse interconnected web has spurred her to create a life in which the horizon conforms to her own person and is molded about her desires. For Janie has exploded the dominant culture's view of fixed vistas, which has been turned so horrendously against black women, and she has learned instead that the horizon may shift and shape according to the force of our dream visions. In this novel, unlike realist, naturalist views of the inescapable forces of the external world, the dream is truth and the power of the vision reforms the horizon.

This refusal of external constraints, this uncontained spillage across normative boundaries, also shapes the formal texture of this text. Narrationally, *Their Eyes Were Watching God* is, as Gates calls it, a double-voiced "speakerly text" in which the vernacular richness of Janie's folk speech melds with the more standard voice of the speaker to color the entire narrative. The vernacular-tinged narrational voice exemplifies Afro-American culture's emphasis on the powers of language and verbal play. Wall among others observes that in Afro-American culture, social power is often asserted through verbal mastery, and this novel is in many respects the story of Janie's coming to voice despite the cultural suppression of women's speech.[58] In this novel, as in Afro-American folk culture, articulation is a source of power; the storytellers in *Mules* comment that the tongue is a sword, and one who wields it well has the law in her mouth.

Hurston's folk-derived views of African-American language disrupt the tyrannies of transparent realist representation, which, like anthropological methodology, often tended to pose nonwhite peoples as object, rather than as subject, of discourse.[59] Like the thematic disruptions discussed above, Afro-American verbal play challenges the basic assumptions of literary realism in which transparent language is supposed to passively convey the objective realities of the external world, transmitting a "true" portrait of a unitary "reality."

In "Characteristics of Negro Expression," Hurston explains that black expressive forms emphasize the play of the art media rather than its invisibility, as she believes to be the case in Western arts. Hurston notes that the Negro uses of adornment, dramatization, stylization all emphatically call attention to themselves and the artistry of the expression. Hurston explains that the playful, generative, decorative aspects of expressive forms, more than literal transmission, are prized in Afro-American culture, for "there can never be too much beauty, let alone enough" (Sanctified Church, 53). Hurston notes that African-Americans embellish language through the use of double descriptive verbs, metaphors, "signifying." They adorn dance with angular, stylized motions, dramatic innuendo, and changing rhythms. Hurston comments that through these stylistic improvisations, African-Americans have been able to reshape practices of the dominant white culture and thus claim them as their own: "While he lives and moves in the midst of a white civilization, everything that he touches is re-interpreted for his own use. . . . Thus has arisen a new art in the civilized world" (Sanctified Church, 58–59).

Gates would later expound a similar view of black art in his highly influential The Signifying Monkey, which argues that while Western verbal expression has depended upon literal interpretation of language, black verbal artistry has realized the complex figurative, contextual, ambiguous, and therefore more elastic and open-ended interpretive possibilities of language and other arts.[60] Such verbal play has the effect, Houston Baker argues in Modernism and the Harlem Renaissance, of "deforming mastery," of destroying Western discourses and patterns of thought that had been used in the enslavement and continued deformation of African Americans. Nonrealist, modernist forms, Baker observes, have political implications for black artists: in deforming mastery, such artists defy the surrounding master narratives of the dominant culture that have been employed to enslave them. Mastery, itself the ground of realist form, must be undermined.[61]

Notably, such a tension between realist concession to the external world and African-American reformations through language is inscribed as gender specific in the opening passages of Their Eyes Were Watching God.

Men, the speaker tells us, are realists, acceding to the exigencies of the external world, waiting passively on the shore for their dreams to wash in or drift past along the horizon. Women, oppositely, actively shape their situation in accordance to their dreams: "Now women forget all those things they don't want to remember, and remember everything they don't want to forget. The dream is the truth. Then they act and do accordingly" (9).[62] In the novel that follows, dreams are indeed truth, and language and stories frequently produce actions and incidents. Figurative and literal workings of language become inextricable as the narration wavers between them in a current that destabilizes their opposition; tropes, images, and figures of speech often reenter the text as literal embodiments, and this textual interplay of figures and literalizations emphasizes the productive powers of language and the impossibility of distinguishing finally between these aspects.[63] The mule, for example, first appears as a trope for the porch sitters and then as a figure for black women in Nanny's speech but soon reappears as the scraggly mule of Starksville that represents Janie's subjugation and Jody's power. The storm originates as a descriptive trope for Nanny's turbulent history but returns as the actual hurricane. The pear tree, which is first introduced as a trope for the complexities of Janie's history and which soon reenters the text as the eroticized pear tree in Nanny's yard, moves back and forth between figurative and literal so many times in the course of this novel as to undermine any clear distinction between these formal modes.

Such moving figure-elements are most often natural phenomena, and the verbal play that textures the narrative serves to denaturalize the operations of realist narrative in which transparent language describes nature as a fixed object. In Hurston's novel, the continuous textual circuit between figurative and literal creates a more mutual and active partnership between word and world, and the play of natural figures and natural elements also suggests that our imaginative stories of nature will produce our relations with the natural-social world. In this novel, then, the verbal play works formally to dislodge the dominant discourse of nature, which has proved so detrimental to black women, and to re-create an alternative, positively playful discourse that fosters Janie's self-creation. Dreams indeed become "truth," because our visions will produce our interactions with what we determine to be the "world"; through the Voodoo-inspired dream of the blossoming pear tree, Janie gains the power to reshape the contours of her life.

In *Their Eyes Were Watching God*, Hurston has used Voodoo spirituality to articulate a vision of black women's self-created possibilities amidst a hostile social order. As in *Tell My Horse,* Voodoo refigures and reforms the limiting terms of the dominant culture. Thus, with these two texts, Hurston recalls the radical possibilities already implicit within indigenous Afro-Caribbean tradition; she remembers the sacred Voodoo tree that continues to thwart Western suppression by offering black women an alternative image of freedom and self-love, rooted within African-derived belief.

3

Returning to the Sacred Tree: Black Women, Nature, and Political Resistance in Alice Walker's *Meridian*

I became aware of my need for Zora Neale Hurston's work some time before I knew her work existed.—*Alice Walker*

The very trees hold our stories.—*Beth Brant.*

ALICE WALKER'S REDISCOVERY of Zora Neale Hurston, who died in obscurity with her innovative writings out of print and out of favor, is now a literary legend. A budding writer, Walker was researching the practices of hoodoo for her short story "The Revenge of Hannah Kemhuff," when she found a reference to Hurston's material on African-derived religions buried in the footnote of a white-authored text on "The Negro and His Folkways and Superstitions" (*Mothers' Gardens*, 11). Walker proceeded to excavate Hurston's out-of-print writings from obscure library collections and took delight in the quality that she calls Hurston's "racial health: a sense of black people as complete, complex, *undiminished* human beings" (*Mothers' Gardens*, 85). Outraged at Hurston's disappearance from the canon of African-American literature, Walker began campaigning to restore Hurston to print and to renewed literary repute, editing *I Love*

Myself When I Am Laughing: A Zora Neale Hurston Reader, which brought excerpts of Hurston's work back into the public eye. In 1973 Walker made a pilgrimage to Florida to plant a tombstone on Hurston's unmarked grave, a symbolic journey that epitomized Walker's mission to unearth Hurston from oblivion and grant her the homage that is her due. Walker admonishes: *"We are a people. A people do not throw their geniuses away.* And if they are thrown away, it our duty *as artists and as witnesses for the future* to collect them again for the sake of our children, if necessary, bone by bone" (*Mothers' Gardens,* 92).

It is more than coincidence that Walker rediscovered Hurston through her interest in African-derived religious practices such as hoodoo, more than coincidence that Walker needed this material for a story in which her character would use root medicine to redress the wrongs of racial inequality. For in Hurston, Walker retrieved not only a scholarly and sympathetic authority on African-derived spiritual practices but, more importantly, a precursor who had written appreciatively about the strength, ingenuity, and artistry of the rural African-American and Afro-Caribbean "folk" and who had seen their cultures as forms of creative rebellion against social injustice. Walker, herself the youngest daughter of southern sharecroppers, found in Hurston a foremother who had prepared the ground for her own literary efforts to describe the various ways that rural black women, scorned and stereotyped by the dominant culture, turn to African-American cultural heritage as a source of strength and inspiration.[1]

I am using the term *return* to represent Alice Walker's literary relationship to Zora Neale Hurston. I define *return* as a dual movement that travels backward to reclaim previous texts and history and that also, simultaneously, veers forward, turning what has been reclaimed in a new direction. Walker makes no bones about her indebtedness to Hurston and other precursors, and she writes essays, poems, and fiction that not only discuss Hurston's works but that also imaginatively recast and respond to Hurston's pre-texts. Walker, who came of age during the heyday of the Civil Rights era and who has since then participated in numerous other social movements such as feminism, American Indian Rights, and environmentalism, turns Hurston's revision of nature, gender, and race toward political action and advocacy on the part of people of color, women, and the natural world.

Beginning with her earliest writings, Walker described the way that southern race relations, particularly the prevailing system of sharecropping, produced a painfully contradictory relationship between African

Americans and the surrounding natural world. As impoverished farmworkers, blacks performed farm labor for white profit, yet, Walker notes that at
the same time, the natural world was also one source of joy for people
deprived of most worldly goods and pastimes. Black women, like her
mother, took great pleasure in gardening and in admiring the beauties of
the lush southern landscape that they could never own.[2] Extending this
analysis, Walker's essays, poems, and novels have become increasingly out-
spoken about the parallels she perceives between the despoliation of the
natural world and the decimation of people of color and women. For example, in her recent novel, *Possessing the Secret of Joy*, the African practice of
female genital mutilation is shown to have been justified through myths
describing God's mutilation and rape of the earth. Walker also emphasizes
the correspondence between social injustice and environmental issues, using cultural analysis to critique our treatment of nature.[3] In a recent essay,
"Everything Is a Human Being," Walker plays upon Hurston's description
of black women as "mule of the world" when she equates the degradation of the natural world with the abuse of women and people of color:
"Some of us have become used to thinking that woman is the nigger of the
world, that a person of color is the nigger of the world, that a poor person
is the nigger of the world. But, in truth, Earth itself has become the nigger
of the world. It is perceived, ironically, as other, alien, evil, and threatening"
(*Living by the Word*, 47).

Like Hurston before her, Walker turns to indigenous cultures for alternative paradigms that might change these destructive social/natural relations. While Hurston was a trained ethnographer, Walker takes a more
eclectic approach, and her writings blend personal history with imaginative
responses to primary and secondary readings on diverse world cultures.
Perhaps more importantly, while Hurston was intent on recording and revaluing cultural tradition, Walker's writings also describe the way that her
exposure to indigenous cultures leads to her involvement in political actions on behalf of embattled peoples and endangered traditions.[4]

In this chapter I will look at Walker's second novel, *Meridian*, as an early
work that clearly returns to Hurston's writings about black women, nature,
and indigenous culture. Not only does *Meridian* echo Hurston's *Their Eyes
Were Watching God*, it also recovers and explicitly politicizes the socially subversive aspect of Voodoo that Hurston had treated openly within her ethnographic study *Tell My Horse* but that she had "embalmed" within the
nature imagery and plot of her novel. *Meridian* restores the historical con-

text and African-derived beliefs that Hurston had hidden within the novel and turns indigenous history and belief toward open political contestation of social oppressions.[5]

In *Meridian*, Walker revives Hurston's view of African-derived spirituality as subverting the negative colonial construction of black women as donkeys, or sexual beasts, but Walker additionally links indigenous animistic spiritualization of nature with civil rights activism against southern racial segregation.[6] *Meridian*, like *Their Eyes Were Watching God*, focuses upon a young black woman's quest to re-create the limited terms of her life within a racist and sexist society. Much as Hurston's *Their Eyes Were Watching God* traces Janie's self-transformation from "mule of the world" to self-possessed, erotically fulfilled woman, *Meridian* chronicles the political transformation of Meridian Hill from a suicidal teenage mother who has been defeated by her lack of options within the Jim Crow rural South into a dedicated activist who uses her body as an instrument to protest social wrongs.

As Hurston's Janie refused Nanny's view of black women as mules, Meridian comes to reject the social geography of racial segregation that impoverishes her people, particularly the black mothers who are driven to desperate straits trying to care for children seen as worthless by the larger society. Much the way that Janie uses her pear-tree vision to counter Nanny's teachings, Meridian will come to understand segregation as historical condition rather than natural fact through two historically marked natural phenomena. The Sacred Serpent Indian burial mound and the Sojourner tree give her access to Native American and African-American counterhistories that challenge the status quo. Furthermore, the mound and tree provide Meridian with indigenous models of spiritual collectivity and animate equality—a vision of different entities dancing together in swirling freedom—that Meridian will translate into action against the fixed social divisions of the Jim Crow South. Whereas Janie enacted her pear-tree vision of marriage in her egalitarian union with Tea Cake Woods, Meridian will eschew sexual relations and will transform herself instead by deploying her body in the cause of racial equality. The geographical overtones of Meridian Hill's name assure us that, indeed, Meridian returns to indigenous views of social/natural alliance in order to strive toward a more egalitarian social geography of the racially stratified South.

Much as Hurston in *Tell My Horse* had described the negative colonial representation of African-Caribbean women as talking donkeys, *Meridian* describes Jim Crow racial segregation as continuing the objectification of black women that had originated under the system of chattel slavery in which blacks had been treated as human cattle. In this system of agricultural slave labor, the negative association of African women and nature was reinforced as black women were "put in the ground" to perform arduous field labor. Paula Giddings notes that as slavery replaced indentured servitude, field labor became the distinguishing division between black slaves and white servants, a sign of the innately bestial character of black women. Giddings quotes the Virginia colonist John Hammond, who concluded that while most women are suited to domestic work, "Yet som (black) wenches that are nasty and beastly and not fit to be so employed are put in the ground."[7] Through self-serving circular logic, slave women assigned to "the ground" were then construed by white colonists as innately subhuman beasts of burden. Even after the legal abolition of slavery and the initial period of more egalitarian social changes following the Civil War, the white conflation of blacks with lower nature was incorporated both implicitly and explicitly within racist stereotypes and ideologies about white superiority and black inferiority. Blacks were construed as savages essentially foreign to Western civilization, and it was argued that blacks were best suited to labor "in the ground" as agricultural serfs.

The Jim Crow laws enforcing racial segregation that were introduced in the 1870s and increasingly adopted by southern states at the turn of the century once again legally reinforced blacks' less than fully human social status. C. Vann Woodward, in *The Strange Career of Jim Crow*, observes that white supremacy and black subordination were to be maintained by curtailing any sort of egalitarian cross-racial social exchange. The laws mandated social and geographical segregation of the races in matters such as housing, employment, schooling, churches, eating and drinking, public and state facilities, public transportation, parks, and other entertainment facilities. Black and white were to live virtually separated except for blacks who performed services in white arenas. Fraternization between the races was forbidden by law. Interracial marriage was a punishable crime, and children of admittedly mixed parentage could be seized by the states. (Of course this law was constantly overlooked in the frequent instances of the rape of black women by white men.) Even the verbal mention of racial kinship in tropes such as "the brotherhood of man" was legally forbidden. Jim Crow legislation also disenfranchised blacks through poll taxes and property and literacy requirements for voting that left all governmental powers in the hands of whites.

Meridian articulates the way that this social geography of racial segregation and white supremacy *dispossesses* blacks of any secure relationship to
homeland, history, and self-determination. Ironically, the historical conflation of blacks with nature severs them from any secure relationship to
southern land; while blacks continue to be seen as innately suited to agricultural labor, as serfs they are unable to purchase the land they worked.
Walker describes this state of structural *disinheritance* in an essay: "If it is true
that land does not belong to anyone until they have buried a body in it,
then the land of my birthplace belongs to me, dozens of times over. Yet the
history of my family, like the history of all black Southerners, is a history of
dispossession. We loved the land and worked the land, but we never owned
it; and even after we bought land, as my great-grandfather did after the
Civil War, it was always in danger of being taken away, as his was, during
the period following Reconstruction" (*Our Mothers' Gardens*, 143). Meridian's
family will be dispossessed from their family farm in just this way when it
is made into a public park that, because of segregation, does not permit
them to set foot on their former land. Such geographical dispossession re-
sults in hardship for the poor rural blacks whose sustenance is often closely
tied to land and farming. Most of the people described in *Meridian* struggle
with extreme poverty and tenuous existence, working, for example, as
sharecroppers, factory workers, and domestics, even selling logs rolled of
soiled newspaper. Yet they are encouraged to accept such dispossessions
as natural, even as religiously ordained. Meridian's mother uses an animal
analogy to defend segregated race relations as God's will: "God separated
the sheep from the goats and the black folks from the white" (85).

Within the social landscape of *Meridian*, black women experience a similar dispossession of their own bodies. Walker expands upon the situation
of black women that Hurston had encapsulated within the phrase "the
mules of the world." As Nanny had instructed Janie in *Their Eyes Were Watching God*, men treat black women as "spit cups," or sexual objects. Because of
this, black women's sexuality often leads to danger and ruination, and only
marriage affords a degree of protection from sexual abuses. The women in
Meridian, particularly Meridian herself, illustrate Nanny's grim view.[8] Meridian experiences sexual encounters as incursions that rob her of self-
determination and sexual pleasure.

As a girl and a young woman, Meridian is bombarded with the sexual
advances of men such as her boyfriends, the funeral parlor employees, the
Saxon college doctor, and the retired professor, all of whom offer her food

and favors in return for sexual grappling. Meridian views sex as an unequal exchange in which males gain pleasure and women gain a small degree of economic and social security. Like Hurston's Nanny, Meridian views men as an unavoidable danger and believes that a secure sexual alliance offers the only protection from the unwanted advances of other men: "She was . . . always afraid until she was taken under the wing of whoever wandered across her defenses to become—in a surprisingly quick time—her lover. This, then was probably what sex meant to her; not pleasure, but a sanctuary in which her mind was freed of any consideration for all the other males in the universe who might want anything of her. It was resting from pursuit" (62). Having spent much energy resisting such undesired approaches, Meridian becomes unable to surrender her body to sexual pleasure, even within the relatively secure confines of her brief marriage. Since for Meridian sexual relations are a battle between the sexes, women's sexual pleasure, ironically, becomes equated with "giving in," with conceding oneself to male domination, even within the "sanctuary" of marriage: "Much as she wanted to, she—her body that is—never had any intention of *giving in*. She was suspicious of pleasure" (67). Within the framework of unequal power relations, women's sexual pleasure appears a further betrayal of their self-determination.

Meridian unintentionally discovers that heterosexual relations in her society also lead inexorably to pregnancy, further undermining women's already limited self-determination when they assume the overwhelming responsibilities of motherhood within a society that scorns black children.[9] Much as Hurston had described Caribbean women as donkeys, *Meridian* recounts the blighting pain of the poor black mothers whose lives are a debilitating attempt to raise their children in a society that devalues and actively destroys black life and in which women are most often handed entire responsibility for reproduction and sustenance of children. In the precarious struggle to raise children within the harsh conditions of southern segregation, the mother's well-being is often sacrificed in order to secure the existence of her children.

Meridian comes to understand that this painfully perverse maternity is a historical legacy of the system of American slavery in which African-American women were treated as "breeders" who owned neither themselves nor their children.[10] As chattel slaves, black women were considered a certain form of livestock, self-reproducing property whose children would become an additional source of profit for their white owners. A white planter explicitly equates the breeding of black women with the breeding of stock: "As much attention is paid to the breeding and growth of negroes as to that of horses and mules. Further south, we raise them both for use and market."[11] Chattel slavery posed African-American mothers as human cattle rather than persons and valued their children as produce rather than kin. In fact, Hortense Spillers argues that the construction of blacks as property was predicated on this denial of kinship between slaves and their children: in property exchanges, maternal/child relations could and would be severed and paternal/child relations would generally be ignored or denied, particularly when white masters owned the offspring they fathered upon black women. Object status and human kinship were regarded as mutually exclusive. Spillers explains: "Certainly if 'kinship' were possible, the property relations would be undermined, since the offspring would then 'belong' to a mother and a father." Spillers calls the contradictory status of slave mothers who were denied kinship with their children as simultaneously "mother and mother-dispossessed."[12]

In this vein, Meridian comments upon the contradictory relation of slave mothers to their children: "They would not have belonged to her but to the white person who 'owned' them all. Meridian knew that enslaved women had been made miserable by the sale of their children, that they had laid down their lives, gladly, for their children, that the daughters of these enslaved women had thought their greatest blessing from 'Freedom' was that it meant they could keep their own children" (91). Meridian realizes that, having suffered the dissolution of kinship ties under slavery and having made terrible sacrifices in order to maintain families, black women have, of necessity, defined their lives around the continuing struggle to preserve their children amidst a hostile white society. Meridian is awestruck by the mothers' resistive determination, yet she also realizes that black women continue to face unbearable contradiction, because the conditions of motherhood have often required them—both figuratively and literally—to lay down their own lives in an often vain attempt to save their children from overt and covert racial violence.[13]

Much as Hurston, in Tell My Horse, had utilized the trope of the "rooster's nest" to attack the colonial erasure of black maternity, Walker also uses a sequence of ironic natural references in order to interrogate these pathological social conditions misshaping mother/child relations within Meridian's maternal family history. In every generation of Meridian's motherline, the nature of motherhood is shown to be distorted through the impossible

contradiction of being simultaneously "mother and mother-dispossessed."
As in Hurston, Walker's references to nature underscore the *unnatural* context of enslavement and the ensuing racist social relations that turn the
African-American mother/child bond back against itself in a cycle of deprivation.

Meridian's motherline begins during slavery with her maternal great-
great-grandmother, whose children had been sold away from her. She repeatedly stole them back until she was allowed to remain with them on
condition that she provide all their food. She did this only by scavenging
berries, greens, and fish from the woods and by slowly starving herself to
death in order to give her own food to her children. Meridian's great-
grandmother was an artist who bought herself and her children out of slavery with fees earned through her barn paintings: "At the center of each tree
or animal, or bird she painted, there was somehow drawn in, so that it
formed part of the pattern, a small, contorted face" (123), emblem of slavery's commodifying contortion of the mother/child relation. Meridian's
grandmother married a financially secure man with no interest in having a
family, who subsequently beat his wife and children "with more pleasure
than he beat his mules" (123). Meridian's mother is a defeated, self-pitying
woman, who resents her children for depriving her of her former self-
determination and prestige as a self-supporting teacher. She spends her life
making prayer pillows too small to kneel on and artificial paper flowers that
symbolize the smallness of her spirit and the death of any natural maternal
affection. The contorted and distorted natural references within Meridian's
genealogy emphasize that the perverse conditions against which African-
American motherhood must contend, at *unnatural*, even deadly price, originated in the construction of black women as self-reproducing lower nature,
or breeders, for whom object status canceled kinship rights.

The tragic deaths of black children that riddle this novel also emphasize the nearly impossible conditions with which black mothers must contend. Children die through overt racist violence, through the negligence of
a society that devalues their existence, and through infanticide by mothers
overwhelmed by the demands of parenthood amidst such hostilities. One
example in particular makes clear the deadly geography of racial segregation. Because blacks are banned from the "public" swimming pool in Chicokema, they wade in the drainage gullies behind their homes. Each year
numbers of the children drown when the Chicokema reservoir is allowed
to run-off through these gullies, flooding them without warning. When

Meridian presents the decomposing, drowned child's corpse to the town mayor "as if she carried a large bouquet of long stemmed roses" (191), her act exposes the atrocious, and by her standards, unnatural devaluation of black life inhering in the exclusionary policies of white supremacy.

Yet most of the women in the novel view their sufferings as inevitable and inescapable, natural rather than historically conditioned. Meridian's mother voices typical resignation. Viewing the burdens of motherhood as a just punishment for sexual promiscuity, she admonishes Meridian: "Everyone else that slips up like you *bears* it" (88). Endorsing sacrificial motherhood as women's god-given role, her mother comments, "If the good lord gives you a child he means for *you* to take care of it" (87). In contrast, Meridian experiences the demands of teenage motherhood as "enslavement." She is overwhelmed with murderous impulses toward her unwanted child and with suicidal despair at her thwarted life. When she is unexpectedly offered a scholarship to attend college in Atlanta, Meridian places her child for adoption in order to save him and herself from the cycle of mutual deprivation. Although she subsequently suffers much guilt at her failure to live up to the self-sacrificing motherhood of her forebears, Meridian begins the difficult process of redefining herself outside of the destructive conceptions of black women that prevail in the segregated South. She will do so by revising the negative association with nature that underlies black women's object status.

The name "Meridian Hill" and the page of definitions of the geographical term *meridian* that prefaces the novel[18] suggest that Meridian will redefine the relationship between human and nature in order to revise the social geography of the segregated South. In the prefatory page of definitions, *meridian* has many variant meanings, including "noon," "the highest point of power, prosperity and splendor," "southern," and "a great circle of earth passing through the geographical poles." As this list signifies, the word *meridian* is a discursive term used to construct the measure and meanings of the physical earth. As such, *meridian* indicates what Donna Haraway calls the "artifactuality of nature," by which she means that we know nature not directly but only as "mediated" or even *"made"* by discursive systems. Haraway argues the need to replace the Enlightenment-derived Western model of "reification and possession" that turned nature into an object of consumption with new discursive systems that view the human relation to the natural world as one of mutually interactive "co-production." She comments: "If the world exists for us as 'nature' this designates a kind of relationship, an achievement among many actors, not all of them human, not all of them organic, not all of them technological. . . . Nature is made but not entirely by humans; it is a co-construction among humans and non-humans."[14]

Meridian's name—the "noon," or "highest point"—indicates her role as exemplary reinterpreter of nature who will *return* to indigenous animistic views of nature that correspond to Haraway's notion of "co-construction" in order to denaturalize the divisive geography of southern segregation. Meridian's return is analogous to Haraway's definition of nature as a "turning" trope: "(Nature) is a figure, construction, artifact, movement, displacement. Nature cannot pre-exist its construction. This construction is based on a particular kind of move—a *tropos* or 'turn.' Faithful to the Greek, as *tropos* nature is about turning. Troping, we turn to nature as if to the earth, to the primal stuff—geotropic, physiotropic. Topically we travel toward the earth, a commonplace. In discoursing on nature, we turn from Plato and his heliotropic son's blinding star to see something else, another kind of figure."[15] As the meridians circle the earth, Meridian's name indicates her role as one who "turns," in Haraway's terminology, to the earth, to nature. "Turning" to nature in the form of the mound and the tree, Meridian will discover indigenous "figures" that might replace the Platonic severance of subject and object, human and nature, that has proved so detrimental to black women. Thus Meridian's *return* is politically symbolic. By realizing what Haraway terms the artifactuality of nature, Meridian will be able to reframe the geography of southern racial relations: as variant definitions of her name indicate, she will regenerate a "southern" "circle of earth passing through the geographical poles" in which the "polar" separations of white and black will be "passed through," and race relations equalized. Reconstructions of nature in the form of the Sacred Serpent Mound and the Sojourner tree will offer Meridian the means of reforming her culture.

Meridian's quest for a means to reinterpret southern social geography corresponds to Walker's own quest for information about African-American folk religion and culture that culminated in her rediscovery of Hurston. Because the dominant culture has successfully suppressed most African-derived culture and knowledge, Meridian has no ready access to her own people's history and heritage that is now masked behind the Christian meekness and resignation that her mother exemplifies.[16] Meridian seeks other, more "martial" spirits, but the only traces that she can find are the marks that previous inhabitants have left upon the land itself. In the same

way that Walker excavated Hurston's ethnographic material, Meridian un-
earths shards of indigenous cultural history buried in the southern landscape.

The Sacred Serpent Indian mound that rises out of Meridian's family
farm, and the Sojourner tree growing at the heart of Saxon college, are
both historically marked natural phenomena, the repository of suppressed
histories and resistive Native American and African-American cultures;
both the mound and the tree are literally gravesites, memorializing the
dead that the dominant white culture denies. The mound and tree function
as what Toni Morrison calls "sites of memory" that allow Meridian to imaginatively "lift the veil" still cloaking much of the history of the enslavement
and extermination of Native American and African-American peoples and
thus to reconstruct counterhistories omitted from the dominant discourse.
As Morrison explains, the "site of memory" affords access to what is otherwise lost: "It's a kind of literary archaeology: on the basis of some information and a little bit of guesswork you journey to a site to see what remains were left behind and to reconstruct the world that these remains
imply." [17]

During her childhood, Meridian has no direct access to African heritage, but she grows up in a Georgia landscape still riddled with traces of
the original Native American inhabitants. By comparing the situation of
African Americans to that of the Native Americans who once peopled the
land on which she lives, she comes to understand racial segregation as historical dispossession rather than natural condition. The quotation from
Black Elk that Walker uses for the epigraph of the novel describes the destruction of Black Elk's tribe at the battle of Wounded Knee as an assault
upon all that had defined them as a people. They are displaced from their
homeland, they are murdered or dispersed, and, finally, the spiritual vision
central to their culture is violated: "I did not know then how much was
ended. . . . I can still see the butchered women and children lying heaped
and scattered all along the crooked gulch as plain as when I saw them with
eyes still young. And I can see that something else died there in the bloody
mud, and was buried in the blizzard. A people's dream died there. It was a
beautiful dream. . . . The nation's hoop is broken and scattered. There is
no center any longer, and the sacred tree is dead." This epigraph signals
Walker's interest in the parallels between Native American and African-
American histories of displacement from both homelands and native culture and community. By acknowledging the destruction of Native Ameri-

cans, Meridian begins to historicize the similar subordination of African-Americans, masked within the racist assumption of the natural superiority of whites.

Although the Indians had long ago been driven from their southern homelands and are now all but forgotten, Meridian and her father think of Indians as they tend their family garden planted on the banks of the Sacred Serpent Indian burial mound, growing vegetables enriched, as her father explains, by the Indians' bodies. Even though the Indians have been forcibly removed, the mound had been formed by them and contains their remains: the mound is a "site of memory" that is both evidence of the Indian presence on this spot and constant reminder of their dispossession. The mound emblematizes the white disinheritance of native peoples, as Meridian's own family will later be disinherited when the Sacred Serpent mound is made into a public park that, because of racial segregation, does not permit African-Americans or Native Americans to set foot on their former land. While the dominant culture has erased the history of the Indians and the usurpation of their lands, the land itself is marked by this history and thus the land offers Meridian access to a counterhistory absent from the dominant historical narratives. As Walker explains in an interview, "In Georgia there are so many remnants of (Indian) presence that there is a real kinship with these people who were forced off the land that was theirs."[18] Even though the disinheritance of Indians and blacks has been effectively naturalized as a given within the institutionalized exclusions of the segregated South, the Sacred Serpent mound historicizes these race relations, teaching Meridian that she, too, lives in historical rather than natural conditions and that social patterns can be resisted and, hopefully, changed. Throughout the novel, Meridian weighs her knowledge of the Indians' fate against the complacent resignation of people like her mother who accept their "disappearance" as "progress" and segregation as a god-given fact.

The mound also represents an alternative mode of animistic spiritual belief that challenges the hierarchies of southern race relations. The "beautiful dream" that Black Elk refers to is a vision of community between human and nature that he describes as a shared "dance": "The leaves on the trees, the grasses on the hills and in the valleys, the waters in the creeks and in the rivers and the lakes, the four-legged and the two-legged and the wings of the air—all danced together to the music of the stallion's song."[19] This "dance" of shared life and spirit binds together all of existence through partnership and collective movement. As Black Elk laments, the destruction of Indian peoples also destroyed the sacred hoop of partnership between human and nature when the settlers imposed divisions between themselves as sovereign subjects and nature and native peoples as objects. Turning back to the sacred tree, Meridian will recuperate Black Elk's vision of spiritual kinship as the basis of renewed political resistance to white dominance and destruction. Like Hurston before her, Walker returns to animistic spirituality as a paradigm that challenges the dominant culture's objectification of people of color. Specifically, the vision of the sacred hoop unifying all of existence offers Meridian a model of expansive collective identity that challenges the enforced boundaries of racial segregation, for in Black Elk's "dance," all entities move together, rather than remaining fixed and apart.

Black Elk's image of the sacred tree as spiritual center echoes Janie's pear tree and foreshadows Walker's rehistoricization of that image in the Sojourner tree, linking African and Native American animistic beliefs.[20] Walker explains: "If there is one thing that African Americans and Native Americans have retained of the African and ancient American heritage, it is probably the belief that everything is inhabited by spirit" (*Our Mother's Gardens*, 252).[21] Meridian discovers this heritage of animistic spirituality through legends of her paternal great-grandmother, Feather Mae, and through her own mystical experiences at the Sacred Serpent mound. It is significant that this animistic heritage is transmitted to Meridian through a female ancestor, because, as Feather Mae demonstrates, this spiritual legacy enables the transformation of black women from sexually exploited objects into inspirited sexual subjects. Native American writer and theorist Paula Gunn Allen notes that actual serpent mounds, such as Snake Mound in Ohio, were most likely sacred to Native American creation goddesses such as Serpent Woman and were significant sites of worship for Native American medicine women.[22] Such mounds, then, signify Native American belief in sacred female creativity and divine female power, in direct contrast to the Western denigration of nonwhite women as carnal objects.

Feather Mae, whose name may signify her "slight and harmless madness" (57) and also her spiritual kinship with the Indians, discovers the secrets of the Serpent Mound, which is viewed by the other local farmers only as a strange hill that makes planting difficult. Feather Mae had spent her girlhood afternoons sitting astraddle the curving length of the mound: "Meridian's great-grandmother dreamed, with the sun across her legs and her black, moon-bright face open to the view" (57). She had also experienced ecstatic transports within the curved chamber hidden in the coiled tail of the serpent mound. The mound transforms her life: "She felt renewed as from some strange spiritual intoxication. Her blood made warm explosions through her body. . . . Later, Feather Mae renounced all religion that was not based on the experience of physical ecstasy . . . and near the end of her life she loved walking nude about her yard and worshipped only the sun" (57). Such religious experience, in which the spiritual is manifest through the physical, particularly the sexual, echoes Hurston's portrayal of Janie's inspirited sexuality in the pear-tree vision of *Their Eyes Were Watching God*, as well as the ceremonial Voodoo worship of female genitalia as the sacred source of life, described in *Tell My Horse*. Like those of Janie and the Caribbean Voodoo adherents, Feather Mae's animistic vision merges spirituality and sexuality and translates her from the historical role of sexual object into a sexual subject who enjoys her own ecstasy. She brings the physical ecstasy of her sacred trance to her marital relations, and she is said to be so "hot" that her husband is enthralled and controlled by her sexual gifts.

Feather Mae's pleasure emphasizes the dire sexual experience of the other women in this novel. She stands as the sole image of egalitarian, nonoppressive sexual relations that might be possible outside the conditions that trouble the other women's lives. In Walker's novel, black women's sexual lives remain problematic. There is no Tea Cake in this novel, only the deeply flawed Truman, whom Meridian forgives and befriends and who finally assumes Meridian's political and spiritual struggle in the closing scene. There is no muck in *Meridian*, no folk community apparently outside the bounds of racism and sexism. In fact, when Meridian becomes pregnant during her brief, disastrous involvement with Truman, who abandons her to marry a white northern exchange student, Meridian has an abortion and then has herself sterilized—and from then on eschews sexual relations for political comradeship. In fact the fleeting political camaraderie of the civil rights activists is the closest that Meridian will come to any sort of idealized community. While Janie achieves health and wholeness through romantic love and the play of folk culture, Meridian heals herself through acts of political resistance and service to her people in the small southern towns she makes home.

Much as Janie's pear tree becomes the standard of her life, Meridian's experience at the Sacred Serpent mound will mold her political activism. Her own mystical trance within the mound teaches her of spiritual connectedness and freedom: "It was as if the walls of the earth that enclosed her rushed outward, leveling themselves at a dizzying rate, and then spinning wildly, lifting her out of her body and giving her the feeling of flying. And in this movement she saw the faces of her family, the branches of trees, the wings of birds, the corners of houses, blades of grass and petals of flowers rush toward a central point high above her and she was drawn with them, as whirling, as bright, as free, as they. . . . It seemed to her that it was a way the living sought to expand the consciousness of being alive" (58–59). As Janie's pear-tree vision of intermingled polarities challenges the dominant model of hierarchic binaries, Meridian's mystical experience offers her the sense of expansive collectivity beyond the artificial racial strictures of the segregated South. In the trance the "enclosing" walls open, permitting unbounded "free," "bright" "movement," and Meridian senses the interconnectedness of all living and nonliving things—"family," "birds," "branches," and even "houses"—"whirling" together, as in Black Elk's dream of the sacred dance. Unlike Western objectification of nature and nonwhite peoples, in which all who are different from the white male norm are treated as less-than-human resources for consumption, Meridian's trance enlivens all that it embraces, regarding even grass and the corners of houses as vital parts of the whirling freedom. In contrast to the historical construction of black slaves as virtual objects, as a form of property that might, as Spillers notes, be listed for sale along with land, furniture and other inanimate possessions, Meridian's vision animates all that it encompasses.[23] Walker explains her interpretation of Native American animism in an essay: "Whereas to the Wasichu, (white man), only the white male attains full human status, everything to the Indian was a relative. Everything was a human being" (*Living*, 150–51).

Contemporary legal theorist Patricia Williams, who writes in *The Alchemy of Race and Rights* about issues of race and law, employs a similar animistic framework in her argument for the utility of a radically extended view of civil rights for black Americans who have continued to be deprived of rights. Williams argues that because the denial of rights to enslaved African Americans was justified by their construction as legal objects, or chattel property, it is necessary to radically challenge *all* objectifications, not only of people of color, but also of any entity posed as human object. She counters such historical objectification with an animistic view of the spiritual worth of all entities that is very similar to the model that Walker takes from Native American animistic belief. Williams argues the need to reframe property rights as mutual civil rights shared by all, and, mirroring Walker, she speaks of "the animating spirit of rights mythology":

> The task is to expand private property rights into a conception of civil rights, into the right to expect civility from others. . . . Society must *give* (rights) away. Unlock them from reification by giving them to slaves. Give them to trees. Give them to cows. Give them to history. Give them to rivers and rocks. Give to all of society's objects and untouchables the rights of privacy, integrity, and self-assertion; give them distance and respect. Flood them with the animating spirit that rights mythology fires in this country's most oppressed psyches, and wash away the shrouds of inanimate-object status, so that we may say not that we own gold but that a luminous golden spirit owns us.[24]

As Walker sees it, such an "animating spirit of rights" flooding all of existence levels the Wasichu model of hierarchical status. Meridian's vision of enlivened kinship provides a radical model of civil rights comparable to the one proposed by Williams. Walker explains in an essay: "Everything has equal rights because existence itself is equal" (*Living*, 148).[25] Meridian's vision destabilizes humanistic ranking systems, such as the Great Chain of Being, that pose man as the standard measure; she realizes that existence itself is democratizing—in direct contrast to the unequal separations naturalized within Jim Crow segregation. In Meridian's vision, equality, kinship, and animation counter hierarchy, division, and objectification. As the 1954 *Brown vs. School Board* Supreme Court decision desegregating public education found, enforced racial separation contradicts equality. The court stated: "The doctrine of 'separate but equal' has no place. Separate educational facilities are inherently unequal."[26] Meridian's notion of animistic equality corresponds to the purpose and praxis of the Civil Rights movement; as demonstrators move toward social equality against the objectifying hierarchies of segregation, they enact Meridian's vision of potential freedom from fixity and enclosure, and they demonstrate the egalitarian spiritual partnership of all that exists.

Thus, Meridian's first glimpse of the civil rights workers, who boldly defy the rigid restrictions of the southern order, corresponds to her trance vision of expansive, shared movement and freedom. This scene occurs within a chapter ironically entitled "The Happy Mother" that describes the dissolution of Meridian's marriage and the murderous despair she feels toward her son and herself. The appearance of the civil rights workers affords Meridian an awareness that her own situation is historically conditioned and that segregation can be challenged, even though the dominant culture will violently defend the old order. Civil rights activism offers Meridian an antidote to the pathological race and gender relations that cause her suffering, because the civil rights workers cross the lines upon which the old order rests, enacting the "freedom" and "movement" of Meridian's trance:

> On the day he left, she had walked past a house . . . where—since it was nearly summer—all the doors and windows were open. People, young people, were everywhere. They milled about inside, shouted out of windows to those outside, looked carefree (as childless young people, her own age, always looked to her) and yet as if sensitive to some outside surveillance beyond her own staring. . . . And she stopped to look only because it was a black family's house, in a black neighborhood, and there were several young white people. And all of the young people were strangely dressed and looked, really, funny and old-timey in the overalls and clodhoppers they wore. Even the girls (and she noticed especially a white girl with long brown hair) were dressed in overalls *with bibs!* (72)

The civil rights workers transgress the structural boundaries of the segregated South, opening a space for nonhierarchical racial and gender identities. They have thrown open the doors and windows of the house, breaking through the walls that enclose Meridian, and they move freely between inside and outside, symbolically denying the spatial divisions of the Jim Crow order that pose blacks as perennially outside of white domains. Whites and blacks mix freely and equally in this household, coming together in unity of common purpose that counters racial separation and polarization. This scene of interracial social interchange transgresses the basic white supremacist assumption that black and white must never interact as social equals. Gender polarity is diminished here as well, since men and women wear identical overalls and clodhoppers and interact in a carefree manner, in contrast to the incessant sexual conquest by which Meridian is objectified.

This household also symbolizes the historic return of urban and north-

ern black and white students to the rural South from which many blacks
had fled earlier in the century. Donning "old-timey" clothes, the young
people reclaim the traditional garb of the rural South as a symbol of new
political ends. The return of the northern students enacts Meridian's own
sense of being "held by something in the past" (27), her sense that a revolutionary future must be true to the spirit of the older generations of African
Americans who still, in a sense, preserve the roots of black experience in
America. Paula Giddings notes that the young SNCC civil rights workers,
who carried the movement to southern backwaters, closed a circle, reuniting northern urban blacks with those who had remained in the rural south:
"History was coming full circle as young urban students and rural folk of
the South peered at each other across the generations and gulf of life experience. But they found the link to complete the circle, a thing called freedom. And that link led to common ground."[27]

This return gave momentum to the mass movements for civil rights
forming throughout the South. Masses of southern blacks united with
northern blacks and with white sympathizers to fight against segregation
through large-scale, sustained civil protest actions, marches, school deseg-
regation, and voter registration campaigns. Such mass movement in which
black and white, rural and urban, northern and southern, male and female
are united in the cause of freedom enacts Meridian's mystical vision of a
whirling collective freedom available beyond the enclosing walls. The very
term *movement* implies transformative possibility in which people move
against the fixed structures and assumptions of hegemonic society and in
so doing demonstrate human changeability. As Hurston's Janie is able to
enact her pear-tree vision of nonpolarized relations within the folk community of the muck, Meridian momentarily glimpses her Sacred Serpent
vision of collective freedom within the political community of the
movement.

Only after Meridian escapes home and motherhood through her scholarship to Saxon College does she encounter a "site of memory" that gives
her access to her own African heritage and history. Like the Sacred Serpent
mound, the Sojourner tree growing at the heart of the college campus
embodies a counterhistory of African culture, suffering but yet resisting
American enslavement. The bitter story of the slave Louvinie and her Sojourner tree emblematizes the history of African women brought as slaves
to the New Land, and the tree is the obvious site of Walker's return to
Hurston. The Sojourner tree not only echoes Janie's blossoming pear tree,

the central icon of Janie's growing self-possession in *Their Eyes Were Watching God*, but also exhumes the Voodoo spiritual beliefs that Hurston had "embalmed" within that image. In effect, Walker's Sojourner resituates the image of the sacred tree within the context of African-derived spirituality and represents the tree as openly resistant to Western decimation of black peoples, particularly black women.

Legend has it that the Sojourner tree, now gracing the Saxon college campus, bears the spirit and history of Louvinie, a grim-faced slave reputed never to have smiled, who had been placed in charge of the plantation kitchen garden because she was considered too ugly and dour for household duties. Louvinie refused to countenance the imposed conditions of slavery, much as Meridian rejects sexual pleasure as delusory within unequal relations. The daughter of African storytellers whose tales were used to settle tribal disputes by divining the guilty party, Louvinie, upon demand, told the master's children horrific stories of Africans tormenting white children. Her tales, like her inability to smile, belied the ideologies of slavery, overturning white fantasies of the happy slave woman fondly caring for white charges. Without intention, Louvinie frightened to death the master's defective-hearted only son with one of her stories, thus effectively employing African tradition in order to end the master's paternal line.[28] As punishment, Louvinie's tongue was clipped out at the root. Knowing that "without one's tongue in one's mouth or in a special spot of one's own choosing the singer in one's soul was lost forever to grunt and snort though eternity like a pig" (44), Louvinie mutely begged for her clipped tongue. She smoked this "thick pink rose petal, bloody at the root" (44) and then buried it at the base of a scrawny magnolia tree.

In African traditions, trees were believed to be intermediaries between human and natural worlds, and between physical and spirit world. Robert Thompson notes that trees were customarily planted on graves to "signify the spirit" as "their roots literally travel to the other world." Thompson quotes a Kongo elder who explains that "this tree is a sign of spirit on its way to the other world." In Haiti the tree signifies the continuity of spirit even after death: "Trees live after us: death is not the end." Accordingly, the Sojourner tree bridges human and natural worlds and keeps alive Louvinie's spiritual resistance. Like the Sacred Serpent mound that is a reminder of Indian presence and removal, the magnolia is a repository for the spirit of opposition that was so violently torn from Louvinie. Fertilized by Louvinie's verbal powers, fed by her African heritage, the Sojourner tree grows to magnificent size. As Thompson notes, the well-being of the grave-tree was equated with the well-being of the spirit: "If the tree flourishes, all is well with the soul."[29] Louvinie's magnolia tree not only flourishes, it is also believed to act in Louvinie's spirit of resistance: "Even before her death forty years later the tree had out-grown all the others around it. Other slaves believed it possessed magic. They claimed the tree could talk, make music, was sacred to birds, and possessed the power to obscure vision. Once in its branches, a hiding slave could not be seen" (44).

The story of the Sojourner strikingly echoes the legend of the sacred palm tree that Hurston had recorded in *Tell My Horse*. Like the palm tree that repulsed the priest's ax and remained a shrine even after it was finally leveled by the church, the Sojourner tree embodies remnants of African heritage and belief forcibly suppressed under slavery yet stubbornly flourishing. In the same way that the Voodoo tree remained a shrine where black women sought healing from the ailments inflicted by colonialism, the Sojourner tree offers balm to the young Saxon women entrapped in the contradictions surrounding sexuality and pregnancy. Louvinie's African-derived tales and traditions contest the abuses of slavery, even turning them back against the enslaver, in the same way that the Voodoo tree turned the ax back against the attacking priest. Louvinie's legend is one of resistance, even renewal, amidst suffering and travail. The Sojourner tree is Meridian's means of regaining the oppositional force of African-derived culture in order to redeploy that heritage as political contestation.

The animistic fusion of Louvinie and the tree poses a challenge to the assumptions underlying Western views of nature and native peoples as passive objects of white human dominion. As a natural phenomenon that exhibits Louvinie's social agency, the tree articulates Donna Haraway's notion of cyborgian human/nonhuman interpenetration that troubles the essential division between human and nature. As a collective entity, neither totally natural nor fully human, the Sojourner defies prevailing Western dichotomies between spiritual and carnal, human and nature, subject and object, that had functioned in the enslavement and continuing objectification of black women. The Sojourner also illustrates what Haraway calls "social nature," meaning that nature and society are mutually producing coconstructors, a blended collectivity of human and nonhuman actants.[30] The Sojourner's miraculous growth in response to the burial of Louvinie's tongue demonstrates that natural phenomena are marked by historical conditions, and the tree's sheltering of runaway slaves also demonstrates that historical conditions are marked by nonhuman actors. Moreover, in the legend of Louvinie and the Sojourner tree, we can see the process by which natural phenomena might come to function as Morrison's "site of memory," through which those whose history has been silenced and erased can imaginatively excavate what has been omitted from dominant histories. In the Sojourner tree legend, Louvinie's African heritage and her counterhistory of resistance to enslavement are literally driven into the ground, only to resurface in the form of the tree, which continues to function as symbol of the simultaneous suppression and survival of Louvinie's *memory*. A site of memory, then, signifies both loss and reconstruction of history. Walker's Sojourner tree implies that not only are nature and history mutually produced, nature may also act as site of contestatory counterhistories and counterparadigms that were forced "into the ground," as the African slaves had been.

In particular, the Sojourner, like Feather Mae's experiences at the Sacred Serpent mound, contests the historic sexual exploitation of black women and challenges their construction by the dominant culture as sexual and reproductive objects. Like its namesake, Sojourner Truth, who fought for the linked causes of race and gender freedom and equality, the Sojourner acts in defense of women trapped in contradictory sexual roles. The tree, which is now growing at the heart of (Anglo) Saxon college, subverts the assimilationist school policies requiring young black female students to be asexual virgins—"pure as the driven snow"—in imitation of acceptable white standards of ladyhood and in direct contradiction to the realities of the larger world that still exploits them as sexual objects.[31] The Sojourner, believed to shelter clandestine lovers from policing eyes, offers the young women a place to act as sexual subjects, pursuing their own desires, until school authorities saw off the lower branches to prevent access to this safe space.

Furthermore, the tree offers the young women solace from the devastating effects of unwanted pregnancies, for in the Saxon philosophy, pregnancy means ruination. This is illustrated by the cautionary tale of Fast Mary of the Tower, the student who secretly gave birth at Saxon and then murdered her infant, flushing the dismembered body down the toilet. The crime was discovered and Mary was publicly flogged, then locked in a room at home where she hanged herself. Mary's grave tale is in many ways a more tragic version of Meridian's own experience of motherhood, emphasizing the unbearable self-contradiction that remains a legacy of enslavement. Even now, these young women know that pregnancy will metaphorically or literally end their lives. The Sojourner was said to have been "Mary's only comfort and friend on the Saxon campus" (45), and the tree is the center of a yearly May Dance commemorating Mary that is performed by all the Saxon girls who have ever prayed for the arrival of their period. Notably, this ceremonial acknowledgment of their shared sexual vulnerability equalizes social differences and unites the young women in a May *dance* circling the tree, reminiscent of Black Elk's collective dance of spirit: "There was only one Sojourner ceremony, however, that united all the students at Saxon—the rich and the poor, the very black-skinned (few though they were) with the very fair, the stupid and the bright—and that was the commemoration of Fast Mary of the Tower. . . . It was the only time in all the many social activities at Saxon that every girl was considered equal. On that day, they held each other's hands tightly" (45).

And so it is most appropriate that when the funeral of the pregnant street waif Wild Child, whom Meridian had attempted to aid, is banned from the Saxon chapel, the girls carry her to the tree. The tree, which is described here as gently maternal toward Wild Child and the other Saxon girls, points toward positive female subjectivity and maternal/child relations rooted in African traditions:

> The pallbearers picked up the casket and carried it to the middle of the campus and put it down gently beneath the Sojourner, whose heavy, flower-lit leaves hovered over it like the inverted peaks of a mother's half-straightened kinky hair. Instead of flowers the students, as if they had planned it, quickly made wreaths from Sojourner's fallen leaves, and The Sojourner herself, ever generous to her children, dropped a leaf on the chest of The Wild Child, who wore for the first time, in her casket, a set of new clothes.
>
> The students sang through tears that slipped like melting pellets of sleet down their grieved and angered cheeks:
> We shall overcome . . .
> We shall overcome . . .
> We shall overcome, someday . . .
> Deep in my heart, I do believe . . .
> We shall overcome, someday. (47)

This passage, which clearly echoes Janie's pear tree and the Caribbean Voodoo tree, reinscribes the sacred tree as emblem of the saving powers of African culture and belief that have been dismembered and buried but yet have risen in new form. Walker's Sojourner, in which nature embodies a history excised by the hegemonic culture, clearly rewrites and recontextualizes Hurston's pear tree. While the pear tree appears as a personal revelation that prompts Janie's individual quest for full personal identity, the Sojourner tree is markedly historicized and functions as a collective rather than individual symbol. Walker's novel insists that Meridian must address the collective history of enslavement and resistance. She seeks to alter the problematic social conditions that mar the lives of black women in general. Thus the young women sing an anthem of political rebellion at Wild Child's funeral, translating personal grief into political contestation.

Unfortunately, though, when the students subsequently riot against the Saxon officials who banned Wild Child's funeral, they attack the very tree that had granted them succor and shelter: "That night . . . students, including Anne-Marion, rioted on Saxon campus for the first time in its long placid, impeccable history, and the only thing they managed to destroy was The Sojourner. Though Meridian begged them to dismantle the president's house instead, in a fury of confusion and frustration they worked all night and chopped and sawed down, level to the ground, that mighty, ancient, sheltering music tree" (47–48). Their "frustration," which, as Meridian argues, should be rightly expressed against the Saxon authorities and the inequities of the larger society, is misdirected against the very tree that has nurtured their rebellious spirit. The destruction of the tree foreshadows the moment when the nonviolent Civil Rights movement will be replaced by more militant black power organizations and when Meridian will part company with the northern cadre over the question of revolutionary violence, which she believes to be as self-mutilating as the leveling of the tree. Unlike those who believe that white violence must be answered by black violence, Meridian retains the conviction that revolutionary praxis must preserve the spiritual integrity of the southern people who have resisted white supremacist abuses without violent retaliation. Her attempted defense of the Sojourner tree demonstrates her continued return to the indigenous cultural heritage embodied by the tree and the Sacred Serpent mound, her refusal to adopt the violently divisive Western model that she sees imitated by the northern group. In Meridian's animistic paradigm of encompassing spiritual collectivity, violence is a form of self-destruction, as exemplified by the women's dismantling of the Sojourner tree.[32]

Throughout the novel, both during the heyday of the Civil Rights movement and after its dispersion, Meridian holds to non-violent activism and service as a praxis that preserves the spiritual legacy that she has excavated from the Sacred Serpent mound and the Sojourner tree. Through her political work, Meridian translates her body from the Western definition of black women as mules of the world into the animistic view of herself as inspirited agent moving within a dancing collectivity. In civil actions, Meridian's black, female body—which was historically construed as subhuman object, or chattel property—is redefined as the agent of social change, moving against the oppressive social boundaries of Jim Crow segregation.

Meridian is able to translate her body from a sexual and maternal object into a political agent as she works to repossess southern lands and political rights for the disinherited southern folk. The civil rights struggle against racist exclusion was most often carried out through various forms of peaceful protest in which African Americans and allied whites physically crossed the boundaries of segregated space, using their bodies to protest legalized racial exclusion. As Meridian participates in marches and demonstrations that defy the Jim Crow laws, as she goes frequently to jail and frequently submits to brutality and beatings, and as she walks from door to door through the rural countryside urging black people to register to vote, she continually employs her body as a political instrument. Meridian physically moves her black, female body across the boundaries that she can no longer tolerate, using her body to defy the dominant view that physical difference justifies racial divisions. Thus, Meridian redefines her body, which has suffered the objectifications of segregation, as a political agent who challenges the socially enforced borders.

Her body, which manifests the unnatural objectifications of her society as bouts of paralysis and illness, also becomes an agent of personal and social health. Christian notes that the mind/body unity enacted through civil disobedience is connected to animistic belief: "By describing her quest as a search for health, Meridian insists that to be whole, there must be unity of body and mind. So too the central action of the Civil Rights Movement, body resistance to manifest protest of the mind, attempted to demonstrate this oneness."[33] Meridian's animistic sense of shared history and spiritual collectivity impels her struggle to re-create a less bounded and more egalitarian social geography. Patricia Williams argues in *The Alchemy of Race and*

Rights that in order to end racism, false boundaries must constantly be challenged: "I think that the hard work of a nonracist sensibility is the boundary crossing, from safe circle into wilderness: the testing of boundary, the consecration of sacrilege. It is the willingness to . . . break an encompassing circle, to travel from safe to unsafe. The transgression is dizzyingly intense, a reminder of what it is to be alive."[34] In acts of civil disobedience, Meridian demonstrates the "whirling freedom" she first experienced within the Sacred Serpent mound, and she renews her certainty of African Americans' full humanity, surpassing arbitrarily imposed boundaries.

In particular, Meridian contests the oppressive terms of race and gender that have posed black women as the mules of the world. Many of her acts of protest and service are undertaken on behalf of suffering black women, such as the pregnant street waif Wild Child, the rural women whom Meridian encourages to register to vote, the dying woman whose family she feeds, and the thirteen-year-old girl incarcerated for murdering her baby whom Meridian visits in prison. It is in her encounter with Miss Treasure that we can most clearly view Meridian's revision of the terms of black women's relation to nature and bodily agency, her translation of their Western construction as mule of the world into the animistic perspective that *treasures* nature and black women's subjectivity.

Miss Treasure is an old spinster who fears that she will lose her farm and her family name because she believes that she has been impregnated by a house painter who was briefly her lover. Even though she is clearly beyond her child-bearing years, Miss Treasure has been convinced by her sister that sexuality will lead inevitably to pregnancy and loss. In the following passage Miss Treasure is trapped between the standard Western conjunction of sexuality, animality, and dispossession and the alternative animistic view of nature and native peoples that offers her means of repossession of self, sexuality, and homeland: "She had been a virgin until Rims came into her life, filling it with fluttery anticipation and making her body so changed, so full of hurting brightness she had known it was a sin for which she would be punished. She lay on the hot ground like a lost child, or like a dog kicked so severely it has lost its sense of smell and wanders about and leans on the tree it otherwise would have soiled" (210).

Miss Treasure's sexual experience is a conflicting blend of the Western view of black women's sexual objectification and the alternative experience of animistic sexual pleasure that Feather Mae had taken from her ecstatic trances. The phrase "hurting brightness" melds the painful experience of sexual exploitation that has been the lot of most women in this novel to the ecstatic experience of inspirited sexual pleasure of Feather Mae. The description of Miss Treasure rolling on the ground like a beaten dog articulates the history of sexual abuse that black women have suffered from their equation with lower nature; yet, paradoxically, this moment of utter abjection also becomes a moment of transformative possibility when the dog "wanders about and leans on the tree it otherwise would have soiled." This movement from "soiling" the tree to "leaning" against the tree corresponds to Meridian's transformative return to the indigenous animistic spirituality of the Sacred Serpent mound and the Sojourner tree as a means of rewriting the Western degradation of nature and native peoples. The tree, which has been "soiled" through the negative Western objectification of nature, may also become the source of support and contestation. The sacred tree, as Meridian has discovered, may be utilized to reframe black women's relation to nature and to reframe sexual pleasure not as debasement, not as objectification, but as "treasure." In assuring Miss Treasure that she is not pregnant and that she can be sexual without shame and disinheritance, Meridian breaks the cycle of dehumanization and dispossession that has been black women's lot throughout this novel, opening a space for a return to renewed relation to southern land and self.

When, at the close of the novel, Meridian is sent a photograph of a new sprig sprouting from massive circle of the Sojourner's hewn trunk, the image symbolizes Meridian's struggle to preserve African-American and Native American heritages and to revive indigenous views of partnership with nature as the basis of an alternative, less divisive American geography. By exhuming the native cultures that had been buried within the southern landscape, Meridian has replanted a missing branch on the genealogical family tree of the diverse ancestral cultures of America. Walker's novel rewrites the relations between nature, gender, and race as explicitly political, directly related to mass movements for social reformation—a direction that will be continued in the work of Leslie Marmon Silko, as discussed in the next chapter.

The revision of nature in this novel is manifest, as well, within the narrative form. Narrationally, *Meridian* enacts a rebellion from coherent, linear, realist narratives that formally inscribe the Western relationship between male writer as sovereign subject and world as feminized passive natural object, or "not me," that has proved so detrimental in the construction of black women. This realist model is exemplified by the Emersonian poetry and philosophy discussed earlier, wherein he argues that the male poet finds God's truth mirrored in feminized nature, and then captures that transcendental truth in transparent prose. In the Emersonian model of realism, a solitary, masculine, unitary subject discovers the single transcendent truth of a passive, foreign natural world and creates a poem transmitting this transparent unitary interpretation. As I have previously argued, this model is problematic for women writers, particularly women of color, who have been, in Emerson's terms, excluded from the act of writing, posed as passive natural objects, and whose own histories and cultures have generally been subsumed by the assumed veracity of master narratives promoting the interests of the dominant culture. Alice Walker's novel revises this narrational paradigm, demonstrating that other models may be more appropriate to the pursuit of more accurate and encompassing histories and less divisive and hierarchical social relations that this novel envisions.

In its narrational structure of short, disconnected chapters arranged in nonchronological order, *Meridian* rebels against the predominant narrative structures of history and realist literature that fail to provide accurate and useful accounts of the besieged native peoples of America. In this novel Walker enacts an answer to a question she had asked herself while teaching black history to middle-aged black women who had been taught that they had no history beyond the shameful history of enslavement and inferiority: "How do you teach . . . the significance of their past? . . . How do you show a connection between present and past when, as eloquent but morally befuddled Faulkner wrote, 'the past is not even past'?" As Walker ascertains: "It should have been as easy as handing them a mirror, but it was not" (*Our Mothers' Gardens*, 28). Narratively, *Meridian* enacts this dilemma: How can a writer locate and "mirror" more accurate and encompassing historical narratives when prevailing discourses still suppress, erase, and distort the very history that one needs to articulate and understand—when one lives and writes within the very forces that one wishes to stand against? Bell hooks describes this dilemma as the difficult leap from "subjection" to "subjectivity": "Opposition is not enough. In that vacant space after one has resisted there is still the necessity to become—to make oneself anew . . . becoming subjects. That process emerges as one comes to understand how structures of domination work in one's own life, as one develops critical thinking and critical consciousness, as one invents new, alternative habits of being, and resists from that marginal space of difference inwardly defined."[35] The narrative of *Meridian* performs this dual process of resistance to the structures of domination and reinvention of alternative subjectivity.

While early critics of this novel found it maddeningly confusing because of the brief and enigmatic chapters, shifting perspective, and nonlinear plot—techniques that were read as failings of the author rather than as intentional rebellions from the hegemony of realism—[36] Christian argued that Walker's "quilt" narration, in which scraps of story are "pieced" together, was an appropriate vernacular form for a black woman writer, one that invoked Walker's own use of the quilt to figure black women's creative employment of limited artistic resources in their daily lives.[37] I would argue further that this quilt narrational mode, with its short, inconclusively parablelike chapters (often bearing ironically discordant or pointed titles) denaturalizes the supposed transparent objectivity of realist historical narrative by accentuating the dissonance between Meridian's experience and prevailing cultural narratives and by signifying the tenuous process of building subjectivity in such a contradictory world; moreover, the scraplike, purposefully inconclusive progress of the plot signifies the difficulty of piecing together alternative histories without committing similar falsifications. The novel enacts Meridian's wariness of the false totalizations of standard histories and political doctrines, a wariness that compares to Donna Haraway's description of the movement from the "God-view" model of traditional objectivity, which assumes that the usually Western, usually white, usually male scientist's vantage point is a universal perspective, to a more accurate paradigm of "situated objectivity" that entails acknowledging the specificity of one's subject position as a knower and speaker, as well as admitting that each of our many diverse positions can provide us only "partial knowledge," rather than "whole" transcendent and unchanging truths.[38]

Haraway argues the necessity of admitting that knowledge is piecemeal, fragmentary, and greatly determined by the social and political location of the knower. The narrative of *Meridian* performs this model of "situated objectivity" and "partial knowledge" as Meridian excavates fragments of archaeological evidence from "sites of memory" and as she narrationally reconstructs history piece by piece—never to make a whole cloth. Meridian's continual denaturalization of societal assumptions in her pursuit of answers to revolutionary questions is enacted in the partiality, gaps, and possibilities of the stubbornly nontotalizing narration. Walker's quilt-piece narrative corresponds to the slippages and formal *play* of Dickinson's poetry, and the narrative play here clearly serves Walker's denaturalization of blind and blinding master paradigms: her formal rebellion from the realist paradigm of fixed universalized truth and subject/object bifurcation clarifies the way that this sort of literary mastery has been related to the hierarchies of social mastery and white/nonwhite division enacted within white supremacist race relations. In order to articulate another history, from the perspectives of those historically posed as racial Others, Walker has utilized a fragmentary narrative form, eschewing narrative and ideological mastery in favor of partiality, movement, and a shifting pattern of significance and meaning.

Moreover, Walker's quilted narrative performs the paradigm of animate partnership and movement that Meridian exhumed from the mound and the tree. Walker's fragmentary, syncretic narrative calls for an active partnership between text and reader in which meaning is, as Haraway would term it, coconstructed rather than authoritatively presented as fixed and supposedly preexistent, as in the Emersonian realist paradigm. Walker's collation of brief, parablelike chapters pieced between chronological schisms and plot gaps leaves spaces for the reader to assemble the many swatches of narrative into variable interpretations, and thus the reader assumes a role of active partnership with the text. Because of the multiple arrangements possible amongst the disjointed chapters, the text moves instead of remaining fixed, much as civil protestors moved against the fixed mores of southern society. The narrative, in which distinct segments move with and against each other in many possible patterns, corresponds to Meridian's trance vision of the distinct and different things—people, houses, blades of grass and birds—moving together in the "whirling freedom" beyond the enclosing wall. The narrative rebellions and innovations of Meridian make assertions about the nature of narrative and of history.[39]

4

Contested Ground: Nature, Narrative, and Native American Identity in Leslie Marmon Silko's *Ceremony* and *Almanac of the Dead*

The Myth of the Frontier is our oldest and most characteristic myth . . . According to this myth-historiography, the conquest of the wilderness and the subjugation or displacement of the Native Americans who originally inhabited it have been the means to our achievement of national identity, democratic polity, an ever-expanding economy, and a phenomenally dynamic and progressive "civilization."—*Richard Slotkin*

The ear for the story and the eye for the pattern were theirs: we came out of this land and we are hers.—*Leslie Marmon Silko*

But after you hear this story, you and the others prepare by the full moon to rise up against the slave masters.—*Leslie Marmon Silko*

LESLIE MARMON SILKO, a contemporary writer of mixed Laguna, Mexican, and Anglo descent, who was raised within the tribe at Laguna Pueblo, calls upon tribal storytelling and spiritual traditions in order to reframe the seemingly irresolvable clash between Native American and Euro-American cultures that has prevailed since their earliest encounters on this continent. Like many of her fellow Native American writers, Silko traces the crippling effects that centuries of intense interracial conflict have had upon the indigenous peoples of America; yet as a person of mixed descent, whose own intertwined family achieved a more harmonious cultural amalgamation, Silko also articulates the very difficult but hope-inspiring process of moving beyond violent enmity toward intercultural resolution.[1] In her novels *Ceremony* and *Almanac of the Dead* it is most often characters of mixed blood and transculturation, those who dwell in the uncomfortable margins between embattled cultures, in that uncertain region that Chicana theorist Gloria Anzaldua terms *borderlands*, who are impelled to redress the hostility and disparity between white and native societies.[2]

To begin this cultural reconfiguration, Silko revisits the American mythos of the conquest of the continent from a Native American vantage point. While *Ceremony* and *Almanac of the Dead* are set, respectively, in the recent past and the near future, Silko's characters come to realize that both the desperate ills of reservation life and the corruptions poisoning mainstream American society result from the way in which American national development has been predicated over and against Indian inhabitation of the land.[3] Her characters must unravel the polarizing mechanism that historian Richard Slotkin calls that "fatal opposition" through which Euro-Americans justified the displacement of Native Americans from their homelands: "Even at the source of the American myth (of conquest) there lies the fatal opposition, the hostility between two worlds, two races, two realms of thought and feeling."[4]

Silko argues that this fatal opposition is not, as the settlers believed, an essential and irresolvable racial enmity, but rather a struggle between irreconcilable notions of land use and land tenure, a struggle between differing cultural orientations to the natural world. She utilizes Laguna story-tradition to reframe the fatal opposition as a story war; when Europeans arrived in America, two conflicting stories about the human relationship to nature were thrown into confrontation, and the European story of human dominion over nature authorized white settlers' ruthless subjugation of the Indian peoples, who viewed themselves as kin to the spirits of the land. Furthermore, Silko asserts that the European story of conquest was itself a fatal opposition—an ideology through which settlers alienated themselves from the American landscape, posing themselves as separate and superior to the natural world and native peoples whom they took as lifeless objects of their expansionist desires. In Silko's novels, then, the social relation to nature is contested ground, the ground of conflict between these embattled cultures.

Employing traditional Laguna views of the power of stories to produce and to reproduce social relations and relations between humans and the natural world, *Ceremony* and *Almanac of the Dead* present the struggle of Indian-identified characters to regain their imperiled connection to the land through reconstruction and reassertion of the traditional stories relating tribe to nature and through the creation and enactment of new stories reframing this historic conflict of cultures—stories that can offer a means of moving beyond the fatal opposition that, as Silko so eloquently argues, is proving so deadly to both races. In *Ceremony*, Tayo, a mixed-blood, mentally anguished veteran of World War II, comes to understand that the devastations wrought by the war, the ills suffered by his tribe, and ravages of the drought-struck southwestern landscape all result from the Euro-American mode of opposition that fears otherness and turns everything beyond its ken into "dead things." Tayo begins to heal himself and his people through a ceremonial reconstruction of traditional stories that reassert the spiritual union of tribe and natural world. In her recent dystopian novel *Almanac of the Dead*, Silko expands upon the circuit of story and history, when the reconstruction of fragments of an ancient Indian almanac rouses the dispossessed peoples of the Americas to revolt against their endlessly corrupt conquerors. Again in this novel, the prevailing sick materialism by which a few individuals profit from the sufferings of the masses is shown to be the final fruition of the conquest mode that objectifies all in its wake, turning the natural world and native peoples into dead resources for consumption. In *Almanac* ancient native stories that view nature as a living, inspirited entity stir the peoples from despair to revolt against the masters. In both of these novels Silko's insistence upon the constructive powers of stories corresponds to feminist theorists Evelyn Fox Keller and Donna Haraway's argument that in order to move beyond the ills of colonialism we must replace our destructive models of social/natural relations with more egalitarian and life-affirming designs. Silko's writings suggest that the Laguna story of the inspirited kinship between human and nature could offer a corrective to current social systems that objectify all persons and entities deemed less than fully human.

In order to redress the violent ethos of conquest that permeates the American dream of nationhood, Silko's characters call upon the traditional Laguna belief that stories are the heart of tribal culture through which tribal identity is reproduced and disseminated and through which Indian peoples continuously reconstruct their relationship to nature, which in Laguna thought is the site of the sacred as well as the source of physical survival.[5] In an essay entitled "Landscape, History, and the Pueblo Imagination," Silko explains that in Laguna tradition stories are the means of creating a collective culture in which humans and their natural surroundings are bound together in meaningful relation, into what Donna Haraway would call a co-constructed social/natural collectivity. Silko suggests that stories may still be used as a powerful antidote to the centuries of Indian displacement and dispossession. As one of the frame poems of *Ceremony* states: "I will tell you something about stories,/ . . . They aren't just entertainment./ . . . They are all we have, you see,/all we have to fight off/illness and death./You don't have anything/if you don't have the stories" (2).

Silko observes that the tribe forms and reforms itself as a social entity through its stories; in Laguna culture the transmission of stories is a collective project in which all members of the tribe participate: "The remembering and retelling were a communal process" ("Landscape," 111). Every tribe member learns portions of the traditional oral stories for recitation and transmission and learns to view his or her own history as a strand within the web of traditional, family, and personal stories.[6] This web of stories binds the tribe into a collectivity in which the well-being of each member is a communal concern and in which the members fulfill what Paula Gunn Allen calls "complementary" male/female roles within generally egalitarian and participatory social structures.[7]

The stories also bind the tribe into the context of the larger natural world. In Pueblo religious tradition the natural world was created and is continuously re-created through the stories (or thoughts) of Thought Woman, the primordial creation deity also known as Spider Woman, the weaver who spins the world out of herself. Allen notes that "the seamless web of life . . . is simultaneously the oral tradition and the thought of Old Spider Woman." In the stories Thought Woman's consciousness animates the natural world and connects humans to other natural entities in much the same fashion as in Black Elk's vision of the collective dance of spirit that was discussed in the previous chapter. Allen explains that in the Laguna view of spiritual collectivity, "each creature is part of a living whole. . . . All the life forms we recognize—animals, plants, rocks, wind—partake of this greater life."[8] Within the collectivity of "this greater life," the spiritual, natural, and human realms are co-joined and interpenetrating. In many traditional stories, beings shape-shift from one realm to another—for example, humans may assume animal form or vice versa—and many gods and goddesses are simultaneously deities who are also incarnated within the natural entities that bear their names. Many stories tell of sacred liaisons between a tribemember and a nature god or goddess, such as Bear Man, Snake Man, or Deer Woman. Sexual congress between human and deity/creature is sacralized in the stories, and such unions are often the means through which sacred power is transmitted from goddesses and gods to the tribe.[9]

Laguna stories originally formulated the relationship between tribe and the western terrain, for wise adaptation to natural conditions was the key to survival in an area of scarce resources. Emergence stories, which chronicle the Laguna people's emergence from the Fourth World into the newly created Fifth World (which is the current, physical world) through the aid of animals, articulate this view of mutual dependence, according to Silko:

> The human beings could not have emerged without the aid of antelope and badger. The human beings depended on the aid and charity of the animals. Only through interdependence could the human being survive. Families belonged to clans, and it was by clan that the human being joined with the animal and plant world. Life on the high arid plateau became viable when the human beings were able to imagine themselves as sisters and brothers to the badger, antelope clay, yucca, sun. Not until they could find a viable relationship to the terrain, the landscape they found themselves in, could they *emerge*. Only at the moment when the requisite balance between human and *other* was realized could the Pueblo people become a culture, a distinct group. ("Landscape," 115)

The cultural identity of the Laguna people was predicated on their constructing "a viable relationship" of familial bonds and reciprocity with the natural surroundings. This Laguna sense of themselves as "clans" "joined with the animal and plant world" corresponds to Haraway's formulation of the co-construction of social/nature in which humans and natural entities interactively produce their collective existence.[10] Silko observes that unlike Euro-Americans, who conceive of themselves as separate from the landscape, Laguna people locate themselves within it: "Viewers are as much a part of the landscape as the boulders they stand on. There is no high mesa edge or mountain peak where one can stand and not immediately be part of all that surrounds. . . . The land, the sky, all that is within them—the landscape—includes human beings" ("Landscape," 109). This belief that "we are the land" is the founding principle of Indian religion, notes Allen.[11] Environmental historian Carolyn Merchant argues in *Ecological Revolutions* that the Indian belief in "symbiosis" of human and nature translated into rituals and taboos governing hunting and agriculture that "constituted an environmental ethic that operated to hinder overexploitation" of the natural resources, which the Indians regarded as spiritually animate "gifts" offering themselves to the people, rather than as resource objects.[12] Within this ethic, nature was disturbed as little as possible, and only what was necessary for comfortable tribal survival was harvested from the land. Merchant explains that among the eastern tribes the settlers first encountered, agriculture was a communal endeavor largely performed by women. Crops were planted unobtrusively in forest clearings and along rivers, and farming sites were shifted periodically so that the land could replenish itself. Agricultural and hunting processes were the focus of many religious stories and ceremonies emphasizing the partnership of human and nature.

But during the conquest and resettlement of the Americas, the American Indian stories of human/natural collectivity were violently confronted by contrasting European stories of the hierarchical division between human and nature, in which nature and all that was identified with the natural world were assumed as resource commodity for human consumption, as I discussed in the introduction. Judeo-Christian belief in a transcendent God, superior to and separate from the physical realm, who had granted mankind dominion over the natural world, were combined with the mechanistic perspective of the scientific revolution, which posed nature as a grand machine to be manipulated for human progress. In this appropriative perspective, human beings were subjects radically divided from an increasingly objectified natural world. The growing European social emphasis upon competitive individualism, capitalist acquisition, and nationalist conquest further authorized the commodification and objectification of all deemed a lower form of existence.[13]

The identification of Indians with the American land served the quest of the Euro-American conquerors to, as Slotkin phrases it, assert an "emotional title" to the American continents.[14] The vision of Native Americans as part of the landscape became a key argument for their removal from territories coveted by settlers.[15] Although the representations of the character of both land and Indians have shifted in accordance with the prevailing ideologies of different historical periods,[16] the white equation of the two has remained a founding premise of American national identity, as the nation defined itself through the cultivation and civilization of wild land and untamed native peoples.

Beginning with Columbus's report to the Spanish court on his discovery of the Bahamas, in which he observed that the fecund resources of the lands and the ready generosity of the Arawak people made these islands prime for Spanish subjugation,[17] the equation of native peoples and natural resources of the New World would continue to be manipulated as justification for conquest. Other early explorers and travel writers continued in the vein of representing the abundant generosity of American land and aboriginal peoples in order to encourage European immigration to the New World. As I mentioned in my introduction, promotional literature enticing settlers to leave familiar settings for new lives in the New Land often portrayed America as an Indian maiden, graciously offering her territory for European entry "with all love and kindness and . . . as much bounty," as noted by Arthur Barlowe's 1584 account of his travels.[18] Ironically, Europeans transformed the Native American stories about the sacred union between the female spirit of the land and tribespeople into a new myth of erotic encounters between white men and American land that masked the actual violence of the conquest of America. The vision of America as the unspoiled *virgin land* conveniently erased the many centuries of Indian habitation, symbolically easing the usurpation of American land by white colonists. In graphic and decorative arts as well, America was imaged as an Indian queen or as an Indian princess who was represented as a loyal daughter of Britannia, or later, after U.S. independence, depicted bearing the national flag.

Anthropologist Sam Gill argues that the extremely popular legend of Pocahontas worked in similar fashion to justify the European settler's subjugation of American land and aboriginal peoples. In this historically-based legend, the Indian princess Pocahontas intervenes to save the British Capt. John Smith from execution at the hands of her tribe. Several years later Pocahontas marries another Englishman, converts to Christianity, and follows her husband to England, where she dies of smallpox. Gill explains that the popularization of her story reveals the contradictory relationship of white men to American land and native peoples: "Pocahontas, the Indian princess who is the American earth, gives up her native lineage, even betraying it, to join in sexual union with the white American, notably and obviously male. . . . The story of Pocahontas captures that peculiar ambiguity of the American story: in the acquisition and cultivation of the American soil, the land is conquered and civilized by the white masculine Americans, but in its domestication and civilization there remains the poignant suggestion of subjugation, destruction, and death."[19]

But most often, particularly during the early centuries of European colonization, white Americans' conceptions of American land and Indians were decidedly hostile, replacing the image of fertility and generosity with a harsher view of land as a wasteland that must be cultivated and of Indians as slothful savages who must give way before the improvements of civilization. Such comparisons used the Indian identification with animals in order to prove their subhuman status and thus served to justify the incursions of civilized white men upon the continent.[20]

In this manner, the early Puritan settlers, whose vision was determined by the perspective of their biblical stories, conceived of America as a threatening wilderness peopled with wild, barely human savages who were clearly of the devil's party.[21] The Puritan colonists believed it their religious mission to transform the wilderness into a fruitful garden and to rid the land of the Indians who were Satan's minions. The Indians might either join the Puritans in preparing the garden or they must give way before the people who would fulfill God's will.

The agrarian republican vision of America as a nation of independent farmers also depended upon the denigration of Indians as savages squandering the land. This republican ideal—based on Euro-American belief in private property, individual labor, progress, and improvement—viewed the Indian agricultural and hunting practices as a wasteful misuse of natural resources that impeded proper settlement and utilization of the land. As Benjamin Lincoln commented in his journal in 1793: "When I consider that to people fully the earth was in the original plan of the benevolent deity . . . I am confident that sooner or later . . . no men will be suffered to live by hunting on lands capable of improvement, and which would support more people under a state of cultivation. So that if the savages cannot be civilized and quit their present pursuits, they will in consequence of their stubbornness, dwindle and moulder away." Lincoln came to grim acceptance of the fatal opposition between Euro-American and Indian relations to nature: "Civilized and uncivilized people cannot live in the same territory." After an 1839 survey of Indians remaining in the Midwest, Thomas Farnum sadly concluded: "The Indian's bones must enrich the soil, before the plough of civilized man can open it. . . . The sturdy plant of the wilderness droops under the enervating culture of the garden."[22]

And so the republican story would continue, until all of the eastern tribes had been decimated through governmental policies of extermination, removal to western territories, or confinement to reservations, leaving the lands that the settlers coveted open to cultivation and improvement. Merchant notes that to the displaced Indians, such improvements often appeared instead to be the arbitrary division and commodification of natural surroundings as private property, the stripping of forest lands through clear-cut logging, the extermination of animals through overhunting and trapping, and the depletion of soils through intensive, nonreplenishing methods of agriculture.[23]

Silko's novels *Ceremony* and *Almanac of the Dead* address the violent history of this fatal opposition between the aboriginal stories of partnership and reciprocity with nature and the Euro-American stories of detachment and dominion. By focusing upon the productive and destructive effects of the contrasting stories, Silko argues that the historic white/Indian confrontation is not an essential racial enmity but a conflict of opposing paradigms that could be renegotiated and rectified. The protagonists of these novels must construct new stories that redress the fundamental disagreements between native and white cultures.

As Tayo realizes in *Ceremony*, contact with Euro-Americans has irrevocably entered into Laguna traditions: "The fifth world had become entangled with European names: the names of the rivers, the hills, the names of the animals and plants—all of creation suddenly had two names: an Indian name and a white name. . . . Now the feelings were twisted, tangled roots, and all the names for the source of this growth were buried under English words, out of reach. And there would be no peace and the people would have no rest until the entanglement had been unwound to the source" (68–69).[24] Paradoxically, this painful "entanglement" of cultures will offer the very means of undoing the fatal opposition between white and native America. In Silko's fiction it is often people at the margins of tribal/dominant culture—people of mixed descent, or of mixed acculturation, those who bear the conflict between cultures in their own persons and who must inevitably negotiate the entanglement of competing cultures—who are driven to create new stories that reframe the relations of native culture and dominant white culture by reaffirming the reciprocal relation of humans to nature. Paula Gunn Allen notes that mixed-blood, or half-breed, protagonists are a recurrent feature of contemporary Native American literature, as these characters, lost between two opposing cultures, embody the alienation endemic to living as a Native American in the midst of a hostile white society. These characters realize that "there is no way to be acceptably Indian (with all the pain that implies) and acceptable to whites at the same time."[25] While Silko's characters of mixed descent certainly struggle with alienation, they also serve the additional purpose of finding ways to negotiate between the warring native and white cultures, utilizing their painfully gained knowledge of the white world in order to reformulate Indian stories and practices that can counter the destructive practices of the dominant culture.

These characters of mixed descent and acculturation inhabit Gloria Anzaldua's *borderlands*, a place of unsettling contradiction that challenges the false boundaries the dominant culture has imposed between itself and all other cultures: "A borderland is a vague and undetermined place created by the emotional residue of an unnatural boundary. It is in a state of constant transition. The prohibited and the forbidden are its inhabitants. *Los atravesados* live here: the squint-eyed, the perverse, the queer, the troublesome, the mongrel, the mulatto, the half-breed, the half dead; in short all those who cross over, pass over, or go through the confines of the 'normal'. . . . Tension grips the inhabitants of the borderlands like a virus. Ambivalence and unrest reside there."[26] Those mixed-breed characters who reside in this borderland between native and white call into question the belief in essential white/Indian racial identities because, for them, originary racial identity is an impossibility. Therefore, as these characters illustrate, identity becomes a fabrication or an amalgamation, a construction of self through the choice of positions and perspectives—a choice of the stories that one will live by.[27] Through these characters, Silko shifts the historic polarity of white/native so that it becomes an adoption of one or the other contrasting relations to nature, instead of an opposition between biologically determined identities. It becomes a matter of competing paradigms, conflicting stories, rather than of blood. Through this shift, change and movement beyond the fatal opposition become a possibility.

Silko's first novel, *Ceremony*, employs and affirms the Laguna view of the restorative power of American Indian stories to challenge the dominant society's ethos of detachment from nature that has decimated the Laguna tribe and the natural and social worlds. *Ceremony* is a multilayered novel, constructed of frame poems surrounding a contemporary plot. Interspersed through the body of the novel are a number of tribal story-poems containing traditional legends about threats to the natural world and to Laguna people. The stories in these poems correspond to the central plot of Tayo's quest to save his tribe and end the drought. The reverberations between the layers of story-poems and main narrative in this novel enact the Laguna belief that stories produce the tribe by articulating relations between human, spirit, and nature. The contemporary plot echoes the story-poems, the poems offer an interpretive framework for the plot, divine entities from stories appear in the plot, and the protagonist learns how to construct and enact new stories that will produce new relations. In this vein, Silko introduces *Ceremony* with a poem that presents the novel as a manifestation of Thought Woman's stories: "Thought-Woman,/ is sitting in her room/ and whatever she thinks about/ appears./ . . . She is sitting in her room/ thinking of a story now/ I'm telling you the story/ she is thinking" (1).

Ceremony addresses the embattled uncertainties of contemporary Laguna reservation existence in the face of the everpresent loss of native lands and in the midst of an actively hostile dominant culture that constantly works to undermine tribal traditions and native people's cultural identities. Tayo, the protagonist of the novel, returns home to the reservation in a state of severe shell shock and cultural confusion. Tayo suffers waves of physical illness and disturbing visions in which the Japanese enemies whom the Allies killed in the Philippines appear to be Tayo's uncle Josiah, who died on the reservation while Tayo was away at war. Similarly, Tayo believes that the drought that is decimating the Laguna reservation has been caused by his cursing the incessant Philippine jungle rain that he blamed for his wounded cousin Rocky's being put to death by Japanese soldiers. Tayo is disturbed by the irrational associations of his visions in which the normal logical boundaries of the modern Western world—such as between family and enemy, home and foreign territory, mental curses and external conditions—fail to hold. During the course of the novel he will come to use his madness as a vision from the borderlands, a vision in which the unbounded, traditional Indian vision of the collective nature of events has run up against the wall of Euro-American conceptual oppositions. Tayo's cure will lie in untangling this conflict of paradigms.

The usual power imbalance of white/native relations has also been aggravated by the war, and the ambiguity of Tayo's half-breed status continues to haunt him upon his return to the reservation. Tayo continues to be denied complete acceptance within the tribe, yet he has always been excluded from the white world off the reservation, which only temporarily deemed Indians real Americans while they were in military uniform, fighting Asians for the good of the nation. The other full-blooded Laguna veterans enjoyed this fleeting taste of white power, white acceptance, and white women, and now that they are once again second-class citizens confined to the reservation, they drown their sense of the white world's betrayal through drinking, fighting amongst themselves, and feeling gnawing envy of white entitlement, which they direct against Tayo because of his mixed descent. The drought that is killing the tribespeople's livestock and crops only adds to the veterans' scorn for tribal ways. Tribal elders are at a loss for an effective means of curing the veterans and the drought-struck land.[28]

Ceremony describes the process of Tayo's healing as he comes to use his cultural confusion and ambiguous social position in order to renegotiate the relations between Indian and white cultures through a ceremonial reconstruction of the traditional Laguna relationship to the land. Tayo's exposure to the brutal hostilities of World War II that culminated in the atomic bombings of Japan have taught him the extreme devastation inherent within the Euro-American model of division and dominion. His ensuing shell shock and madness force him to comprehend the unbearable contradiction between the Indian belief in reciprocal relatedness and the white mode of destructive detachment. During Tayo's ceremonial healing under the direction of the unorthodox half-breed medicine man Betonie, he discovers and enacts new, empowering stories that alter the power imbalance between whites and natives and restore the partnership between tribe and nature. Much as *Meridian's* civil rights activism demonstrated the political application of African-American animistic tradition, the process of Tayo's healing reaffirms the viability of traditional Indian animistic culture as a means of rectifying the ravages wrought by the white world. During the ceremony that Tayo performs throughout the course of the novel, he comes to perceive potentiality and renewed life where the white world has wrought only sterility, drought, and death.

Tayo's cure begins with his growing comprehension of the way that the white conquest of tribal lands underlies Indian social subordination and the threatened dissolution of tribal culture. The seizure of native lands— which, as I have argued above, was justified by white claims of cultural superiority and divine mandate to people the wilderness—has come to be interpreted by whites and certain Indians as sign of the superiority of the Euro-American model of private property and progress over the Indian model of nonexploitative partnership with nature. In a twist of circular logic, as whites violently usurp more and more land, fulfilling their vision of productive progress, their conquest becomes self-endorsing: white predominance upon the land comes to signify white superiority. Whites and even many Indians interpret the hardships of reservation life that are actually directly related to the loss of prime farming and hunting grounds—such as economic impoverishment, lack of higher education and professional positions, overwhelming unemployment, "backwards" subsistence farming methods, as well as the accompanying emotional hardships, such as drunkenness and depression—as a sign of Indian racial inferiority and inability to survive the rigors of the white world. For many of the tribespeople of *Ceremony*, the loss of land leads to bitter cultural self-doubt and growing accession to white ways. Tayo realizes that Auntie's Christianity, Rocky's emulation of the white mainstream image of success, and even the veterans' self-destructive envy of white entitlement all stem from the omnipresent loss of ancestral lands: "They were never the same after that: they had seen what the white people had made from the stolen land. . . . Every day they had to look at the land, from horizon to horizon, and every day the loss was with them; it was the dead unburied, and the mourning of the lost going on forever. So they tried to sink the loss in booze, and silence their grief with war stories about their courage, defending the land already lost" (169).

Worse yet, white encroachment upon native ancestral lands threatens the reciprocity between humans and nature. Tayo describes the tribespeople's painful realization that they cannot protect the natural entities whom they regard as spiritual kin from abuses at the hands of whites. When former tribal lands that have been seized by the government are sold to ranchers and loggers, the land is stripped for profit and the animals are exterminated for sport: "The loggers had come, and they stripped the canyons below the rim and cut great clearings on the plateau slopes. . . . The loggers shot the bears and mountain lions for sport. And it was then the Laguna people understood that the land had been taken, because they couldn't stop these white people from coming to destroy the animals and the land" (186). The inability of the tribe to prevent this wanton desecration leads to terrible sorrow and guilt.

Tayo's illness accentuates the necessity for the Laguna people to redress this omnipresent loss of land and reciprocity so that the tribe might heal from crippling guilt and self-hatred. Central to Tayo's ceremonial healing and to Silko's unsettling of the fatal opposition is a story-poem that the healer Betonie recounts to Tayo about Indian sorcerers' creation of white people as implements of destruction who believe themselves to be separate from nature and who thus ravage everything and everyone associated with the natural world. Not only does this poem reinterpret the European dis-

junction from nature from a Laguna point of view, the poem also reframes
the European conquest of America as the product of an Indian witchery
story, since "white skin people" are conjured into existence when the witch
speaks this poem. In this story-poem the conflict between Indian and European paradigms is reframed within a larger conflict between beneficent Indians who claim kinship with nature, and maleficent Indian sorcerers, or
witches, bent on fomenting death and destruction, who employ "white skin
people" as tools for their diabolical work. Within this poem, the social and
political power that the Indians have lost during the white conquest of
America is effectively restored, as Betonie tells Tayo: "We can deal with
white people, with their machines and their beliefs. We can because we
invented white people" (132).

This story-poem tells of a witchery contest during which a witch con-
jures the white-skin destroyers by recounting a story-poem about their decimation of the natural and native worlds. The witch introduces the poem
with the warning, "as I tell the story / it will begin to happen" (134), demonstrating the power of stories to set things in motion, for good or ill. Thus
the witchery poem is testament to the Indian belief in the productivity of
stories, even as it recounts the decimation of the Indian world through the
advent of the white settlers' dangerous new story of detachment from and
destruction of nature and native peoples. The witch tells the following
story of witchery, white people, and ultimate destruction:

> Caves across the ocean
> in caves of dark hills
> white skin people
> like the belly of a fish
> covered with hair.
>
> Then they grow away from the earth
> then they grow away from the sun
> then they grow away from the plants and animals.
> They see no life. . . .
>
> They fear
> They fear the world.
> They destroy what they fear.
> They fear themselves.

The wind will blow them across the ocean
thousands of them in giant boats
swarming like larva
out of a crushed ant hill.

They will carry objects
which can shoot death
faster than the eye can see.

They will kill the things they fear
all the animals
the people will starve.

They will poison the water
they will spin the water away
and there will be drought
the people will starve.

They will fear what they find
They will fear the people
They kill what they fear.

Entire villages will be wiped out
They will slaughter whole tribes.

Corpses for us
Blood for us
Killing killing killing killing.

And those they do not kill
will die anyway
at the destruction they see
at the loss
at the loss of the children
the loss will destroy the rest.

Stolen rivers and mountains
the stolen land will eat their hearts
and jerk their mouths from the Mother
The people will starve.

They will bring terrible diseases
the people have never known.
Entire tribes will die out
covered with festered sores
shitting blood
vomiting blood
corpses for our work.

Set in motion now
set in motion by our witchery
set in motion
to work for us.

They will take this world from ocean to ocean
they will turn on each other
they will destroy each other
Up here in these hills
they will find the rocks,
rocks with veins of green and yellow and black.
They will lay the final pattern with these rocks
they will lay it across the world
and explode everything.

Set in motion now
set in motion
to destroy
to kill
objects to work for us
objects to act for us
Performing the witchery (134–36)

In effect, the witchery poem realigns the historic American antagonism between the Indian mode of relationality of human to nature and the supposedly superior Euro-American mode of detachment and dominion. While white and Indian modes are still shown to be dichotomous in this poem, whites are described as agents of destruction and puppets of witchery rather than as divinely ordained bearers of enlightened progress, as their historic self-descriptions would have it. In this poem, white-skin peoples' detachment from nature causes all of their violent actions. When the white-skin people "grow away" from the earth and the sun and all other beings, and when they come to regard natural entities as dead things with no life, their alienation leads to fear and enmity toward nature and those peoples still associated with the natural world. The poem describes the white objectification of nature as inherently destructive: because whites believe that natural entities and native peoples are dead things, they deaden them through violent assault, thus enforcing their story about the lifelessness of the surrounding world. Each act of violence leads to greater and greater destruction, and, as the world is made ever more dead and alien, the devastation eventually circles back upon the white destroyers as enmity toward fellow whites and, ultimately, as a final, all-encompassing debacle of nuclear immolation. Thus the witchery poem reframes the historic fatal opposition as truly fatal to all involved, since the white mode of thought and behavior is based upon a fatal denial of life to anything perceived as Other. In the poem, the white mode of objectification and domination is itself shown to be a fatal opposition between subject and object that produces alienation, fear, and death.

The deadly divisiveness at the core of the white-skin paradigm corresponds to the radical separation of subject and object that feminist analysts of science find responsible for the objectification of nature within the Western model of scientific objectivity. Keller notes: "Having divided the world into two parts—the knower (mind), and the knowable (nature)—scientific ideology goes on to prescribe a very specific relation between the two . . . one of distance and separation. It is that between a subject and an object radically divided. . . . Nature is objectified."[29] Keller explains that this radical division is the basis of the traditional scientific stance of dominant mastery, in which nature and people identified with nature—such as women and people of color—are to be forcibly appropriated in the service of Western development. Haraway further analyzes the appropriative dynamic between omnipotent knower and passive, inert object within the Western analytic tradition:

> The analytic tradition, deeply indebted to Aristotle and to the transformative history of "White Capitalist Patriarchy" . . . turns everything into a resource for appropriation, in which an object of knowledge is finally itself only matter for the seminal power, the act of the knower. Here, the object both guarantees and refreshes

the power of the knower, but any status as *agent* in the production
of knowledge must be denied the object. It—the world—must, in
short, be objectified as thing, not as an agent; it must be matter for
the self-formulation of the only social being in the productions of
knowledge, the human knower. . . . Nature is only the raw material
of culture, appropriated, preserved, enslaved, exalted or otherwise
made flexible for disposal by culture in the logic of capitalist colonialism.[30]

Haraway notes the power imbalance through which the object of analytic
knowledge becomes only "matter," or as Silko puts it, "dead thing," that
shores up the all-consuming subjectivity of the knower. In this epistemological model, nature is "objectified," "enslaved," and "disposed of," in a
manner analogous to the white-skin "deadening" of the natural world and
native peoples in Silko's witchery poem. This critique of the exploitative
dynamic within traditional models of objectivity, which is crucial to feminist scientists' efforts to theorize more egalitarian, accountable, and mutually interactive subject/object relations for the sciences, corresponds to the
exposure of the whites' fatal opposition to nature in the witchery poem,
which is similarly crucial to Tayo's struggle to reconstruct less exploitative
and hostile relations between the two races and between the tribe and the
natural world.

Through the witchery poem Tayo comes to understand that the hostilities and divisions that he sees everywhere—the enmity of white and Indian, of rich and poor, of Japanese and American, the division of the natural
world into exclusive tracts of private property, and the growing separation
of humans from an increasingly plundered and degraded natural environment—are all the result of this fatal opposition between alienated subject
and objectified world. Through the poem Tayo comes to attribute polarization to the witchery rather than to the white-skin invaders and to regard
whites as tools of a greater evil, rather than as evil in themselves. After
hearing this poem, Tayo understands that Indians, too, may fall prey to this
divisiveness, and he will perceive Emo and other veterans as menacing
agents of the witchery. He realizes that polarization itself, rather than any
group of people, is the core problem. But before any widespread resolution
can occur, whites, too, must face the racial polarity inhering in the founda-
tional American mythos that assumes that Euro-Americans are the innocent
civilizers of a land lost to Indian savagery—a mythos that serves the witch-

ery by keeping both peoples divided and turned against each other. The "lie" of white manifest destiny and Indian savagery now threatens to destroy everyone: "If white people never looked beyond the lie, to see that theirs was a nation built on stolen land, then they would never be able to understand how they had been used by the witchery; they would never know that they were still being manipulated by those who knew how to stir the ingredients together: white thievery and injustice boiling up the anger and hatred that would finally destroy the world: the starving against the fat, the colored against the white" (191).

The witchery poem and the plot of the novel, which links the uranium mines on the reservation to the nuclear bombing of Japan, assert the very real threat that the destroyers' paradigm will come to final fruition through nuclear annihilation; yet this final threat of nuclear destruction reforms humans into a new collectivity that subsumes social differences into a new clan, united by shared danger:

> Trinity Site, where they exploded the first atomic bomb, was only three hundred miles to the southeast. . . . And the top-secret laboratories where the bomb had been created were deep in the Jemez Mountains, on land the Government took from Cochiti Pueblo. . . . There was no end to it; it knew no boundaries; and he had arrived at the point of convergence where the fate of all living things, and even the earth, had been laid. From the jungles of his dreaming he recognized why the Japanese voices had merged with Laguna voices, with Josiah's voice and Rocky's voice; the lines of cultures and worlds were drawn in flat dark lines on fine light sand, converging in the middle of witchery's final ceremonial sand painting. From that time on, human beings were one clan again, united by the fate the destroyers had planned for all of them, for all living things; united by a circle of death that devoured people in cities twelve thousand miles away, victims who had never known these mesas, who had never seen the delicate colors of the rocks which boiled up their slaughter. (245–46)

The magnitude of the witchery's final pattern of nuclear holocaust confounds divisions between races, nations, species, and geographical distances, reuniting all earthly entities into a global "circle of death." The witchery story comes full circle when the final pattern of destruction reen-compasses all within its deadly plot. Paradoxically, the very scope of the destroyers' deadly power has made human beings "one clan again," de-creating the boundaries that the witchery story had originally set in motion and thus opening a space for the alternative Laguna story of collectivity and interconnection.[31]

In light of this revelation, Tayo can reinterpret his madness and confu-sion in which the Japanese and Laguna people are identical and his curse against the Philippine jungle rain has led to the southwestern drought as an alternative vision of genuine interconnections available outside of the false boundaries of the witchery. Tayo realizes that the uranium used for the bombing of Japan has been mined on the Laguna reservation, and so the fate of the Laguna and the fate of the Japanese are truly intertwined.[32] Upon recognizing this, Tayo can reassert the Laguna faith in the intercon-nectedness of all life within the ordering vision of the stories: "He cried with relief at finally seeing the pattern, the way all the stories fit together— the old stories, the war stories, their stories—to become the story that was still being told. He was not crazy; he had never been crazy; he had only seen and heard the world as it always was; no boundaries, only transitions through all distances and times" (246).

It devolves upon the mixed-breed characters such as Tayo, Betonie, and Uncle Josiah's mysterious lover, the Night Swan, those who have dwelt in the painful borderlands produced by racial polarization and who have personally borne the negative consequences of these divisive boundaries, to move beyond the fatal opposition toward less polarized stories of merg-ing boundaries, fluid transitions in culture, and transracial social adaptation. Appropriately, Tayo's ceremonial healing takes the form of a quest to find his uncle Josiah's lost herd of hybrid Mexican wild cattle, interbred to sur-vive desert conditions. Josiah's experimental herd, which might bring the Laguna tribe a means of farming the arid land during years of drought, symbolizes the way that Tayo might reenvision the borderlands as a prom ising site of productive intermixing and flexible adaptation to the shifting realities of an always-evolving American landscape composed of many in-teracting creatures and cultures. Tayo's ceremonial quest is, in essence, an act of recovery of all that has been "stolen" by the witchery. In tracking the Mexican cattle, which have been taken by a rich white rancher, Tayo will find the mountain and woman that Betonie has envisioned, and through

them he will recuperate the power of traditional stories to renew the collectivity of tribe and land.

Tayo's cure is fulfilled through his relationship with the mysterious
woman named Ts'eh, who helps him to recover Josiah's cattle and whose
love and guidance teach Tayo how to regain his health and protect himself
from Emo's violent witchery. Ts'eh, whose storm-cloud patterned blanket
has the power to conjure storms and whose medicine work with plants and
stones renews the drought-struck landscape, appears to be human being,
natural entity, and supernatural being at once—a mountain goddess incarnate in a woman's form. Allen notes that the name Ts'eh echoes the Laguna
name for Mount Taylor, which is a tribal sacred site known as Tse-pi'na, or
Woman Veiled in Clouds.[33] Ts'eh is a sacred shapeshifter, in the tradition
of spirit beings such as Buffalo Man and Sun Man, who appear in the traditional Laguna stories that Silko collected in *Storyteller* and that she discussed
in the essay "Landscape" quoted above. Such shapeshifters convey spiritual
knowledge to the tribe by momentarily assuming human shape in order to
form unions with tribespeople. The nature gods and goddesses act as lovers
and teachers, offering their human partners sacred knowledge and sacred
items that aid the entire tribe.[34] Thus, these relationships epitomize the
Laguna belief in the reciprocal spiritual kinship of human and nature, the
belief, discussed above, that the Laguna *became* a people when they articulated a partnership relationship to the surrounding landscape.

As Tayo's lover, protector, and teacher, Ts'eh restores Tayo's faith in the
veracity and viability of the old stories of the loving union between tribe
and natural world even in the face of white antagonism to this mode of
relation.[35] For Tayo, Ts'eh is living proof of the spiritual animation of nature, of the living presence of the sacred beings of the tribal stories.
Through the love of Ts'eh, Tayo is able to renew the bond that tribal stories
had articulated between human and nature: "The ear for the story and the
eye for the pattern were theirs; the feeling was theirs; we came out of this
land and we are hers. . . . They had always been loved. He thought of her
then; she had always loved him, she had never left him, she had always
been there" (255). Through Ts'eh, Tayo realizes that despite the tribe's displacement from the land and its inability to prevent white encroachments
upon nature, even despite the omnipresent sense of loss that the tribe has
suffered, the tribe has always retained its compact of reciprocity with nature: "They had always been loved." The "she" who loves in this passage is
clearly Ts'eh, yet this omnipresent "she" is also Old Spider Woman, or

Thought Woman—the primordial Laguna female deity whose thoughts produce the natural world. Through love of Ts'eh, then, Tayo reconstructs and recovers a living relationship to the Laguna sacred principles incarnate in nature, and his rekindled animistic belief absolves the loss and guilt that has plagued the tribe.[36]

Furthermore, the tender, egalitarian, sexual and spiritual relation between the lovers offers Tayo a healing antidote to the witchery's mode of antagonistic objectification that has sickened him. Tayo's relationship to the shapeshifter Ts'eh defies the diseased disjunctions at the heart of the white-skin mode. Within herself Ts'eh intermingles much that the whites deem to be essentially opposed; she is what Haraway would call a cyborgian entity at once goddess and woman, mountain and human, supernatural and natural, sacred and sexual, timeless and momentary. Tayo's union with Ts'eh teaches him the falsity of the many sorts of boundaries that the white world has imposed across the American continent—the fences dividing the landscape into private plots, the reservations quarantining the Indians into their allotted place, the indiscriminate plundering of nature. But the lovers reconstruct the Indian mode of animistic relation as potent medicine against the deadening witchery that the whites have unwittingly wrought. As Ts'eh teaches Tayo, the struggle for an ending to the story of the fatal encounter between whites and Indians is not yet settled, and it is vitally necessary to counter the witchery story with an alternative story of kinship, life, love, connection, and renewal. Ts'eh teaches Tayo that the way to end the witchery is not to engage the agents of witchery, such as Emo, in fruitless physical battle, but to refuse to participate in the violent antagonisms the witchery has fomented.[37] While the witchery "can't be called back" and while the Indian mode of relation cannot be returned to some precontact purity, Ts'eh insists that the outcome of the Laguna/white encounter can be rewritten if Tayo adheres to the alternative story of loving collectivity.

The function of the animistic story as antidote to the witchery is analogous to the articulation by feminist analysts of science of alternative, more positive relations between human and nature, subject and object, as antidote to the polarizations that they see still predominating in the sciences. While neither Keller nor Haraway makes claims for the spiritual animation of nature that Silko describes, the feminist analysts do articulate alternative models of coconstructive interactions between knower and nonhuman actors that closely correspond to Silko's representation of the egalitarian

mutuality between Tayo and Ts'eh. Keller describes the transformative possibility of such a paradigm of interdependent subject/object relations by
arguing, as I mentioned in my discussion of Dickinson's nature poetry, that
if one claims kinship with a complex and resourceful natural world, rather
than viewing it as inferior and alien, one's questions and conclusions will
shift accordingly.[38] This model of kinship between human knower and resourceful nature echoes the Laguna belief in reciprocity between tribe and
surrounding natural world.

   Similarly, Haraway argues that the existing paradigms of science that
promote Western domination of nature and of native peoples might be
contested through the articulation of alternative models of collectivities
of human and nonhuman actors, as I have mentioned in the chapters on
Dickinson and Walker. Haraway suggests that "perhaps our hopes for ac-
countability for techno-biopolitics in the belly of the monster turn on revi-
sioning the world as coding trickster with whom we must learn to
converse." Haraway's notion of a "conversation" with the world as coding
trickster who acts with some form of agency and intelligence is reminiscent
of the Laguna view of nature spirits as loving teachers who offer the tribe
vital knowledge, as Ts'eh "converses" with Tayo. In fact, Haraway often
refers to nature specifically as "coyote," in reference to the Indian trickster
god of that name, citing the Indian view of the natural world in her own
articulation of nature "as witty actor and agent." Haraway finds in Indian
animistic beliefs a useful model of nature as "active" "partner" and "co-
constructor" of the complex human and nonhuman collectivities within
which we live. Like Silko, Haraway finds the borderlands to be a region of
hopeful disturbance of false polarities. She proclaims: "We *are all* in chias-
matic borderlands, liminal areas where new shapes, new kinds of action
and responsibility, are gestating in the world."[39]

   The relationship of Tayo and Ts'eh is an articulation of this gestation
of new shapes and new kinds of actions and responsibilities spawned by
traditional Laguna animistic beliefs and incubated during the centuries of
white siege and seizure. For the image of the mountain/goddess/woman in
loving relation with the half-breed Indian man is not a simple, naive, and
innocent recapitulation of the precontact Laguna stories. It is instead a
canny, conscious redeployment of the Laguna image of sacred female presence in nature—the very image that the whites had early on appropriated
in order to justify white settlement of the virgin land. Silko's reappropria-
tion of this image, like Walker's return to buried African and Indian animis-

tic traditions, turns this image of the land-as-native-woman back against the white-skin conquerors' commodification of native peoples and nature. Silko's land-as-native-woman entrusts herself only to those who acknowledge her as living presence, rather than as passive object of their desires, and to those who will care for her, rather than ravage her for profit and the perverse pleasures of wanton destruction. Significantly, she entrusts herself to a mixed-breed inhabitant of the borderlands. Rather than being a sentimental metaphor, Silko's Ts'eh is a contestatory recuperation of Laguna story tradition as that which might aid us—as a nation—to escape our continued entrapment within a deadly national mythology.

The relationship between Tayo and Ts'eh is an instance of Keller's and Haraway's calls to us to articulate collectivities composed of human and nonhuman agents in order to counter the deadly traditional "God View" of white master disjunct from the passive world that he has forcibly overpowered. Furthermore, Silko's image insists that in the complex, long-embattled American context, there is no essential innocent position from which we might assume what Haraway calls "new actions and responsibilities."[40] There is truly no way to "untangle" the snarl of white/native relations, nor to disown the witchery. Tayo's union with Ts'eh is historically contextualized against the realities of Indian participation in World War II and Indian complicity in nuclear weaponry through concession to uranium mining on reservation lands. Only by claiming his responsibility for participating in the witchery can Tayo resituate himself within the alternative paradigm embodied in his union with Ts'eh.

At the conclusion of the novel Tayo assumes his own place in the living web of the Laguna oral tradition. He relates the story of his encounter with the mountain/woman to the tribal council, who receive his words as a sign of divine blessing of the tribe. The old men cry: "'A'moo'ooh'/You have seen her/ We will be blessed/again" (257). Tribal life will be reinvigorated by Tayo's reconstruction and enactment of this new yet perennial story that renews tribal relations to land and sends the witchery back upon itself. Through Ts'eh, Tayo has brought the tribe the sacred knowledge that the witchery story is its own trick; if one sees "no life" in the natural world, the witchery will ascend, but if one proclaims the spiritual life animating the natural world, then the witchery is defeated. The concluding poem of *Ceremony* confirms: "Whirling darkness/ started its journey/ with its witchery/ and/ its witchery/ has returned upon it/ . . . It is dead for now./ It is dead for now/ It is dead for now./ It is dead for now" (261). *Ceremony* insists that, for better or worse, we will re-create the world in the image of our stories.

I close my study with a brief discussion of Silko's recent epic dystopian novel *Almanac of the Dead*, for in this text many of the themes that I have discussed become the impetus for political confrontations, that, in Silko's vision, have the potential to restructure the social and natural worlds of the Americas. In *Almanac of the Dead* the historic conflict between Indian animism and the witchery's fatal opposition will erupt into an undeclared war between the hordes of dispossessed peoples and the ruling elite Destroyers, a guerilla war that will rage across the Americas in many forms of subversion and strife, perhaps clearing a space for a new, truly democratic America that might actually be of the people, for the people, and that might live in keeping with the forces of Mother Earth.

While *Ceremony* ended optimistically with the temporary defeat of the witchery and the reinvigoration of the tribe, the witchery is reigning full force in mainstream America by the opening of *Almanac of the Dead*, which is set around the beginning of the twenty-first century. Focusing on the world outside of reservations, tracing scores of non-native characters, as well as characters of partial native descent and partial native acculturation who can only reconstruct an Indian perspective, the novel presents the America of the future as a wasteland in which Tayo's nightmare vision of the witchery-prompted war between "have nots and haves" has erupted. *Almanac* describes a world almost totally within the maw of the "Death Eye Dog," the Mexican Indian god of blood-lust and destruction, who in this novel has spiritually reigned over the Americas during the five-hundred-year period since Mexican Indian witches summoned the Conquistadors to these shores to share in their blood sports. Like the witchery poem of *Ceremony*, *Almanac of the Dead* reframes the history of the twin American continents as a fatal opposition between those primarily native inhabitants who uphold the reciprocal animistic compact with Mother Earth and those Destroyers bent on turning everything into a waste, an object, a commodity for their profit and perverse pleasures. In this bleakly satiric characterization of millennial America, the witchery is clearly in ascendancy.

Silko describes the ruling Destroyers as those who, like the white-skin people of the witchery poem in *Ceremony*, see "no life," in the larger world and who thus can feel no empathy for other living beings. The Destroyers' main pleasures lie in acquiring wealth, engaging in violence, and wreaking death—all practices that de-create a living world into inert object—and the Destroyers are characterized by reckless disregard for the integrity of the natural world and native peoples who are their prime targets of destruction.

Leah Blue, for example, is a real estate magnate (married to an assassin), whose grandest development scheme is a re-creation of Venice that she is building in the deserts of Arizona, complete with canals that she plans to fill by draining the underground aquifers that sustain all life in the region, particularly the nearby Indian reservations. Trigg, Leah's lover and business partner, constructs hospitals and treatment centers. He supplies these facilities with human blood, skin, and organs that he has "harvested" from local homeless people by literally draining and dismembering these displaced persons into commodifiable body parts. For the Destroyers, violence is the ultimate pornographic thrill, and Beaufrey has found it profitable to film the torture of South and Central American political prisoners, as well as to collect footage of last trimester abortions and of rapes and murders of women and children, which he distributes to the pornographic film industry.

The Destroyers' disregard for nature, native peoples, and women converges in Serlo's experimental research into the production of Artificial Earths that might sustain a few wealthy aristocratic white men in indefinite orbit when the planet Earth becomes so degraded that it can no longer sustain human life. Serlo, who despises the human touch and believes that women are worthless creatures whose physical and emotional proximity taints children, is also experimenting with cloning himself and other perfect male specimens—in ferociously parodic enactment of Luce Irigaray's observation in *Speculum of the Other Woman* that Western phallogocentric culture is in fact a continuous chain of male self-replication in deep denial of men's actual births from out of the wombs of women and from out of the womb of nature, or earth.[11] Serlo's scientific projects exemplify the Destroyers' wish to be rid of all that is perceived as natural, native, essentially Other, categories that unfortunately happen to include most forms of life on this planet. As the Destroyers, many of whom are prominent political, military, and economic figures, accumulate ever more wealth and commit ever more exaggerated acts of violence and perversion and as they drain the resources of their nations in vampirelike predatory gluttony and degrade the natural environment to such an extent that many regions become nearly uninhabitable, the general populace becomes ever more deprived and desperate, ever more cognizant of Karl Marx's revolutionary dictum that they have nothing to lose but their chains.

As in *Ceremony*, this dramatic imbalance of power is countered through the evocation of stories that frame alternative relations between human/ nature and subject/object; but unlike the resolution of Silko's earlier novel, in which Tayo is able to turn the witchery back upon itself by refusing to participate in its bloody struggles, the stories in *Almanac* serve to rouse the dispossessed to various forms of combative actions against the Destroyers. Central to the novel's title and plot is an old Indian woman's transmission of the tattered Almanac of the Dead to her twin granddaughters, who begin translating into English this fragmentary, cryptic, five-hundred-year-old record begun by the Indians who fled north to escape the advent of the Death Eye Dog Destroyers.

The granddaughters' transcription of the almanac sets in motion the eclectic, anarchic, but steadily converging waves of uprising that gather force throughout this novel. Like the tribal stories threading through the narrative of *Ceremony* that offer Tayo an alternative to the witchery, the almanac exemplifies the power of indigenous stories to spur resistance to the dominant forces of the Destroyers. But while Tayo has access to the verbal heritage of the Laguna tribe, the Mexican Indian tribe that produced the almanac was dispersed by the Destroyers, and all that remains of their history and culture is this fragmented written record, pieced together again and again by the many who have handed it down through the generations. This document—partial, raggedly transmitted, and imaginatively reconstructed—represents the fractured relationship that the dispossessed have with their native cultures within this novel. For the most part, these characters are peoples of the borderlands who have been largely severed from tribal cultures, and the indigenous stories in *Almanac* are no longer communally produced and transmitted throughout a united tribe but have been dispersed by the Destroyers and must be painstakingly exhumed, reassembled, and then broadcast to peoples so desperately in need of direction and renewed hope.[42]

Yet even under these circumstances, the stories fulfill their traditional Laguna function of articulating collectivities of humans and nature, for in *Almanac* stories of resistance and stories of animistic partnership between human and nature stir the dispossessed to revolutionary resistance against the reigning Destroyers. An entry from the almanac describes this revolutionary function of stories: "One day a story will arrive in your town. There

will always be disagreement over direction—whether the story came from
the southwest or the southeast. The story may arrive with a stranger, a
traveler thrown out of his home country months ago. Or the story may be
brought by an old friend, perhaps the parrot trader. But after you hear the
story, you and others prepare by the new moon to rise up against the slave
masters" (578).

Old Yoeme, the keeper of the almanac, believes that "power resides in
certain stories" (581). Each retelling of stories of resistance, such as stories
of Indian uprisings against European settlers or stories of African-American
slave rebellions, increases the revolutionary spirit of the people. As Clinton, the African-American leader of the homeless veterans resistance movement, believes: "If the people knew their history, they would realize they
must rise up" (742). In fact, like Clinton, several of the Indian characters in
this novel believe that the spirits of their peoples literally live within the
stories, and thus the transmission of stories preserves these revolutionary
spirits.[43] The transmission of these stories serves to gather the listeners into
communities of resistance, once again forming the people into collectivities, even though the communities of Almanac are, for the most part, loosely
eclectic congregations rather than homogenous, originary tribes.

As in Ceremony, the stories of resistance circulating throughout Almanac
encode the traditional animistic compact of reciprocity between tribe and
inspirited natural world. Unlike the Destroyers, who turn natural entities
and other humans into objects of prey, the stories of the revolutionaries
emphasize the spiritual integrity of nature and the loving partnership between natural world and human inhabitants. Much as Ts'eh emblematized
this animistic paradigm in Ceremony, the revolutionary stories of Almanac
urge the people to come to the defense of Mother Earth, the sacred prin
ciple of the planet who is being ravaged almost beyond repair by the
Destroyers. The stories intone: "We must protect Mother Earth from destruction. . . . We want our mother the land" (518–19). And the stories pro-
claim a war of the dispossessed to reclaim Mother Earth from the
destroyers: "The dispossessed people of the earth would rise up and take
back lands that had been their birthright, and these lands would never
again be held as private property, but as lands belonging to the people
forever to protect" (532). For the spirits of the earth urge the dispossessed
to rescue them from destruction and to reestablish the animistic paradigm:
"Tribal people would retake the Americas; tribal people would retake ancestral land all over the world. This was what the earth's spirits wanted: her

indigenous children who loved her and did not harm her" (712). As the representation of Ts'eh in loving union with Tayo unsettled white claims of title to the land in *Ceremony*, the evocation of Mother Earth throughout *Almanac* is clearly oppositional, rather than sentimental, representing the contrasting visions of the animistic dispossessed and the objectifying Destroyers. The revolution between the "haves and have nots" will be a war for Mother Earth.[44] The tribal stories have become a call to arms.

The revolutionaries who finally converge at the close of this expansive novel are an eclectic assortment of renegades, social outcasts, and social objectors whose resistance to the Destroyers will eventually draw them together into a syncretic, wildly varied army. Clinton realizes that "nothing could be black only or brown only or white only anymore. . . . This was the last chance the people had against the Destroyers and they would never prevail if they did not work together as a common force" (747). Even though their primary concerns range widely from homelessness, the plight of veterans, tribal rights, and poverty, to environmental defense, all these characters see a connection between the restoration of the earth and social justice, and all engage in acts of subversion against the ruling order of the Death Eye Dog Destroyers.

In contrast to *Ceremony*, there is no sense that the reaffirmation of the animistic vision will suffice to defeat the Destroyers; yet this novel, too, asserts that the Destroyers will be defeated through their own destructiveness, and much of what the revolutionaries do is to turn the forces that have been deployed against them back against the Destroyers. The revolution will be fought in all sorts of ways; some tribal peoples will reassert tribal beliefs and practices, but many of the revolutionaries who come from the borderlands will utilize their knowledge of the dominant culture to fight against it. The Mexican parrot people will begin their walk to reclaim Mother Earth for tribal people, but Angelita La Escapia will reappropriate Marxist theory in order to reframe the history of indigenous Indian resistance and will use contraband military rockets to defend the marching tribes. Zeta, one of the twin granddaughters, will defy national boundaries by smuggling goods across the borders, and she will supply military weaponry to the resistance fighters. Clinton will rouse an army of homeless veterans. Awa Gee, a computer hacker, will use his skills to transfer monies and shut down electric companies, literally subverting the powers that be. Eco warriors will sacrifice their lives to blow up electric dams and protect rivers and forests.

But perhaps most crucial to the cause of the revolution, nature is arising in acts of natural disaster that wreak havoc with the structures that the Destroyers have imposed and thus speed the return of the land to the peoples who believe it to be alive and inspirited:

> The time had come when people were beginning to sense impending disaster and to see signs all around them—great upheavals of the earth that cracked open mountains and crushed man-made walls. Great winds would flatten houses, and floods, driven by great winds would drown thousands. All of man's computers and "high technology" could do nothing in the face of earth's power.
>
> All at once people who were waiting and watching would realize the presence of all the spirits—the great mountain and river spirits, the great sky spirits, all the spirits of beloved ancestors, warriors and old friends the spirits would assemble and then the people of these continents would rise up. (424–25)

These powerful acts of natural disaster are signs of the falsity of the Destroyers' conception of nature as passive object, or virgin land at their disposal.[45] In the same way that T'seh defies the witchery by enacting the Laguna view of the nature as cyborgian, inspirited, active entity, the earth's rebellious upheavals dislodge the structures that the Destroyers' have imposed upon the landscape and rekindle the peoples' belief in nature's inspirited animation.

By making the conflict between the Destroyers and the dispossessed so extreme, Silko emphasizes the severity of the philosophical and political clash between those who articulate a partnership of human and nature and those who view nature and people identified with nature as dead objects of dominion. By imagining an actual war between these contrasting groups, Silko unmasks the pervasive violence that has been so endemic to American conflicts concerning nature and she also makes it very clear that constructions of nature do not exist in isolation from other social concerns (as some environmental groups would have us believe) but are instead historically intertwined with issues of race, ethnicity, gender, and national identities.[46] *Almanac* insists that conflicting conceptions of nature are not dead history; these arguments ground very real, very current social issues, such as native sovereignty, racism and environmental racism, environmental degradation and environmental poisoning, homelessness and classism, sexism and assaults upon women's bodies. The novel exemplifies Patricia Limerick's observation that we still live within the legacy of conquest, by which she means, as I explained in my introduction, that the institutional and ideological structures of oppression that the American conquerors imposed upon the conquered still adversely mold our social, political and national relations.[47]

Silko's novel insists that if we want to alter social relations, we must shift the ground upon which they have rested—the Euro-American conceptions of nature and those identified with nature as dead object of consumption. As this dystopian novel insists, such an alteration would be an enormous and revolutionary task, since conquest has been one of the primary bases of American national identity. In Silko's dystopian America it will take sustained acts of resistance and opposition to replace the stories and structures of domination with alternative stories and structures of enlivened relationality. Yet the novel illustrates Haraway's comment that alternative stories of nature are crucial to those who wish to counter many sorts of social oppression. *Almanac of the Dead* culminates my argument that our conceptions of nature are always deeply social, grounding in particular our constructions of gender and racial difference.

Afterword

what would it feel like to know
your country was changing?—
You yourself must change it.—
Though your life felt arduous
new and unmapped and strange
what would it mean to stand on the first
page of the end of despair?
—*Adrienne Rich*

I OPENED THIS BOOK with a segment of an earlier Adrienne Rich poem setting forth the problematic negative association with nature that American women have needed to revise in order to refashion more positive social identities. In the epigraph above, from "Dreams before Waking," Rich again urges us to embrace the work of remapping our social ties and remaking our country.[1] Dickinson, Hurston, Walker, and Silko have undertaken just this task: to revise the troubling formulation of America as nature's nation, a script that casts women, Native Americans, African Americans, and the natural continent itself as what ecofeminist Val Plumwood calls "terra nullius," or empty background, available for annexation in service to the needs of nation. The four writers make it clear that if we desire to change our country, as Rich enjoins us to do, we must revise the ground upon which it has rested: the conquest of the natural continent and the social hierarchies that colonization entailed. Through their visions of alternate social/natural coconstructions, Dickinson, Hurston, Walker, and Silko have challenged our colonialist arrangements and reimagined American geographies that offer us places to "stand on the first page of the end of despair."

By examining the four authors within the context of ecofeminist theory, I have been able to track the contours of their new geographies as well as demonstrate the applicability of this burgeoning theoretical field to the interpretation of American literature. While many ecocritics turn their attention toward our effects upon the natural world, I have been more concerned with examining the social consequences of our discourses of nature, and ecofeminist theory has offered me the means to do so. My analysis of textual conjunctions of nature, gender, and race has been inspired by the ecofeminist axiom that questions of nature are always also deeply social concerns embedded within complex histories and that recourse to "nature" has often been used to naturalize disturbing colonialist social arrangements. In particular, Donna Haraway's and Evelyn Fox Keller's critiques of the gender politics within scientific discourse have guided my analysis, and their speculations about more egalitarian human/natural interactions have helped me to articulate the full implications of women writers' subversions of colonializing paradigms.

Although they write in different eras and from differing social positions, and while on the surface their works are strikingly varied, Dickinson, Hurston, Walker, and Silko share a common underlying purpose. Reading their works within an ecofeminist framework makes it clear that each of the writers is engaged in her own version of the story war that Silko's novels describe in which the enlivened stories of marginalized cultures must struggle against master narratives that pose certain peoples as essential objects, part of the natural realm open to conquest and exploitation. While the writers address various instances of negative conflation with nature, they uncover a similar dynamic at work. It becomes clear that the root of the problem lies within the mode of hierarchical polarization that Plumwood describes, through which all that is viewed as natural Other is emptied of intrinsic value and drafted into service to the dominant party. It is this disjunctive polarization of master versus ground, of human versus nature, that the writers must dismantle, and they do so by incorporating popular and indigenous conceptions of human/natural interdependent coconstruction that attribute agency to both parties. In rewriting nature as active partner rather than passive object, the writers are able to unsettle hierarchic polarity, to dislodge the very notion of null ground, and therefore to call extremely limiting racial and gender formations into question. Thus, the four women's writings bear out Haraway, Keller, and Plumwood's premise that by acknowledging the interactive mutuality, or interpenetrating amalgamation, of human and nature we might also promote more egalitarian and nonexploitative social interrelations.

Let me briefly sum up the common process through which the writers accomplish their revisionary projects. First, they must expose the alienating system of unequal opposition through which gender and racial difference are cast in terms of nature and then interpreted as the natural basis for social divisions and stratifications. Accordingly, Emily Dickinson traces parallels between masculinist appropriation of nature-as-woman current in Transcendental and Puritan thought and the Victorian confinement of middle- and upper-class women to the strictly domestic sphere. In the same way that nature is assumed to be the servant of God and man, so women, who are believed to be more immersed in the natural cycle of reproduction, must be subordinated to male authority, excluded from the masculine public professional sphere. Analogously, Zora Neale Hurston's ethnography and fiction expose the insidious effects of the prevailing representation of black women as animals in the early decades of the twentieth century. In *Tell My Horse* Hurston acerbically comments that under colonialism, white male ascendancy is naturalized by denigrating black women as sexual beasts, talking donkeys fit for no more than brute labor and sexual service. She notes that Caribbean social ranks and divisions operate through this false, colonialist "rooster's nest" logic that elevates white masculinity by objectifying black women.

Alice Walker describes the same dynamic still operating within the Jim Crow racial segregation of the southern United States in the years preceding the Civil Rights movement. The title character of *Meridian* comes to understand that as a result of chattel slavery, which denied kinship ties within slave families, black women continue to be dispossessed from sexual and maternal subjectivity since they must often lay down their own lives as they struggle to raise children amidst violent white supremacy. So, too, Tayo, the protagonist of Leslie Marmon Silko's *Ceremony*, must unravel the mechanism of the fatal opposition through which agents of the witchery dominate and destroy all that is perceived as natural and therefore threateningly Other, culminating in the heinous rampage and atomic bombings of World War II. In *Almanac of the Dead* these Destroyers have gained ascendancy in the Americas, plundering the natural continents and exploiting the masses of the dispossessed in order to sate their violent frenzy for power and possessions. Silko's dystopian epic paints a more extreme scenario than any of the previous writings, but in many ways *Almanac* merely expands and satirically broadcasts the pattern of appropriative oppositionality already implicit within the preceding texts.

Once the writers have delineated these intersections between conceptions of nature, gender, and race, they proceed to denaturalize these problematic ideas by demonstrating that they are interpretive fictions, social constructs, rather than natural fact, as those in power would have them believe. They demonstrate this constructedness by incorporating contrasting models of social/nature that dislodge the grounding assumptions of the dominant discourse. In various ways, all of these models emphasize relationality, partiality, and mutuality between human and nature and within social ties. Where the dominant discourse poses nature and those deemed nature incarnate as resource object, the writers' stories restore personhood and intrinsic worth to those who have been devalued, and substitute border-crossing flux and change in the place of division and fixity.

In this fashion, Dickinson's reinscriptions of nature challenge the tenets of female subordination and instead attribute primacy and uncontainable power to nature-as-woman and actual women. Utilizing the positive sentimental identification of women and nature, Dickinson reimagines nature as a primary, independent, and omnipotent figure whose playfulness, willfulness, and mystery defy masculine mastery and juggle realist certitudes into flux. Hurston describes Afro-Caribbean Voodoo as offering black women a spiritual practice that subverts colonial dominance. Not only does Voodoo sacralize nature and black women's sexuality, Voodoo belief and ritual also enact a cyborgian intermingling of the binary oppositions that inform colonial hierarchies; furthermore, spirit-possession permits black women to temporarily cross the boundaries of race, class, and gender, redefining themselves in more fluid and positive terms. Walker's protagonist excavates images of spiritual collectivity, kinship, and movement within the Sacred Serpent mound and the Sojourner tree, and these images fuel her defiance of the racist divisions that make the lives of black women so painfully difficult. In similar fashion, Silko's Tayo reconstructs Laguna stories of the interdependence between the tribe and the surrounding natural world, enacting this reciprocity within his union with Ts'eh, the cyborgian mountain/goddess who in herself reconciles what the witchery would divide.

Furthermore, through formal innovations the writers also subvert the realist narrational model, which they show to be implicated in the mastery and objectification of nature. Instead, the writers employ narrative positionality, partiality, and play, and they inscribe a positive identification of speaker with nature that is more conducive to egalitarian exchange. Dickinson pioneers this formal subversion, opening a space for women to reconstruct more hospitable literary patterns. Dickinson's poetic innovations, such as the use of dashes, skewed word sequence, and omissions, all work to break down the fixed order of the prevailing realist paradigms in which a masculine subject finds God's truth revealed within feminized nature's passively transparent face. Replacing the standard bifurcation of subject and object with a model of identification, slippage, and confused overlap between speaker and nature, Dickinson is then able to slide past the fixed boundaries of Victorian decorum, imaginatively freeing herself from the confines of gender segregation. Dickinson's riddling approach is crucial, for it demonstrates that nothing is as clear as advocates of nature's nation might believe. Along the same lines, Hurston's *Tell My Horse* manifests discomfort with the social scientist's stance of detached observation. Hurston's authorial waverings between detached description and partisan commentary signal her dissension from the realist model of objectivity that she sees implicated in the colonial objectification of black women. In this vein, she incorporates the play of African-American folk speech within the narrative voice of *Their Eyes Were Watching God*, emphasizing the plastic, productive qualities of language as a source of resistance and self-recreation.

So, too, *Meridian*'s narrational "quilt" signals Walker's distrust of the master narratives that have dispossessed native peoples. Walker's narrative disjunction and dissonance function similarly to Dickinson's formal play, replacing fixed master plots in favor of partiality and movement. Silko, echoing Dickinson, foregrounds the fictive artifactuality of her novels, which are narrative circuits in which traditional story-poems set the plots into motion. Silko's layered and circling narratives enact the Laguna philosophy that everything exists within a web of stories binding us to the natural world and to each other. Her novels demonstrate the enormous power of stories to blind us, control us, rouse us, and renew us. For Silko, the choice of stories that one lives by is *the* crucial choice.

Most importantly, the writers articulate the liberatory effects of replacing the deadly discourse of nature's nation. In rewriting social/nature, the writers prompt individual and social transformations that illustrate how deeply doctrines about nature have permeated social categories. Their new stories of mutually productive social/natural interrelations foster more egalitarian and fluid gender and racial identities, proving that we must re-examine these underlying conjunctions if we wish to institute genuine, positive change. By freeing nature-as-woman from her subordination to the male gaze, Dickinson is able to challenge sexist theological and social doctrines, to redefine gender in less polarized terms, to cannily express her highly transgressive ideas, and to authorize herself as serious poet. Similarly, in Hurston's *Their Eyes Were Watching God* Janie finds self-fulfillment by pursuing her Voodoo-inspired image of marriage as an interpenetration of polarities onto the muck, where colonial divisions fall by the wayside and Janie achieves voice, freedom, and playful partnership.

Where Dickinson's poetry and Hurston's fiction present personal transformations, the novels of Walker and Silko extend into the greater social and political arena, asserting that widespread social reformation and revolution will be necessary to institute general reconstructions of nature, gender, and race. Walker's *Meridian* enacts a political praxis based upon indigenous spiritual collectivity, engaging in civil rights protests that defy the divisions of racial segregation. Crossing Jim Crow lines, Meridian transforms herself into a political subject and reclaims her body as an agent of resistance and revolutionary service. *Meridian* indicates that indigenous spirituality may spark revolutionary political change in keeping with black heritage.

Silko's novels demonstrate the Laguna belief in the curative power of stories. In *Ceremony* Tayo's loving relationship with the mountain/goddess Ts'eh revives stories of mutuality and restores health to Tayo and his tribe. His rejection of the fatal opposition temporarily defeats the witchery that has been decimating his people and allows him to make a new ending to their story. In *Almanac of the Dead,* when the reconstruction of the ancient text rouses the dispossessed peoples of the Americas to resist their corrupt conquerors, the story war becomes a literal guerilla war raging across the twin continents. By portraying an actual war between those persons who believe in violent mastery and those who wish to liberate Mother Earth, Silko emphasizes how deeply the conquest paradigm is rooted within mainstream American culture, sending tenacious tendrils into all areas of life; in her dystopian future, the premises of nature's nation will only be overturned through a war fought on many fronts. Through this civil war, Silko also makes it very clear that she views the outcome as critical to human and ecological survival, to the very sustenance of planetary life.

While Dickinson, Hurston, Walker, and Silko revise varied aspects of the discourse of nature, gender, and race, their writings resonate in clear chorus, each one adding a distinct note to the chord, each one harmonizing with the other voices raised, like Walker's civil rights workers', in anthems of rebellion against the prevailing order. These anthems invite us to sing America in a new key, lamenting a painful history, but also rejoicing in visions of greater liberation and reaffirming the many diverse cultures that indeed make up our nation. When we listen to the writers in concert, we can hear the reverberations sounding between them, building in timbre, perhaps even trembling sympathetically in our own bones. The four women's writings stir me to new hope that in discerning the underlying patterns of a damaging mythology, we might learn to re create social/natural relations based upon something other than fear, objectification, and destruction. Their new American geographics lead us toward what Haraway calls a "politics of hope," which she explains in an interview: "It's not about optimism, but about the belief that movement is always possible in principle and practice. . . . It's that fine line between describing the systems of domination relentlessly and refusing to believe them. In a politics of hope, things are always more complicated, there are always more cracks."[2] Dickinson, Hurston, Walker, and Silko assure us that, while we are still entrapped within a deadly legacy, the diverse cultures of America offer invaluable tools for mining the cracks in the story of nature's nation, for prying open crevices where hope may take root. All four writers demonstrate that alternative stories of nature and nation have always also been part of the American fabric, marginalized, yet still available to those who seek them.

Like the eclectic forces of resistance gathered by the end of Silko's *Almanac of the Dead*, my book, too, is an assemblage of assorted treatments of one sweeping pattern, pieces that accumulate collective force even in their separate movements. It is crucial that we acknowledge that the work of reimagining our social/natural fabric has taken many forms that, although disparate, do finally converge, as Silko imagines in her novel. In her portrait of America, the hope lies in revaluing our painfully entangled cultures as rich and frightening borderlands from which we might reconstruct a new sort of nation founded within the recognition of our inextricable, sometimes monstrous, interconnection to each other and the natural world. Taken together, Dickinson, Hurston, Walker, and Silko's writings shift the ground of American identity in this way, overturning the appropriative dynamic of master versus ground and mapping out more fertile social/natural geographies within which women, particularly women of color, may redefine themselves in more expansive, mobile, and life-sustaining terms. May the writers' potent visions encourage us to cultivate a new American mythology in which nature and nation might be joined in moving and mutual embrace.

Notes

Introduction

1. See Gill, *Mother Earth*, 33–34, and Kolodny, *Lay of the Land*, 5, for descriptions of such images.

2. Scholarship articulating the connections between nature and American national identity includes Perry Miller, *Nature's Nation* and *Errand*, Henry Nash Smith, *Virgin Land*, Marx, *Machine in the Garden*, Nash, *Wilderness*. Scholarship examining intersections between the American conquest of nature and the oppression of those persons identified with nature includes Pearce, *Savagism and Civilization*, Slotkin, *Regeneration*, Kolodny, *Lay of the Land*, Merchant, *Ecological Revolutions*, Frederick Turner, *Beyond Geography*, Norwood, *Made from This Earth*, Morrison, *Playing in the Dark*.

3. See Limerick, *The Legacy of Conquest*, in which she argues that the history of the west is the history of various interrelated conquests of land, natural resources, and native peoples. Limerick observes that such intercultural conflicts continue to shape national policies, social relations, and environmental issues.

4. Rich, *Fact of a Doorframe*, 215–16.

5. Writers who also might be read in this context include Sarah Orne Jewett, Willa Cather, Mary Austin, Gertrude Stein, H. D., Linda Hogan, Luci Tapahanso, Cherrie Moraga, Pat Mora, Toni Morrison, Gloria Naylor, Ntozake Shange, Toni Cade Bambara, Adrienne Rich, and Terry Tempest Williams, among others.

6. See Perry Miller, *Nature's Nation*, 201–6.

7. Jehlen, *American Incarnation*, 3.

8. While my emphasis is upon the contours of the dominant mythos, I do not mean to imply that there were no exceptions, variations, or vehement objections to this pattern. The American view of nature has been rich and complex—one of the most fully articulated analyses of the interconnections between nation and natural world—and thus it has been woven of many, varied views. I am tracing a general trend noted by many historians and cultural critics, but I am by no means saying that this was the only form that these issues took.

9. See Perry Miller, *Errand*, 5–11, and Henry Nash Smith, *Virgin Land*, 51–70.

10. Quoted by Henry Nash Smith, *Virgin Land*, 254. I discuss the problematic workings of the gender imagery of such passages below.

11. See Merchant, *Ecological Revolutions*, 100–103, and Turner, *Beyond Geography*, 171–99.

12. Turner, *Beyond Geography*, 184.

13. Perry Miller, *Errand*, 6.

14. Turner, *Beyond Geography*, 238.

15. Merchant, *Ecological Revolutions*, 63.

16. Ibid.

17. See Merchant, *Death of Nature* for a discussion of the workings of this gendered imagery of nature in scientific and other discourses.

18. Jordanova, *Sexual Visions*, 36.

19. Kolodny, *Lay of the Land*, 9.

20. Quoted ibid, 12.

21. Quoted by Henry Nash Smith, *Virgin Land*, 121.

22. Kolodny, *Lay of the Land*, 26.

23. See Norwood, *Made from This Earth*, 2–12 and 172–76, for discussion of the import of conceptions of nature upon American gender roles.

24. Quoted by Pearce, *Savagism*, 8.

25. Quoted ibid, 21, 57.

26. Quoted ibid, 5, 12. Pearce's views are extended in the writings of Richard Slotkin and Patricia Limerick, among others. Slotkin, *Regeneration* and *Gunfighter Nation*, argues that Euro-Americans regenerated themselves through violent conquest of other American peoples. He exposes the violent heart of the national mythos of the conquest of the wild frontier. Limerick, *Legacy of Conquest*, traces the conquest of American territories held by other peoples. She reveals the ways that such conquests still shape American policies toward groups such as Native Americans and Latinos.

27. See Turner, *Beyond Geography*, 127–43, and Slotkin, *Regeneration*, 10–18.

28. Quoted by Jordan, *White over Black*, 69.

29. Morrison, *Playing in the Dark*, 6–13 and 31–39, argues that American notions of "whiteness" were conceptualized as antithetical to negative formulations of African Americans, which she terms "American Africanist." She argues that whiteness was defined through its negative converse, "Africanism" in much the same way that Pearce notes that settlers defined "civilization" against Indian "savagery." Thus Morrison reads constructions of race within literary images of whiteness and darkness. Many of these images are of natural phenomena, such as Melville's white whale, and I would argue that the discourse of nature is here giving away the way that it has underpinned the American discourse of race.

30. For example, Sojourner Truth's famous address to the Ohio Women's convention, in which she repeats the refrain "Ain't I a Woman?" detailed such abuses in order to challenge both the mistreatment of black women and the falsity of Victorian definitions of *woman*.

31. Williams, *Alchemy*, 17–19, uses the history of her enslaved great-great-grandmother in order to interrogate the brutal contradictions of the legal concept of "chattel personal."

32. Gates, *Figures in Black*, 11–14 and 104–5, explains that because slaves were denied the trappings of Western culture, black literacy, particularly in the form of slave narratives, was frequently utilized by abolitionists to demonstrate the humanity and intelligence of blacks.

33. Kolodny, *Land before Her*, xiii.

34. See Norwood, *Made from This Earth*, 172–92.

35. Ibid, xv.

36. For example, while Thoreau writes positively about American Indians in *Walden*, he admires their "savage" immersion in nature, but does not realize that this was the very argument used to endorse settlers' encroachment upon their lands. Similarly, in advocating for national parks as a

means of protecting wilderness areas, Muir and Abbey seem unconcerned that the creation of parks frequently displaced native inhabitants. All three writers rely upon the feminization of nature and exclude women from their visions of men at one with the wilds. In *Desert Solitaire* Abbey is particularly virulent upon this point.

I should note that white women writers, too, even those who challenged constructs of gender and nature, often overlooked the intersections of conceptions of nature with those of race. For example, Dickinson does not openly question white supremacy, although her light/dark imagery might be read as destabilizing white superiority. Also see Morrison, *Playing in the Dark,* 18–28, for an interesting critique of Willa Cather's constructions of race.

37. Two broad-ranging ecocritical texts are Buell, *The Environmental Imagination,* and Glotfelty and Fromm, *The Ecocriticism Reader.* The latter contains a very useful reading list of books and periodicals on the subject.

38. A sampling of pertinent ecofeminist books includes: Daly, *Gyn/Ecology,* Devine, *Woman and Nature,* Diamond and Orenstein, *Reweaving the World,* Gaard, *Ecofeminism,* Griffin, *Woman and Nature,* Haraway, *Simians,* Keller, *Reflections,* King, *What Is Ecofeminism?,* Merchant, *Death of Nature,* Mies and Shiva, *Ecofeminism,* Murphy, *Literature, Nature, and Other,* Plant, *Healing the Wounds,* Plumwood, *Feminism and the Mastery of Nature,* Shiva, *Staying Alive.*

While there are a great variety of ecofeminists and while ecofeminism has received a very mixed response including charges of essentialism from the larger feminist community, I find persuasive the ecofeminist analyses of the ways that women have been socially positioned in terms of nature and of the ways that environmental concerns are inflected by race, class, and gender. Such analyses do not argue for essential gender difference, nor do they presume women to be the angels in the ecosystem.

39. Plumwood, *Feminism,* 4.

40. Haraway, *Simians,* 2.

41. Haraway, "Promises," 309–11; *Simians,* 3.

42. See "The Cyborg Manifesto" and "Situated Knowledges" in Haraway, *Simians.*

Chapter One: Nature Is a Haunted House

1. See Perry Miller, *Nature's Nation,* 199–206, for discussion of the romanticization of nature. See Nash, *Wilderness,* 96–160, for discussion of the revaluation of wilderness in the wake of domestication and industrialization, and also Marx, *Machine,* 145–226, for a study of the relation between the American pastoral and industrialization.

2. See Merchant, *Ecological Revolutions,* 233–60. As I will discuss in the following chapters, women of color, particularly Native American women and enslaved African-American women were still subjected by whites to particularly harsh forms of negative identification with nature. They also continued to participate largely in agricultural labor, either by duress or by choice, but a working knowledge of nature remained an important feature of these cultures. For an interesting account of Seneca women's resistance to the efforts of missionaries to domesticate them, see Joan Jensen's "Native American Women and Agriculture: A Seneca Case Study."

3. Norwood, *Made from This Earth,* 173. Norwood traces the extremely sequestered lives of American women. European women naturalists who visited the states were surprised by the way that American women were often cut off from the surrounding natural world, rarely venturing beyond the space of the garden into wilder territory.

4. See ibid. for a detailed discussion of women's botanizing, nature journals, flower painting and instruction.

5. Quoted by Wolff, *Emily Dickinson*, 79.

6. Wolff, *Emily Dickinson*, 93–94, and Sewall, *Life*, 353–67, discuss Dickinson's theologically scientific training in Amherst and at Mount Holyoke. Wolff, 282–365, presents an extensive and convincing reading of many of Dickinson's nature poems as challenging the rigid theological certitudes of typological interpretations of nature. She argues that Dickinson's poems often express disappointment and anger at the failure of natural types to offer any certain assurance of salvation or life after death. Both biographers also describe the depth of Dickinson's lifelong interest in gardening and horticulture.

7. Wolff, *Emily Dickinson*, 167.

8. Dobson, *Dickinson*, xi.

9. Rich, *Lies*, 161.

10. See Tompkins, *Sensational Designs*, xi–xix.

11. It is clear that Dickinson was highly indebted to preceding and contemporary women poets, primarily of the sentimental tradition, as many feminist studies have established. I can here note only a few that have most influenced my interpretations. Gilbert and Gubar, *Madwoman in the Attic*, treat Dickinson's nature writing as one aspect of her struggle to mythologize, perform, and thus gain control of the many forms of social, psychological, and literary containment to which Victorian women were subjected. Watts, *Poetry of American Women*, places Dickinson's work within the primarily sentimental tradition of women's nature writing and contrasts her against her more appropriative and pompous male contemporaries. Bennett, *Emily Dickinson*, in this same vein, further develops Dickinson's positive engagement with the flourishing sentimental tradition. Ostriker, *Stealing the Language*, emphasizes Dickinson's verbal "duplicity" as a means of simultaneously employing and subverting typically feminine decorous locutions. Dobson, *Dickinson*, similarly traces Dickinson's physical and verbal "retirement" within the spectrum of women's strategies for responding to gender strictures.

12. See for example Diehl, who reads Dickinson as attempting but failing to enter the Romantic tradition, and Wolff, who reads much of Dickinson's nature poetry as expressing her disappointment with the exclusions of the Puritan theological tradition.

13. Homans, *Women Writers*, 31, quoted in Homans, *Women Writers*, 31.

14. See Jordanova, *Sexual Visions*, for a provocative discussion of the prevalent sexualized imagery of nature-as-woman unveiling herself before the gaze of the male observer. Jordanova discusses this paradigm within science, philosophy, art, and literature.

15. Homans, *Women Writers*, 37, 188, Emerson quoted in, 37, 37, 16.

16. Emerson, *Selections*, 35.

17. Ibid, 424.

18. Ibid, 23–56. For instance, Emerson feminizes the figure of nature throughout the essay "Nature." For example: "Nature never wears a mean appearance. Neither does the wisest man extort her secret, and lose his curiosity by finding out all her perfection" (23). Or: "Nature stretches out her arms to embrace man, only let his thoughts be of equal greatness" (29).

19. Brooks, Lewis, and Warren, *American Literature*, 105–7.

20. While I by no means wish to dismiss the numerous realist women writers nor to deny that many women continue to write in this mode, I am interested in the underlying gender politics

implicit in the assumed gendering of nature and knower upon which realism is based; and while I do not by any means wish to imply that everyone experimenting with nonrealist expressive modes is of necessity interested in restructuring this gendered paradigm of nature and knower, I do argue that the women writers under study here *are* refashioning this paradigm both formally and thematically and that their work is of interest because of the political and epistemological implications of these revisions. Friedman and Fuchs, *Breaking the Sequence*, is a collection of critical essays pursuing this connection between gender and experimental form in twentieth-century fiction.

21. Homans, *Women Writers*, 200.

22. Christanne Miller, *Emily Dickinson*, 2–4.

23. Homans, *Women Writers*, 177–93, also discusses Dickinson's use of figurative and contradictory, non-hierarchical language to undercut realist appropriation of woman and nature. Yet I find problematic Homans's repeated assertion that women writers will be silenced by any identification with nature, particularly "mother nature." See Homans, *Women Writers*, 16. This view seems marred by the same masculinist othering of nature which Homans so cogently analyzes throughout her text.

24. Haraway, *Simians*, 190. Keller, *Reflections*, 117, 167.

25. Christanne Miller, *Emily Dickinson*, 172.

26. Wolff, *Emily Dickinson*, 461.

27. Ibid, 462.

28. I agree with Wolff's view that Dickinson's letters and poems describe her spiritual struggles as a "wayward" Christian who is distressed by many theological questions, rather than a disbeliever. Yet I find Dickinson to be much more radical than Wolff perceives her, in her questioning of God's authority and in her willingness to reimagine other divinities and other spiritual paths as in "Some keep the Sabbath going to church/ I keep it staying at home/ . . . So instead of getting to heaven at last—/ I'm going, all along" (324).

29. Bennett, *Emily Dickinson*, 32.

30. Homans, *Women Writers*, 196, discusses Dickinson's use of the child's voice but finds it a "stultifying" failed strategy in such nature poems. Wolff, *Emily Dickinson*, 283, decries its naivety as "wishful thinking."

31. Bennett, *Emily Dickinson*, 90.

32. See poems 376 and 338.

33. While Homans, *Women Writers*, 199–200, reads this poem as parodically criticizing Mother Nature as judgmental and ultimately deadly— she interprets the closing silence as death— I believe such a reading is again prejudiced against any positive inscription of nature as maternal. I read Dickinson's parody as directed instead against Puritan doctrine.

34. In "Sweet Mountains" (722), discussed below, the speaker refers to herself as a "wayward nun" in "service" to the feminized mountains, again clearly posing this female-identified worship against more standard God-centered theologies. Wolff, *Emily Dickinson*, 126–36, discusses Dickinson's resistance to conversion and her subsequent withdrawal from organized religion which equated piety with submission and which damned nonconformists.

35. Bennett, *Emily Dickinson*, 88.

36. Gubar, "'Wayward Nun,'" 35.

37. See Kolodny, *Lay of the Land*.

38. Jordanova, *Sexual Visions*, 43–58, traces such cultural constructs. She argues that this sexu-

alized relationship between male observer and eroticized nature is endemic to the natural sciences as evidenced by sexual tropes in scientific discourse, many of which describe nature as a female body laying itself open before the gaze of science.

39. Kolodny's title, *Lay of the Land*, punningly points to this sexualized view of nature.

40. Psalm 121.

41. Haraway, *Simians*, 199–201.

42. In "Song of the Solomon," the mountain is symbol of female sexuality. The male lover says of his desire for the female lover: "Until the day break,/ and the shadows fly away, I will get me to the mountain of myrrh,/ and to the hill of frankincense" (4:6). As a "wayward nun," Dickinson's speaker may have pledged sacred marriage not to the son of God, but to these feminized and sexualized hills.

Martha Nell Smith, "To Fill a Gap," 6–10, Faderman, "Emily Dickinson's Homoerotic Poetry," 19–27, and Paula Bennett, *Emily Dickinson*, 151–84, argue persuasively for homoerotic or autoerotic readings of some of Dickinson's love poems. In "'To Fill a Gap'" Smith notes that tamperings with letters may have disguised Dickinson's most clearly lesbian statements, and she also argues that many supposedly heterosexual poems were sent to women and thus could be read as encoded lesbian desire.

Bennett follows Faderman in pointing out that even in heterosexual poems Dickinson's speakers often identify with the male lover who blissfully "enters" the female, so that the description emphasizes female sexuality and genitalia. Bennett also notes that some of Dickinson's flower poetry may be read as lesbian exchanges. She also argues for autoerotic, "clitoral" readings of some of Dickinson's images, such as crumbs, nuts and peas.

43. See Homans, "Oh, Vision of Language!"

44. Marilyn Farwell, "Heterosexual Plots and Lesbian Subtexts" suggests similarly that a lesbian narrative space would accentuate sameness rather than heterosexual difference and would allow for more fluid movement between subject and object, self and other. She explains: "I believe that only in the space of sameness can this (lesbian) desire emerge. . . . Such a concentration of one woman on another disturbs if not destroys Western dualism. The result is a space defined by fluid instead of rigid boundaries" (97).

I have been arguing throughout this chapter that Dickinson utilizes the feminization of nature to inscribe such sameness between female speaker and nature. While in Dickinson this sameness is not always necessarily homosexual, it is certainly homosocial.

45. In "To Fill a Gap," Martha Nell Smith argues for homoerotic readings of Dickinson love poems and love letters and she discusses Dickinson's relationship with her sister-in-law, Susan Gilbert, as a primary emotional and passionate love relationship. Smith notes that in such poems and letters, Dickinson and Sue are often described as mirroring each other in what Smith describes as a "rhetoric of similarity, not difference" (18). But Smith also notes passages in Dickinson's letter #73 to Sue which ask forgiveness for her sensual desires, and reveal her awareness that such love is socially transgressive (7–10). Following Smith, I would suggest that in poems such as "Sweet Mountains" Dickinson displaces love between human women onto the homoerotic love between woman and nature, as a more socially acceptable means of expressing same-sex desire.

46. Bennett, *Emily Dickinson*, 167, reads the imagery of this poem as describing lesbian cunnilingus, the flower representing the speaker's vulva "sipped" by the reader's "lips," but she also notes that this homoerotic implication may not have been conscious, as Dickinson sent the poem to a

cousin Eudocia Flint. What I find more notable is the intentional confusion between woman and nature which permits this reading.

47. Numerous poems that Dickinson sent accompanying flowers repeat the figure of flower as emissary, presenting the flower as metonymic of the writer's desire and presence, even in her absence. The flower serves as medium for communication between writer and recipient. For example: "The grace—Myself—might not obtain— / Confer upon My flower— / Refracted but a Countenance—For I—inhabit Her" (707); "Beauty is the love she doth— / Itself—exhibit—Mine (558); "Herself, without a Parliament / Apology for Me" (852); "I hide myself within my flower" (903): "Where Roses would not dare to go, What heart would risk the way— / And so I send my Crimson Scouts / To sound the Enemy—" (1582). In these poems, the women's shared identification with the flower-emissary is used to cement relations between the women. Rather than the traditional symbol of flower as woman's sexual offering to man, in Dickinson's usage the flowers are usually part of a homosocial exchange between women and households.

48. Haraway, *Simians*, 199–201.

Chapter Two: Rerooting the Sacred Tree

1. Hurston claimed to be ten years younger, but Wall, *Women of Letters*, 143, has established the year of her birth from census records.

2. Wall, *Women of Letters*, 163–72, discusses the gender politics of this text. She focuses upon Big Sweet as a character who defies sexist limitation and who uses folk language to assert a powerful self amidst a sexist and racist society.

3. Hemenway, *Zora Neale Hurston*, 248–51, describes the lukewarm critical reception of this text.

4. Gwendolyn Mikell, "When Horses Talk," published in 1982, was one of the first positive analyses of Hurston's Caribbean work. Mikell notes that Hurston's ethnographic work was originally dismissed because of her authorial "double vision," through which she eshews anthropological objectivity for historical analysis of social inequalities and insider accounts of religious practices. Yet Mikell argues that this "double vision" is the crucial feature of Hurston's work. She suggests that Hurston's social analysis of class, color, and gender divisions offers readers a social context for interpreting the Voodoo beliefs and ceremonies that Hurston presents from an internal perspective. Mikell views Huston as a forerunner of contemporary ethnography, rather than a failure.

Similarly, Reed, Foreword to the Harper and Row edition of *Tell My Horse*, acknowledges Hurston as a major pioneering Voodoo scholar and protopostmodernist. Reed calls her "skeptical, cynical, funny, ironic, brilliant and innovative" (xv).

More recent positive commentaries include Dutton, "The Problem of Invisibility," and Menke, "The Lips of Books.'"

5. Jordan, *White over Black*, 238.

6. Collins, *Black Feminist Thought*, 170–74, argues that this conception of black women's bestial sexuality still holds sway in the pornographic representation of black women as animalistic sexual objects.

7. See Jordan, *White over Black*, 230–34, for discussion of the contradictions endemic to this conception of black women's sexuality. He notes, for example, that if the women had really been

conceived as subhuman, then miscegenation would have been conceived as bestiality, which it was not.

8. In Haraway's study of primatology, *Primate Visions*, primates are similarly represented as the vector between human and nature. Ironically, Haraway, 52–54, notes that in the master narratives of primate study, the African natives who served as guides and aides during field studies and specimen collecting were usually erased from field notes and histories, so that the confrontation between "human and nature" was portrayed as that between white man and ape.

9. Gilman, "Black Bodies," 90.

10. While Hurston is ironic in her discussion of Caribbean racial identity, this notion of nonessential racial difference is in some ways similar to Hurston's own view that racial classification is reductive.

11. See Irigaray, *Speculum of the Other Woman*, 267–75.

12. Reed, Foreword, xi, notes that Voodoo was driven underground in Haiti shortly afterward, by the time Hurston's study was first published in 1938.

13. Thompson, *Flash*, 163–73, notes that Voodoo blends the gods and rituals of diverse African nations whose peoples were intermixed under slavery. Voodoo is thus both a preservation and an alteration of African religions.

14. See for example the chapter "Religion," *Dust Tracks*, 193–204, where she argues for religious relativity on the grounds that no one spiritual tradition is "truer" than any other, but is merely a reflection of that particular people.

15. Wall and Baker have both written about the empowering effects that hoodoo, the mainland U.S. form of Vodun, has upon black women. Wall, *Women of Letters*, analyzes the gender politics of Hurston's frame tale, her folklore, and her initiations into hoodoo. Wall argues that hoodoo offered women empowerment that offset their lack of social control: "Metaphysically decentered and clerically nonhierarchical, hoodoo offered some women a more expansive vision of themselves than did Christianity. Within hoodoo, women were the spiritual equals of men. They had like authority to speak and to act" (172).

Houston Baker, *Workings of the Spirit*, 72–97, argues that hoodoo heals the violent rifts among black which Hurston describes in the early sections of *Mules*.

Luisah Teish's *Jambalaya* is also of interest here, as a first-person, contemporary account of her empowerment through her experiences as a Voodoo initiate.

16. Thompson, *Flash*, 169–73, argues for a view of Voodoo not as derivative of Catholic iconography, as was stated in many Euro-centric studies, but as a practice which absorbed and transformed these icons, revealing the African symbolism already represented in the images, and thus altering the colonial "reading" of the icons. Like Reed's "jes grew", then, Voodoo is a constantly transformative religion.

17. Haraway, *Simians*, 154.

18. I am struck by the parallels between this service and the numerous Afro-American spirituals that have healing river and water imagery, such as "Down by the Riverside," or "Wash me in the Waters."

19. It is at many points in *Tell* hard to determine exactly where Hurston as speaker is positioning herself in relation to the subjects of her narrative and in relation to Caribbean assumptions. At times she is clearly quoting and criticizing the tone of Caribbean views of race and gender, such as in the passages above about black women as donkeys, but in this passage I am uncertain of exactly how she may using the terms *sordid things*: is this her outsider's view, or this a quotation of

church or colonial views of these bodies? While she has been criticized as an anthropologist for her uneven tone and perspective upon Caribbean culture, I think the unstable tone and position are actually of great interest, revealing her complicated and problematic relationship to this material, and also, as I will discuss below, exposing the impossibilities of detached, objective realist narrative for someone intent on interrogating the effects of colonial objectification.

20. This passage is very like the story of the Sojourner tree in Alice Walker's novel *Meridian*, discussed in chapter 3.

21. I am reminded here of Baby Suggs's sermon in the clearing in Morrison, *Beloved*, 87–89. Baby Suggs enjoins her followers to love their bodies, which are despised and destroyed by the surrounding white culture.

22. Thompson, *Flash*, 187. The Voodoo drawings of the serpents twining the tree that Thompson includes look remarkably like the insignia of the medical profession, and I would wonder if it is possible that this image was transported from Africa to Greece in the cultural exchange that Martin Bernal posits in *Black Athena*.

23. I am struck, in this ceremony, by the convergence of "veneration" and "venereal," both of which stem from the same Latin root.

24. See Hurston, *Mules and Men*, 192–98, for a description of Levau's familiar.

25. The description of Simalo's funeral in *Tell My Horse*, 98, closely parallels the funeral of the mule in *Their Eyes*, 95–97. President Simon hides the body in a coffin and tricks the clergy into giving him Christian burial, much the way the townspeople conduct a funeral service for the mule.

26. Haraway, *Simians*, 152.

27. Spirit-possession is indigenous to African religions. Hurston, *Sanctified Church*, 91–94, notes that a form of possession also occurs in African-American churches in which worshippers "shout."

28. For example, Hurston, *Tell My Horse*, 176, 221–22, describes "horses" who walk through fire, those who perform feats of strength and endurance, and the physical and performative transformations that occur during possession.

Mars, *The Crisis of Possession in Voodoo*, also presents many case studies of possession in which the possessed person is physically altered and performs extraordinary feats. Mars describes possession as a psychological crisis induced by group belief and social circumstances. Like Hurston, he argues that the loa are a reflection of social conditions and psychological states.

Deren, *Divine Horsemen*, includes detailed descriptions of Voodoo ceremonies including possession.

29. Dayan, "Caribbean Cannibals and Whores," analyzes the many forms that the loa Erzulie takes and argues that this contradictory loa both contains and undermines colonial values. Dayan also discusses Caribbean women writers' responses to this loa.

30. Hurston, *Tell My Horse*, 199–204, describes being warned against approaching unfamiliar houngans, as it is impossible to tell whether they may also be associated with feared secret sects.

31. For example, Mars, *Crisis of Possession*, notes a case of possession in which "a young woman became a veritable reptilian acrobat slithering through the branches of a tree for two days. . . . She was possessed by the god Damballah, whose symbol is the snake" (26).

32. In fact, Zombies are the most extreme instance of the black person reduced to "beast" rather than human, and, interestingly, Hurston describes this fate as particularly horrible to the upper-class Haitian who has heretofore escaped brute existence. Zombies level class difference and make everyone "donkeys" in a horrible manner: "Think of the fiendishness of the thing. It is

not good for a person who has lived all his life surrounded by a degree of fastidious culture, loved to his last breath by family and friends, to contemplate the probability of his resurrected body being dragged from the vault—the best that love and means could provide, and set to toiling ceaselessly in the banana fields, working like a beast, unclothed like a beast, and like a brute crouching in some foul den in the few hours allowed for rest and food. From an educated, intelligent being to an unthinking, unknowing beast" (181).

33. Hooks, *Yearning*, 135–43, discusses Hurston's "participant observer" stance as anthropologist, arguing cogently that Hurston was too much a part of the Eatonville community to write about it from a detached "colonial" perspective or reduce this rich cultural heritage to "scientific data." I agree that Hurston intentionally abandons "pure objectivity" for a more complicated modernist narrational stance that acknowledges and includes her own subject position as part of the study, and she thus pioneers the revision of anthropological study now current in the latter part of the twentieth century. In *Tell* her perspective is somewhat different, as she always remains a "foreigner" even when present at ceremonies, and as she is clearly ambivalent about Caribbean culture and religion.

34. See my discussions of the shortcomings of this model of subject/object relation in chapter 1.

35. I take the term "inappropriate/d" from Haraway, "Promises," 299–300, who expands upon Trinh Minh-ha's coinage of the word.

36. Hurston, *Tell My Horse*, 196, notes that the doctors surmise that Zombies may be created by secret African drugs that destroy parts of the brain. As Hurston states repeatedly in *Tell*, 237–38, Voodoo practitioners have extremely potent herbal medicines and poisons, and ceremonial practices which appear to outside observers as mere "superstitions" may have strong physical consequences. For example, she explains that the graveyard dust called for in certain spells may contain deadly bacteria, and thus it is a potent poison as well as a symbol of death. Hemenway, *Zora Neale Hurston*, 247–48, notes that Hurston fled Haiti after a severe abdominal illness, in fears that she may have been poisoned or put under a spell by a malevolent bocor.

37. See Mikell, "When Horses Talk," for an extensive discussion of Hurston's ambivalent stance in *Tell*.

38. Hemenway, *Zora Neale Hurston*, 203, notes the simultaneous research for *Tell* and composition of *Their Eyes*.

39. Du Plessis, *Writing*, 157, discusses the dual implications of the word *embalm*.

40. Hurston's first novel, *Jonah's Gourd Vine*, is similarly ambivalent toward hoodoo; conjure is treated as dark but powerful when Hattie hires a conjure woman to kill John's virtuous wife Amy with a wasting spell. Interestingly, in Hurston's later novel *Moses, Man of the Mountain*, Voodoo is inscribed as the sacred source of Moses' godlike powers. In fact, the novel is based upon the Voodoo reading of Moses as conjure man which Hurston records in *Tell My Horse*, 116–17.

41. Southerland, "The Influence of Voodoo," 179–83, and Wall, *Women of Letters*, 192–95, are suggestive discussions of Voodoo and hoodoo influences in this novel. Southerland touches upon similarities between Voodoo belief and the imagery of *Their Eyes*, and Wall discusses parallels between Hurston's hoodoo section of *Mules* and this novel.

42. While some critics have questioned Hurston's dependence upon the "tragic mulatto" type for Janie, I see her instead as echoing the mulattoes of the Caribbean, and Janie's mixed background as intentionally problematizing biological racial classifications. In contradiction to the Caribbean

mulattoes who deny their black heritage, Janie finds happiness only after she reclaims her cultural heritage with Tea Cake. Here, race, in a sense, becomes cultural and fluid rather than biologically fixed.

43. While this incident has been interpreted variously, often as sign of Janie's lack of racial loyalty and awareness, I see it more in terms of Hurston's argument that intrinsic racial difference is overestimated. It does, however, seem odd that Janie does not feel akin to her grandmother. In fact, her identification with the white children is similar to the mulattoes of the "roosters nest" in *Tell* in that it erases her connection to her black grandmother; but Janie will always resist the social role thrust upon black women in opposition to her grandmother's acceptance of these limits. Perhaps Janie never accepts this racist and sexist identity of black woman, and thus sees it as separate from herself.

44. Wall, *Women of Letters*, 179–80, and Southerland, "The Influence of Voodoo," 177, among others, argue persuasively that this mule image is an echo of the mule image and folktales about racial politics in *Mules and Men*. In fact, Wall argues that *Their Eyes* reframes the mule metaphor so that it refers primarily to gender rather than race.

45. Gates, *Signifying Monkey*, 203, reads the tree as Janie's metaphoric language of desire.

46. Kubitschek, "'Tuh de Horizon,'" 110. While Gates reads the "was" of the final sentence as free indirect discourse incorporation of Janie's dialect, I am more in agreement with Kubitschek's reading.

47. This passage is strikingly similar to Dickinson's flower poetry with its sensuous description of female desire, the identification of female lover with nature, and the intermingling of spiritual and sexual. Dickinson has a number of bee and blossom poems not discussed above, that emphasize the mutual and egalitarian sexual union of male and female lovers.

48. Wall, *Women of Letters*, 188.

49. Gates, *Signifying Monkey*, explains: "Tea Cake not only embodies Janie's tree, he is the woods themselves, the delectable veritable woods, as his name connotes ('Verigible' being a vernacular term for 'veritable') Verigible Tea Cake Woods is a sign of verity, one who speaks the truth, one genuine and real. . . . 'Veritable,' we know, also suggests the aptness of metaphor. Hurston now replaces the figure of the tree as a sign of desire with figures of play, rituals of play that cause Janie to 'beam with light'" (190).

50. Christian, *Black Women Novelists*, 174–75.

51. Marks, "Sex, Violence and Organic Consciousness" 155–59, and Willis, *Specifying*, 48–49, both dismiss the muck as utopian, and Marks sees Hurston's desire for such a community as reactionary in terms of Marxist ideals. Both do discuss the ways that the muck apparently escapes or evades the strictures of capitalism, although both also discuss the failure of this community—its violence, sexism, and hidden racism. Walker, *Our Mothers' Gardens*, 304–6, among others, also discuss the clear limitations of Tea Cake as partner.

52. Wall, *Women of Letters*, 190–91.

53. Du Plessis, "Power, Judgement, and Narrative," 98–108, presents the notion of Hurston's racial "bifocality," or her double-identification with both blacks and whites, which is helpful here, since at the trial Janie will instead identify with the white women, because, ironically, the black community is set against her, out of mistaken loyalty to Tea Cake and out of credulous belief in the classism Mrs. Turner espouses. Racial loyalty is complicated in this problematic situation.

54. Thompson, *Flash*, 181.

55. Hurston, *Tell My Horse,* 166–74, describes with some distaste the animal sacrifices at Petro ceremonies and she relates many stories of pacts with these gods that must be repaid through extreme personal sacrifice.

56. Du Plessis, "Power, Judgement, and Narrative," 118, notes the conflict between the dissolution of the difference and the reassertion of difference in this scene, and reads Tea Cake's comment, "Looks like dey think God don't know nothin 'bout the Jim Crow law," as also simultaneously erasing and asserting racist structures.

57. Motor Boat, who sleeps out the storm in a house carried by the flood, is perhaps most emblematic of the saving non-resistance of the muck dwellers.

58. Gates, *Signifying Monkey,* 170–216, Wall, *Women of Letters,* 139–199.

59. See my discussion of Dickinson's rebellions against the realist assumptions of Emerson in chapter 1. For a discussion of the shortcomings of realist narrative, see Virginia Woolf's essay "The Modern Novel" in *Common Reader,* which rails against the novelists' subjection to mundane external details rather than consciousness.

60. Gates, *Signifying Monkey,* 170–216, is devoted to Hurston's *Their Eyes,* and I see strong correspondences between Hurston's pioneering analyses of black expression and Gates's poststructuralist return to indigenous black cultural traditions as the basis for his theory of the intertextual relations within black literature. While Gates returns to the mythic African and African-American figures of Esu and the Signifying Monkey as inspiration for his perspective, I would pose Hurston's essay as another *significant* intertextual precedent.

61. Baker confines his discussion to male writers and therefore omits any discussion of Hurston as modernist, but he does pose her as central to Afro-American women's literary tradition in *Workings,* 69–101. As I have been arguing throughout this study, "deformation of mastery" works similarly for women writers who also have political stakes in escaping from the detrimental master narratives of their cultures.

62. As will be discussed in chapter 4, this view of dreams and stories is like the Laguna Pueblo philosophy that dreams and stories create or re-create the world and that words connect dreams to realities.

63. Du Plessis, "Power, Judgement, and Narrative," notes that this literalization of figures and speeches endorses the powers of the word which is so much a theme of the novel. She discusses Nanny as a prophet whose words come to pass: "The creative word, the word acting in time, the word able to bring events into being, is a mighty powerful word" (111). The spitcup and mule that Nanny mentions in relation to black women are both literally actualized later in the novel.

Chapter Three: Returning to the Sacred Tree

1. For example, Walker's signature essay, "In Search of Our Mothers' Gardens," enacts this sort of turn toward heritage as Walker searches for black female artistic predecessors and redefines art and genius so that they might include quiltmaking, gardening, singing. In Walker's most famous (and infamous) novel, *The Color Purple,* Celie transforms the extreme hardships of her life through her association with Shug Avery, a blues singer who offers Celie an alternative conception of women, sexuality, God, and creative work.

2. See, for example, a number of the essays in *Our Mothers' Gardens,* such as the title essay, "The Black Writer and the Southern Experience," and "Only Justic Can Stop a Curse." Celie, the protagonist of *The Color Purple* is caught within this contradiction. She develops a sense of self and

pleasure only after Shug helps her to view the natural world as beautiful and imbued with spirit, rather than as just another source of drudging, exploitative labor.

3. This is a method that a number of ecofeminists have pursued. See Di Chiro, "Defining Environmental Justice," Hamilton, "Women Home and Community," and Shiva, *Staying Alive*.

4. A number of the essays in *Living by the Word* describe Walker's participation in political actions, such as attending the trial of Dennis Banks, working to free Dessie Woods from prison, going to a demonstration protesting the deployment of nuclear weapons, speaking at fund-raisers for the International Indian Treaty Council, and opposing oil drilling off the Mendocino coast. Some of these essays explicitly link her concerns with social justice and protections of nature.

5. Christian, *Black Women Novelists*, 207, notes that another obvious source of *Meridian* is Jean Toomer's long poem "The Blue Meridian." In it he envisions an America no longer racially divided and a people of the blue meridian who have transcended racial difference. The poem seeks to heal the dispossession of Native Americans and African Americans through utopian social transformation. Walker reclaims and revises this vision in her novel.

6. This connection between spirituality and political change is a theme emphasized by many other African-American and Native American writers, such as Jarena Lee, James Baldwin, Toni Morrison, bell hooks, Cornel West, Melvin Dixon, Leslie Marmon Silko, and Paula Gunn Allen.

7. Giddings, *When and Where I Enter*, 37.

8. For discussion of the ongoing prevalence of these stereotypes see hooks, *Ain't I a Woman*, 51–86, and *Black Looks*, 61–77, Giddings, *When and Where I Enter*, 85–94, and Collins, *Black Feminist Thought*, 170–74. Such theorists discuss, for example, the way that the stereotype of black women as sexually provocative excused the very numerous rapes of black women by white and black men; the myth of the black matriarch; the Moynihan report's stigmatization of black women's employment and single motherhood. Walker's short story "Porn" describes the current representation of black women as sexual animals in pornographic materials.

9. Wells, *A Red Record*, 395–96, explains that while slave owners had regarded slaves as valuable property, once slavery was abolished, southern whites saw black life as valueless, and all sorts of violence toward blacks, such as lynching, became incredibly common during the Jim Crow era.

10. In the essay "In the Closet of the Soul" in *Living by the Word*, 78–92, Walker argues that sexist relations within black communities originated in black men's imitation of white masters' sexist and racist abuses of black women. Hooks, *Ain't I A Woman*, 51–86, similarly argues that black men's sexual exploitation of black women arose under slavery when black women were subject to rape and forced breeding by first white and then also black men who held positions of relative power.

11. Quoted in hooks, *Ain't I a Woman*, 39.

12. Spillers, "Mama's Baby," 75, 80.

13. Christian, *Black Women Novelists*, 210–22, is an excellent treatment of the subject of motherhood in this novel. Christian views Meridian's ambivalence toward motherhood and her guilt about not living up to the maternal standards of her predecessors as the motivating forces behind her social activism, which Christian reads as an alternative mode of mothering black children and black women.

14. Haraway, "Promises," 269–78.

15. Ibid, 296.

16. While Meridian is deeply moved by the pure voices of the church faithful, she is extremely distrustful of her mother's resigned blindness to injustice. The only time Meridian feels

comfortable in church is toward the end of the novel, when she finds a church that has adopted the "martial spirit" of King's civil rights activism and rhetoric. In fact, it is at this church that Meridian realizes her own revolutionary role as preserver of the song of the people.

17. Morrison, "Site of Memory," 112.

18. Tate, *Black Women Writers*, 179.

19. Niehardt, *Black Elk Speaks*, 35. Willis, *Specifying*, 120–22, discusses the political import of Black Elk's vision of "community" for Meridian's growing political consciousness. While Willis dismisses the connection between spirituality and Meridian's praxis, I argue that Walker bases political change on spiritual vision in this novel—as she also does frequently in her essays.

20. The image of the tree runs through Walker's fiction as an emblem of resistance to social oppression. In *Third Life of Grange Copeland*, 186, Ruth becomes convinced of the racism of public education when she encounters the drawing of the evolutionary tree-of-man with an apelike Negro at the base, waiting to evolve into the higher form of humanity—the Caucasian. In *Temple of My Familiar*, 83–88, this tree is rewritten as an African genesis-tree, with families of apes and pygmies living peaceably in the branches.

21. Walker has increasingly pursued this correspondence between Native American and African-American beliefs. Essays in *Living by the Word*, 41–50, 139–52, discuss Native American beliefs and concerns, and describe Walker's support for Native American political organizations such as the American Indian Movement and international coalitions of native peoples. Walker has also explored the historical correspondence between Native American and African-American peoples in the novel *Temple of My Familiar*.

Other writers and theorists such as bell hooks and Leslie Marmon Silko also discuss such parallels. Hooks, *Black Looks*, contains an essay on black Indians and bears a photograph of a black Indian on the cover. Silko's latest novel, *Almanac of the Dead*, presents the transporting of African slaves to the Caribbean where they were intermixed with Indian natives as the point of convergence for Native American and African spirits and traditions.

22. Allen, *Sacred Hoop*, 257. While the snake has come to be seen as a male sign, symbolizing the phallus in Freudian-derived interpretations, in Native American, African, old European, and Middle Eastern traditions, the snake was either associated with the creative and transformative powers of creation goddesses or was a gender-neutral symbol of spiritual and sexual union and communication. See for example, Thompson, *Flash*, Gimbutas, *Goddesses*, and Stone, *When God Was a Woman*.

23. See Spillers, "Mama's Baby," 73–82, for her argument about the objectification of slave women in particular.

24. Williams, *Alchemy*, 164–65.

25. Several essays in *Living by the Word*, such as "Am I Blue" and "The Universe Responds," use this premise to argue for animal rights. The essay "Everything Is a Human Being" contrasts Native American belief in spiritual partnership with the Wasichu (white) model of domination and division.

26. Quoted in Woodward, *Strange Career of Jim Crow*, 147.

27. Giddings, *When and Where I Enter*, 286.

28. Ibid, 39–42, describes slave women's various forms of violent resistance, including poisoning food and burning homes and property. She notes that punishment of women was often more dramatic and severe than that of men.

29. Thompson, *Flash*, 84, 85, 139.

30. Haraway, "Promises," 310. Haraway takes the term *social nature* from Susanna Hecht and Alexander Cockburn's *Fate of the Forest*, which describes the history of the Amazon rain forest as "social nature" in which the human inhabitant and landscape were mutually productive. The actions of human inhabitants alter the growth patterns of the forest, and the forest affects the living patterns of human and nonhuman inhabitants. Nature is historically produced in the same manner that society is historically produced. Both are "artifacts" rather than originary.

31. The name and assimilationist tendencies of Saxon College echo the school Naxos where Helga Crane taught at the beginning of Nella Larsen's *Quicksand*. Helga, like the young women of Saxon, attempts to negotiate her contradictory position between cultures.

32. In fact, Meridian sees her allegiance to the past and the spiritual heritage as what prevents her from endorsing violence. After the dispersion of the nonviolent movement, she sees herself as belonging to the past rather than to the future, and sees her functions as that of preserving the past in the face of violence. She is to act as the conduit for return: "I am not to belong to the future. I am to be left, listening to the old music, beside the highway. But then, she thought, perhaps it will be my part to walk behind the real revolutionaries—those who know they must spill blood in order to help the poor and the black and therefore go right ahead—and when they stop to wash off the blood and find their throats too choked with the smell of murdered flesh to sing, I will come forward and sing from memory songs they will need once more to hear. For it is the song of the people, transformed by the experiences of each generation, that holds them together, and if any part of it is lost the people suffer and are without soul. If I can only do that, my role will not have been a useless one after all" (201).

33. Christian, *Black Women Novelists*, 211.

34. Williams, *Alchemy*, 129–30.

35. Hooks, *Yearning*, 15.

36. Hite, *Other Side of the Story*, argues that this is often the case with women writers' experimentation; it is interpreted as failed realism rather than as intentional narrational strategy. She argues that realism is assumed to be the dominant, naturalized, narrative mode and that critics fail to consider the strategic deployment and departure from realism that is every writer's prerogative—including women writers.

37. Christian, *Black Women Novelists*, 205.

38. Haraway, *Simians*, 183–202.

39. The political implications of experimental literary forms are, of course, a matter of critical debate, particularly in regard to modernist and postmodernist texts. While I concede that the formal disruption of linearity and mastery is not always born out by substantive revisions of social terms, and while I believe it is reductive always to read innovation as working a certain way, I do tend to read formal experimentation as disrupting the status quo and thus creating a space for social change. I would argue that this is the case for the writers under discussion here. For a cogent summation of this debate over formal innovation see DeKoven, *Rich and Strange*, which traces the critical arguments about modernism.

Chapter Four: Contested Ground

1. Silko discusses her tricultural family in *Yellow Woman*. Perry's interview with Silko in *Backtalk* also contains interesting comments upon her family and intercultural contacts and conflicts.

2. Anzaldua, *Borderlands*, 1–13.

3. While there are debates about the use of the word *Indian* versus the more recent title *Native*

American, I have chosen to use the former term throughout most of this chapter because Silko uses it in much of her writing and because the term predominates in the works of many contemporary Indian writers. Both terms are also debatable because they erase the cultural specificity of the numerous, greatly diverse tribes that they encompass. I will use *Indian* in contrast with *Euro-American,* but I will also specify Silko's particular Laguna Pueblo tribal identity when she is referring to that people. See Dorris, "Native American Literature" for a discussion of these terms.

4. Slotkin, *Regeneration,* 17.

5. For further discussion of Silko's view of Laguna stories, see her collection of tribal, family, and original stories and poems, appropriately entitled *Storyteller.*

6. This making of everything into story is analogous to the convergence of "documentary historicizing" and literary "self-reflexivity" that Hutcheon observes in postmodernist art. She argues that such art is "an exploration of the way in which narration and images structure how we see ourselves and how we construct our notions of self in the present and in the past" (*Politics of Postmodernism,* 7). Postmodernism, she continues, makes clear the "discursiveness of the real" (34) much the way that Laguna stories produce the tribe.

7. Allen, *Sacred Hoop,* 13–26.

8. Ibid, 100, 60–61.

9. Silko has several stories about such unions in *Storyteller.* See for example "Storytelling," "Cottonwood" parts one and two, and "Yellow Woman." A story of a union between a nature goddess and a man is also a central theme of *Ceremony,* as I will discuss below.

10. Haraway, "Promises," 295–300.

11. Allen, *Sacred Hoop,* 119.

12. Merchant, *Ecological Revolutions,* 47.

13. Zinn, *People's History,* 1–22, discusses the conflicting social values of the Arawaks and the Spanish.

14. Slotkin, *Regeneration,* 17.

15. Pearce, *Savagism and Civilization,* argues that the Indians' modes of land use were always construed as "savage," while the settlers' more intensive forms of agriculture and hunting were believed to be essential to "civilization." Conflicts over land use and land ownership were endemic to white/native encounters. Merchant, *Ecological Revolutions,* traces the differing ecological paradigms of the Northeastern Indians and the European settlers to that region. Like Pearce, she too argues that the Indian modes of shifting and nonobtrusive agriculture, communal farming and hunting, and women's control of agricultural processes were all interpreted by the Europeans as signs of the Indians' social inferiority, and consequently were utilized to justify their displacement.

16. Tompkins, "'Indians,'" focuses upon several of the contradictory narrative representations of "Indians" produced during different historical periods and from different interpretive frameworks in order to discuss the issue of "textuality" within historical analysis. Crosby, "Construction of the Imaginary Indian," writes as a Haida/T'simpsian First Nations member about the construction of Indians within different Canadian historical narratives. She discusses the self-serving white representation of the "imaginary Indian" who, while evolving through various historical incarnations is always self-reflective of white interests, rather than accurately or helpfully articulating the situation of First Nations peoples.

17. Zinn, *People's History,* notes that in Columbus's report to the Spanish court, he associates the tropical lushness of the islands with the astounding generosity and "naivety" of the Arawak people: "Hispaniola is a miracle. Mountains and hills, plains and pastures are both fertile and

beautiful ... the harbors are unbelievably good and there are many wide rivers of which the majority contain gold. ... (The Indians) are so naive and so free with their possessions that no one who has not witnessed them would believe it. When you ask for something they have they never say no. To the contrary, they offer to share with anyone" (1–3).

18. Quoted in Kolodny, *Lay of the Land*, 5.

19. Gill, *Mother Earth*, 38.

20. Merchant, *Ecological Revolutions*, 63, discusses the European settlers' insistence upon distinguishing themselves from animals, and their fears that once in the "wilderness" humans reverted to brute savagery. She notes their adoption of extremely strict laws against bestiality in the colonies, and the execution of a number of people accused of this crime. Obviously, this Euro-American "story" of man's essential superiority ran counter to the Indian stories of animal/human clans and sacred sexual encounters between Indians and nature deities, or shape-shifters.

21. See Nash, *Wilderness*, for discussions of the extremely negative connotations of the word *wilderness* as it was originally used in reference to America. He traces the evolving attitudes toward wilderness from settlement until the twentieth-century, arguing that as the actual wilderness receded before settlement and cultivation, Americans came increasingly to romanticize and prize wilderness as essential to the American national character. As Pearce argues, the romanticization of wilderness paralleled the romanticization of Indians as "noble savages"—but as the romanticization of wilderness followed the diminishing of the frontier, so too the romanticization of Indians followed their removal and confinement. Only when "civilization" had prevailed, could "wild" lands and "wild" peoples be revalued.

22. Quoted in Pearce, *Savagism*, 69, 65.

23. Merchant, *Ecological Revolutions*, 29–68.

24. See, for example, Silko's writings in *Storyteller* about her Aunt Susie who transcribed the oral stories into written form in order to save them from disappearing when children were forced by government policy to attend Indian schools far from the reservation, thus breaking the chain of oral transmission of Indian culture. At the schools, the children were acculturated in Western ways and taught to despise their native heritage as false superstition.

25. Allen, *Sacred Hoop*, 136.

26. Anzaldua, *Borderlands*, 3–4.

27. See Owens, *Other Destinies*, for discussion of mixed-blood identities. He cites Silko as the first novelist to write a character able to create a positive, syncretic, mixed-blood identification based on choice of positions rather than bloodlines. He also argues that all Native Americans, no matter their descent, are in the position of negotiating between Euro-American and Native American cultures.

28. Silko, *Ceremony*, 38, refers to the "scalp ceremony" that is a purification ritual performed to cleanse the taint of death from those who have killed in battle. This ritual has failed to reintegrate the veterans back into the tribe. Old Koo'sh, the healer, is at a loss for how to cure these men, but Tayo believes that the medicine fails because the veterans have witnessed destruction on a scale unimaginable to the tribe.

29. Keller, *Reflections*, 79.

30. Haraway, *Simians*, 197–98.

31. Buell, *Environmental Imagination*, 280–96, argues that apocalytic visions, such as this moment in *Ceremony*, are actually founded in the ecological notion of life as an interconnected web within which destruction of one strand will have repercussions upon the rest of the system. Interestingly,

in this section of *Ceremony* the apocalytic vision of total destruction produces the possibility of a renewed ecological sense of interconnection among humans across divisions and emnities.

32. The mine itself is also the crux of confrontation between the Indian and white-skin stories of nature, as Indian reluctance to tamper with the "body" of the earth gives way before Euro-American determination to mine the ore that can produce nuclear power and nuclear annihilation. See Merchant, *Death of Nature*, 2–5, for discussion of these contrasting views of mining. See Matthiessen, *Indian Country*, 293–306, for discussion of internal tribal debates over the sale of mineral rights, and the hazards and consequences of the lack of regulation of radioactive mining practices on sovereign reservation lands.

33. Allen, *Sacred Hoop*, 121. Swan, "Laguna Symbolic Geography," also provides detailed explanations of Laguna religious interpretations of the geographic features of the novel, including Ts'eh's connections to Mount Taylor.

34. Smith and Allen, "Earthy Relations," 174–96, traces such instructive sexual liaisons between Indian women and spirit entities within the works of a number of writers, including Silko. They argue that, in contrast to white views, sexual relations are posed as a convergence of spirituality and carnality, and a convergence of animal, human, and supernatural entities, similar to my interpretation of Haraway's cyborg myth.

35. Allen, *Sacred Hoop*, 118–26, views the relationship between Tayo and T'seh as a restoration of balance between the masculine and feminine elements of the Laguna world. She sees Tayo's illness as the result of his alienation from the feminine landscape and his recovery as following upon the restoration of connection that he gains through T'seh. She traces traditional Laguna patterns of feminine imagery throughout the novel.

36. Tayo's relationship to Ts'eh is evocative of the relationship between speaker and "sweet mountains" in Emily Dickinson's "Sweet Mountains—Ye tell Me no lie—." In Dickinson's poem the fluid identification between speaker and constant, yet moving mountains counters the exclusive polarities of Calvinist doctrines. In both instances, reciprocity between human and natural entity contests dominant oppositional policies.

37. Betonie had expressed a similar opinion of the folly of trying to withstand the superior brutal force of the whites: "We have done as much fighting as we can with the destroyers and thieves: as much as we could do and still survive"(*Ceremony*, 128).

38. Keller, *Reflections*, 117.

39. Haraway "Promises," 298, 314.

40. Ibid, 303–15.

41. See, in particular, Irigaray's parodic analysis of phallogocentrism in "Plato's Hystera." Serlo's projects are also reminiscent of Hurston's description of the Caribbean "rooster's nest" phenomena in which mulatto males deny their black mothers when they legally re-create themselves in the image of their white, English fathers.

42. Silko's articulation of stories as rousing the hopeless hordes of dispossessed to combative and productive actions reminds me of Cornel West's repeated observation that many black youths have lost the sense of spiritual hope that had sustained African-American struggles for economic and social justice. Like Silko, West believes that besieged peoples need such "stories" to offset despair and promote action. See West, *Race Matters*, and hooks and West, *Breaking Bread*.

43. La Escapia, the Mexican Indian revolutionary, rereads Marx's theory of history in light of this belief: "Wherever their stories were told, the spirits of the ancestors were present and their power was alive. . . . Marx had understood stories are alive with the energy words generate. Word

by word, the stories of suffering, injury, and death had transformed the present moment, seizing listeners' or readers' imaginations so that for an instant, they were present and felt the suffering of sisters and brothers long past. . . . He had sensed the great power these stories had—power to move millions of people. Poor Marx did not understand the power of the stories belonged to the spirits of the dead" (*Almanac*, 520–21).

44. Gill, *Mother Earth*, 107–58, argues that the figure of "Mother Earth" emerged in the 1970s as central icon of the American Indian Movement. He argues that although this figure is not indigenous to many tribes, it became a unifying symbol of intertribal commonalities and of differences from dominant white practices and beliefs. "Mother Earth" functions this way in *Almanac*, signifying the common struggles of the dispossessed, and their common differences from the Destroyers.

Similarly, Haraway, "Promises," 317–19, describes her taking part in a "Mothers' and Others' Day" protest against a nuclear power plant located on land treatied to the Shoshone Nation. Haraway observes that the icon of the protest, a photograph of the "whole earth" printed on a T-shirt with the script "Love Your Mother," may be read as oppositional, rather than sentimental, when contextualized against the ominous techno-science that produced the image from space satellites in the first place.

45. The various sorts of natural disasters and extreme weather patterns of the 1990s, from the flooding of the midwestern U.S. and Europe, to devastating earthquakes and tornadoes in the southeastern and southwestern U.S. bear striking resemblance to Silko's dystopian predictions.

46. For analysis of environmentalists' positions on such issues see Darnovsky, "Stories Less Told," and Zimmerman, *Contesting Earth's Future*.

47. Limerick, *Legacy of Conquest*, 17–32.

Afterword

1. Rich, *Your Native Land, Your Life*, 46.

2. Haraway, "More Than You Think," 20–21.

Works Cited

Allen, Paula Gunn. *The Sacred Hoop: Recovering the Feminine in American Indian Traditions.* Boston: Beacon Press, 1986.

Anzaldua, Gloria. *Borderlands: The New Mestiza.* San Francisco: Spinsters, 1987.

Baker, Houston. *Modernism and the Harlem Renaissance.* Chicago. Univ. of Chicago Press, 1987.

————. *Workings of the Spirit: The Poetics of Afro-American Women's Writing.* Chicago: Univ. of Chicago Press, 1991.

Bennett, Paula. *Emily Dickinson: Woman Poet.* Iowa City: Univ. of Iowa Press, 1990.

Bernal, Martin. *Black Athena: The Afroasiatic Roots of Classical Culture.* New Brunswick: Rutgers Univer. Press, 1987.

Buell, Lawrence. *The Environmental Imagination: Thoreau, Nature Writing, and the Formation of American Culture.* Cambridge: Belknap Press of Harvard Univ. Press, 1995.

Christian, Barbara. *Black Women Novelists: The Development of a Tradition, 1892–1976.* Westport: Greenwood Press, 1980.

Collins, Patricia. *Black Feminist Thought: Knowledge, Consciousness and the Politics of Empowerment.* Boston: Beacon Press, 1990.

Crosby, Marcia. "Construction of the Imaginary Indian." In *Threshholds of Difference: Feminist Critique, Women's Writings, Postcolonial Theory,* ed. Julia Emberly, pp. 267–93. Toronto: Univ. of Toronto Press.

Daly, Mary. *Gyn/Ecology: The Metaethics of Radical Feminism.* Boston: Beacon Press, 1978.

Dayan, Joan. "Caribbean Cannibals and Whores." *Raritan* 9 (1989): 45–67.

DeKoven, Marianne. *Rich and Strange: Gender, History, Modernism.* Princeton: Princeton Univ. Press, 1991.

Deren, Maya. *Divine Horsemen: The Living Gods of Haiti.* London: Thames and Hudson, 1953.

Diamond, Irene, and Gloria Orenstein, eds. *Reweaving the World: The Emergence of Ecofeminism.* San Fansisco: Sierra Club Books, 1990.

Di Chiro, Giovanna. "Defining Environmental Justice: Women's Voices and Grassroots Politics." *Socialist Review* 22 (October 1992): 93–130.

Dickinson, Emily. *The Complete Poems of Emily Dickinson*. Thomas Johnson, ed. Boston: Little, Brown, 1960.

———. *Emily Dickinson: Selected Letters*. Thomas Johnson, ed. Cambridge: Belknap Press of Harvard Univ. Press, 1986.

Diehl, Joanne Feit. *Dickinson and the Romantic Imagination*. Princeton: Princeton Univ. Press, 1981.

Dobson, Joanne. *Dickinson and the Strategies of Reticence: The Woman Writer in Nineteenth Century America*. Bloomington: Univ. of Indiana Press, 1989.

Dornovsky, Marcy. "Stories Less Told: Histories of US Environmentalism," *Socialist Review* 22 (October 1992): 57–92.

Dorris, Michael. "Native American Literature in an Ethnohistorical Context." College English 41 (October 1979): 147–62.

Du Plessis, Rachel Blau. *Writing beyond the Ending: Narrative Strategies of Twentieth Century Women Writers*. Bloomington: Univ. of Indiana Press, 1985.

———. "Power, Judgement, and Narrative in a Work of Zora Neale Hurston: Feminist Critical Studies." In Awkward, ed., *New Essays on Their Eyes Were Watching God*, pp. 95–123.

Dutton, Wendy. "The Problem of Invisibility: Voodoo and Zora Neale Hurston." *Frontiers* 13 (1992): 131–52.

Edwards, Jonathan. "Images or Shadows of Divine Things." In Cleanth Brooks, R. W. B. Lewis, and Robert Penn Warren, eds., *American Literature: The Makers and the Making*, pp. 105–9. New York: St. Martin's Press, 1973.

Emerson, Ralph Waldo. *Selections from Ralph Waldo Emerson*, ed. Stephen Whicher. Boston: Houghton Mifflin, 1957.

Faderman, Lillian. "Emily Dickinson's Homoerotic Poetry." *Higginson Journal* 18 (1978): 19–27.

Farwell, Marilyn. "Heterosexual Plots and Lesbian Subtexts: Toward a Theory of Lesbian Narrative Space." In *Lesbian Texts and Contexts*, ed. Karla Jay and Joanne Glascow. New York: New York Univ. Press, 1990.

Friedman, Ellen, and Mirium Fuchs, eds. *Breaking the Sequence: Women's Experimental Fiction*. Princeton: Princeton Univ. Press, 1989.

Gaard, Greta, ed. *Ecofeminism: Women, Animals, Nature*. Philadelphia: Temple Univ. Press, 1993.

Gates, Henry Louis, Jr. *Figures in Black: Words, Signs and the "Racial" Self*. New York: Oxford Univ. Press, 1987.

———. *The Signifying Monkey: A Theory of Afro-American Literary Criticism*. New York: Oxford Univ. Press, 1988.

———, ed. *"Race," Writing and Difference*. Chicago: Univ. of Chicago Press, 1985.

Giddings, Paula. *When and Where I Enter: The Impact of Black Women on Race and Sex in America*. New York: Bantam, 1988.

Gilbert, Sandra, and Susan Gubar. *The Madwoman in the Attic: The Woman Writer and the Nineteenth Century Imagination.* New Haven: Yale Univ. Press, 1979.

Gill, Sam. *Mother Earth: An American Story.* Chicago: Univ. of Chicago Press, 1987.

Gilman, Sander. "Black Bodies, White Bodies: Toward an Iconography of Female Sexuality in Late Nineteenth-Century Art, Medicine, and Literature." In Gates, ed. *"Race," Writing and Difference,* pp. 223–61.

Gimbutas, Marija. *The Goddesses and Gods of Old Europe, 6500–3500 BC: Myths and Cult Images.* Berkeley: Univ. of California Press, 1982.

Glotfelty, Cheryll and Harold Fromm, eds. *The Ecocriticism Reader: Landmarks in Literary Ecology.* Athens: Univ. of Georgia Press, 1996.

Griffin, Susan. *Woman and Nature: The Roaring inside Her.* New York: Harper and Row, 1978.

Gubar, Susan. "'Wayward Nun beneath the Hill:' Emily Dickinson and the Mysteries of Womanhood." In Juhasz, ed., *Feminist Critics Read Emily Dickinson,* pp. 22–44.

Hamilton, Cynthia. "Women, Home, and Community: The Struggle in an Urban Environment." In *A Forest of Voices: Reading and Writing the Environment,* ed. Chris Anderson and Lex Runcinan, pp. 673–80. Toronto: Mayfield Press, 1995.

Haraway, Donna. *Primate Visions: Gender, Race and Nature in the World of Modern Science.* New York: Routledge, 1989.

———. "The Promises of Monsters: A Regenerative Politics for Inappropriate/d Others." In *Cultural Studies,* ed. Lawrence Grossberg, Cary Nelson, and Paula Treichler, pp. 295–337. New York: Routledge, 1992.

———. *Simians, Cyborgs and Women: The Reinvention of Nature.* New York: Routledge, 1991.

———. "More than You Think, Less than There Should Be: An Interview with Donna Haraway." *Praxis* (1991): 1–21.

Hemenway, Robert. *Zora Neale Hurston: A Literary Biography.* Urbana: Univ. of Illinois Press, 1977.

Hite, Molly. *The Other Side of the Story: Structures and Strategies of Contemporary Feminist Fiction.* Ithaca: Cornell Univ. Press, 1989.

Homans, Margaret. "'Oh, Vision of Language!': Dickinson's Poems of Love and Death." In Juhasz, ed., *Feminist Critics Read Emily Dickinson,* pp. 114–33.

———. *Women Writers and Poetic Identity: Dorothy Wordsworth, Emily Brontë and Emily Dickinson.* Princeton: Princeton Univ. Press, 1980.

hooks, bell. *Ain't I a Woman: Black Women and Feminism.* Boston: South End Press, 1992.

———. *Black Looks: Race and Representation.* Boston: South End Press, 1992.

———. *Yearning: Race, Gender and Cultural Politics.* Boston: South End Press, 1990.

———, and Cornel West. *Breaking Bread: Insurgent Black Intellectual Life.* Boston: South End Press, 1991.

Hurston, Zora Neale. *Dust Tracks on a Road.* New York: Harper Collins, 1991.

———. "Hoodoo in America." *Journal of American Folklore* 44 (1931): 317–418.

———. *I Love Myself When I Am Laughing . . . and Then Again When I Am Looking Mean and*

Impressive: A Zora Neale Hurston Reader, ed. Alice Walker. New York: Feminist Press, 1979.

————. *Jonah's Gourd Vine*. New York: Harper and Row, 1990.

————. *Mules and Men*. New York: Harper and Row, 1990.

————. *The Sanctified Church: The Folklore Writings of Zora Neale Hurston*. Berkeley: Turtle Island, 1981.

————. *Tell My Horse: Voodoo and Life in Haiti and Jamaica*. New York: Harper and Row, 1990.

————. *Moses, Man of the Mountain*. Urbana: Univ. of Illinois Press, 1984.

————. *Their Eyes Were Watching God*. Urbana: Univ. of Illinois Press, 1978.

Hutcheon, Linda. *The Politics of Postmodernsim*. New York: Routledge, 1989.

Irigaray, Luce. *Speculum of the Other Woman*. Ithaca: Cornell Univ. Press, 1985.

————. *This Sex Which Is Not One*. Ithaca: Cornell Univ. Press, 1985.

Jehlen, Myra. *American Incarnation: The Individual, the Nation, and the Continent*. Cambridge: Harvard Univ. Press, 1986.

Jensen, Joan. "Native American Women and Agriculture: A Seneca Case Study." In *Women, Culture and Society: A Reader*, ed. Barbara Balliet, pp. 285–98. Dubuque: Kendal Hunt Publishing, 1992.

Jordan, Winthrop. *White over Black: American Attitudes toward the Negro, 1550–1812*. Chapel Hill: Univ. of North Carolina Press, 1968.

Jordanova, Ludmilla. *Sexual Visions: Images of Gender in Science and Medicine between the Eighteenth and Twentieth Centuries*. Madison: Univ. of Wisconsin Press, 1989.

Juhasz, Suzanne, ed. *Feminist Critics Read Emily Dickinson*. Bloomington: Indiana Univ. Press, 1983.

Keller, Evelyn Fox. *Reflections on Gender and Science*. New Haven: Yale Univ. Press, 1985.

King, Ynestra. *What Is Ecofeminism?* New York: Ecofeminist Resources, 1990.

Kolodny, Annette. *The Land before Her: Fantasy and Experience of the American Frontiers, 1630–1860*. Chapel Hill: Univ. of North Carolina Press, 1984.

————. *The Lay of the Land: Metaphor as Experience and History in American Life and Letters*. Chapel Hill: Univ. of North Carolina Press, 1975.

Kubitschek, Missy Dehn. "'Tuh de horizon and Back:' The Female Quest in *Their Eyes Were Watching God*." *Black American Literature Forum* 17 (1983): 109–15.

Larsen, Nella. *Quicksand and Passing*, ed. Deborah McDowell. New Brunswick: Rutgers Univ. Press, 1986.

Limerick, Patricia. *The Legacy of Conquest: The Unbroken Past of the American West*. New York: Norton, 1987.

Marks, Donald. "Sex, Violence, and Organic Consciousness in Zora Neale Hurston's *Their Eyes Were Watching God*." *Black American Literature Forum* 19 (1985): 152–57.

Mars, Louis. *The Crisis of Possession in Voodoo*. Berkeley: Reed, Cannon and Johnson, 1977.

Marx, Leo. *The Machine in the Garden: Technology and the Pastoral Ideal in America*. New York: Oxford Univ. Press, 1964.

Matthiessen, Peter. *Indian Country*. New York: Viking, 1984.

Menke, Pamela. "'The Lips of Books:' Hurston's *Tell My Horse* and *Their Eyes Were Watching God* as Metalingual Texts." *The Literary Griot* 14 (1992): 77–95.

Merchant, Carolyn. *The Death of Nature: Women, Ecology and the Scientific Revolution*. San Francisco: Harper and Row, 1980.

———. *Ecological Revolutions: Nature, Gender and Science in New England*. Chapel Hill: Univ. of North Carolina Press, 1989.

Mies, Maria, and Vandana Shiva. *Ecofeminism*. London: Zed Books, 1993.

Mikell, Gwendolyn. "When Horses Talk: Reflections of Zora Neale Hurston's Haitian Anthropology." *Phylon* 43 (1982): 218–30.

Miller, Christanne. *Emily Dickinson: A Poet's Grammar*. Cambridge: Harvard Univ. Press, 1987.

Miller, Perry. *Errand into the Wilderness*. Cambridge: Belknap Press of Harvard Univ. Press, 1956.

———. *Nature's Nation*. Cambridge: Harvard Univ. Press, 1967.

Morrison, Toni. *Beloved*. New York: New American Library, 1987.

———. *Playing in the Dark: Whiteness and the Literary Imagination*. New York: Random House, 1992.

———. "The Site of Memory." In *Inventing the Truth: The Art and Craft of Memoir*, ed. William Zinsser, pp. 101–24. Boston: Houghton Mifflin, 1987.

Mullane, Deirdre, ed. *Crossing the Danger Water: Three Hundred Years of African-American Writing*. New York: Doubleday, 1993.

Murphy, Patrick. *Literature, Nature, and Other: Ecofeminist Critiques*. Albany: State Univ. of New York Press, 1995.

Nash, Roderick. *Wilderness and the American Mind*. New Haven: Yale Univ. Press, 1967.

Niehardt, John. *Black Elk Speaks: Being the Life Story of a Holy Man of the Oglala Sioux*. Lincoln: Univ. of Nebraska Press, 1979.

Norwood, Vera. *Made from This Earth: American Women and Nature*. Chapel Hill: Univ. of North Carolina Press, 1993.

———, and Janice Monk. *The Desert Is No Lady: Southwestern Landscapes in Women's Writing and Art*. New Haven: Yale Univ. Press, 1987.

Ostriker, Alicia. *Stealing the Language: The Emergence of Women's Poetry in America*. Boston: Beacon Press, 1986.

Owens, Louis. *Other Destinies: Understanding the American Indian Novel*. Tulsa: Univ. of Oklahoma Press, 1992.

Pearce, Roy Harvey. *Savagism and Civilization: A Study of the Indian and the American Mind*. Berkeley: Univ. of California Press, 1988.

Perry, Donna. *Backtalk: Women Writers Speak Out*. New Brunswick: Rutgers Univ. Press, 1993.

Plant, Judith, ed. *Healing the Wounds: The Promise of Ecofeminism*. Philadelphia: New Society Publishers, 1989.

Plumwood, Val. *Feminism and the Mastery of Nature*. London: Routledge, 1993.

Reed, Ishmael. Foreword to *Tell My Horse: Voodoo and Life in Haiti and Jamaica*, by Zora Neale Hurston. New York: Harper and Row, 1990.

Rich, Adrienne. *The Fact of a Doorframe: Poems Selected and New, 1950–1984*. New York: Norton, 1984.

———. *On Lies, Secrets, and Silence: Selected Prose, 1966–1978*. New York: Norton, 1979.

———. *Your Native Land, Your Life: Poems*. New York: Norton, 1986.

Sewall, Richard. *The Life of Emily Dickinson*. New York: Farrar, Strauss and Giroux, 1974.

Shiva, Vandana. *Staying Alive: Women, Ecology and Survival*. London: Zed Books, 1990.

Silko, Leslie Marmon. *The Almanac of the Dead*. New York: Simon and Schuster, 1991.

———. *Ceremony*. New York: Penguin, 1977.

———. "Landscape, History, and the Pueblo Imagination." In *Celebrating the Land: Women's Nature Writings, 1850–1991*, ed. Karen Knowles, pp. 107–17. Cadillac: Northland Publishing, 1992.

———. *Storyteller*. New York: Arcade, 1981.

———. *Yellow Woman and a Beauty of Spirit: Essays on Native American Life Today*. New York: Simon and Schuster, 1996.

Slotkin, Richard. *Gunfighter Nation: The Myth of the Frontier in Twentieth Century America*. New York: Atheneum, 1992.

———. *Regeneration through Violence: The Myth of the American Frontier, 1600–1800*. Middletown: Wesleyan Univ. Press, 1973.

Smith, Clark, and Paula Gunn Allen. "Earthy Relations, Carnal Knowledge: Southwestern American Indian Women Writers and Landscape." In *The Desert Is No Lady*, ed. Vera Norwood, pp. 174–96. New Haven: Yale Univ. Press, 1987.

Smith, Henry Nash. *Virgin Land: The American West as Symbol and Myth*. Cambridge: Harvard Univ. Press, 1950.

Smith, Martha Nell. "'To Fill a Gap.'" *San Jose Studies* 13 (1987): 3–25.

Southerland, Ellease. "The Influence of Voodoo on the Fiction of Zora Neale Hurston." In *Sturdy Black Bridges: Visions of Black Women in Literature*, ed. Roseann Bell, pp. 171–83. New York: Anchor Books, 1979.

Spillers, Hortense. "Mama's Baby, Papa's Maybe: An American Grammar Book." *Diacritics* 17 (1987): 65–81.

Stone, Merlin. *When God Was a Woman*. New York: Harcourt Brace Jovanovich, 1976.

Swan, Edith. "Laguna Symbolic Geography and Silko's *Ceremony*." *American Indian Quarterly* 12 (1988): 229–49.

Tate, Claudia. *Black Women Writers at Work*. New York: Continuum, 1983.

Teish, Luisah. *Jambalaya*. San Francisco: Harper and Row, 1985.

Thompson, Robert Farris. *Flash of the Spirit: African and Afro-American Art and Philosophy*. New York: Vintage Books, 1984.

Tompkins, Jane. "'Indians': Textualism, Morality, and the Problem of History." In Gates, ed., *'Race,' Writing and Difference*, pp. 59–77.

————. *Sensational Designs: The Cultural Work of American Fiction, 1790–1860*. New York: Oxford Univ. Press, 1985.

Trinh T. Minh-ha. *Woman, Native, Other: Writing Postcoloniality and Feminism*. Bloomington: Indiana Univ. Press, 1989.

Truth, Sojourner. "Address to the Ohio Women's Rights Convention." In Mullane, ed., *Crossing the Danger Water: Three Hundred Years of African-American Writing*, p. 186.

Turner, Frederick. *Beyond Geography: The Western Spirit against the Wilderness*. New Brunswick: Rutgers Univ. Press, 1990.

Walker, Alice. *The Color Purple*. New York: Washington Square Press, 1982.

————. *In Search of Our Mothers' Gardens*. San Diego: Harcourt Brace Jovanovich, 1983.

————. *Living by the Word*. San Diego: Harcourt Brace Jovanovich, 1988.

————. *Meridian*. New York: Washington Square Press, 1976.

————. *The Temple of My Familiar*. San Diego: Harcourt Brace Jovanovich, 1989.

————. *The Third Life of Grange Copeland*. New York: Harcourt Brace Jovanovich, 1970.

————. *You Can't Keep a Good Woman Down*. San Diego: Harcourt Brace Jovanovich.

Wall, Cheryl. *Women of Letters of the Harlem Renaissance*. Bloomington: Indiana Univ. Press, 1995.

Washington, Mary Helen. *Invented Lives: Narratives of Black Women, 1860–1960*. Garden City, N.Y.: Anchor Press, 1987.

Watts, Emily Stipes. *The Poetry of American Women from 1632–1945*. Austin: Univ. of Texas Press, 1977.

Wells, Ida B. "From *A Red Record*." In Mullane, ed., *Crossing the Danger Water: Three Hundred Years of African-American Writing*, pp. 395–401.

West, Cornel. *Race Matters*. Boston: Beacon Press, 1993.

Williams, Patricia. *The Alchemy of Race and Rights: Diary of a Law Professor*. Cambridge: Harvard Univ. Press, 1991.

Willis, Susan. *Specifying: Black Women Writing the American Experience*. Madison: Univ. of Wisconsin Press, 1987.

Wolff, Cynthia Griffin. *Emily Dickison*. New York: Knopf, 1987.

Woodward, C. Vann. *The Strange Career of Jim Crow*. London: Oxford Univ. Press, 1965.

Woolf, Virginia. *The Common Reader*. New York: Harcourt Brace, 1948.

Zimmerman, Michael. *Contesting Earth's Future: Radical Ecology and Postmodernism*. Berkeley: Univ. of California Press, 1994.

Zinn, Howard. *A People's History of the United States*. New York: Harper and Row, 1980.

Index